Sacred Trust

Sacred Trust:
The Medieval Church
as an Economic Firm

ROBERT B. EKELUND, JR.

ROBERT F. HÉBERT

ROBERT D. TOLLISON

GARY M. ANDERSON

AUDREY B. DAVIDSON

New York   Oxford

OXFORD UNIVERSITY PRESS

1996

Oxford University Press

Oxford   New York
Athens   Auckland   Bangkok   Bogotá   Bombay
Buenos Aires   Calcutta   Cape Town   Dar es Salaam
Delhi   Florence   Hong Kong   Istanbul   Karachi
Kuala Lumpur   Madras   Madrid   Melbourne
Mexico City   Nairobi   Paris   Singapore
Taipei   Tokyo   Toronto

and associated companies in
Berlin   Ibadan

Library of Congress Cataloging-in-Publication Data
Sacred trust : the medieval church as an economic firm / Robert B.
Ekelund, Jr. . . . [et al.].
p.   cm.
Includes bibliographical references and index.
ISBN 0-19-510337-8
1. Economics—Religious aspects—Catholic Church.   2. Church
history—Middle Ages, 600–1500.   3. Catholic Church—Europe—
History.   4. Europe—Church history—600–1500.   I. Ekelund, Robert
B. (Robert Burton), 1940–   .
BX1795.E27S33   1996
330.94'01—dc20   96-20830

9 8 7 6 5 4 3 2 1

Printed in the United States of America
on acid-free paper

Preface

Obviously, successful books are not written by a committee, so it is incumbent on us to explain the large number of authors involved in this work—to describe, as it were, the nature of the production function. Ekelund and Tollison pioneered the conceptual framework of this book in their work *Mercantilism as a Rent-Seeking Society* (1981). The significance of this earlier work is that it was the first systematic attempt to show how state control of the supply and demand of monopoly rights provided the impetus to the rise of mercantilism and later led to its downfall.

This book pushes the same analytical paradigm farther back into history. Before nation-states emerged, the Roman Catholic Church served as the unifying (and monopolizing) central presence in western Europe. For centuries, after attaining secular power commensurate with its spiritual aspirations, the medieval Christian Church functioned as a quasi-government, providing public goods as well as private goods, but mainly establishing guidelines and standards for individual behavior—from kings to peasants. The Church dominated medieval society. As the most important organizational and institutional force in the Middle Ages, the Church could not help but be a key economic player. Many economic historians and Church historians have recognized this fact and incorporated it into past research. But for the most part, the nature of past research has been to focus on the effect of the medieval Church on the macroeconomy. Thus, on the one hand, we are confronted with the Weber–Tawney view (at least as popularized) that the medieval Church had a negative impact on economic development, while, on the other hand, we are confronted by the alternative Sombart–Schumpeter view that the medieval Church had a net posi-

tive effect on economic development. Despite the problematic nature of
this "big question" in the history of economic thought, we are not aware of
any sustained attempt to resolve the matter by a systematic analysis of the
medieval Church as a microeconomic entity. Hence, the justification for
this book.

The origin of this book occurred in ideas discussed over a decade ago
by Ekelund and Tollison in 1985 and in a graduate seminar on the subject
Ekelund conducted at Auburn University in winter quarter 1986. In 1987
Ekelund and Tollison recruited Hébert to join their research team. The
initial fruits of the research that this new team spawned were published in
a series of articles that appeared between 1989 and 1992. The first article
in this series, "An Economic Model of the Medieval Church: Usury as a
Form of Rent Seeking," was published in 1989 by the *Journal of Law, Economics, and Organization;* the second, "The Economics of Sin and Redemption:
Purgatory as a Market-Pull Innovation?" appeared in 1992 in the *Journal of
Economic Behavior & Organization;* and the third, written with the additional
collaboration of Gary Anderson, entitled "An Economic Interpretation of
the Medieval Crusades," was published later the same year in the *Journal of
European Economic History.*

Anderson's addition to the research team was both natural and logical.
He began his research in the economics of religion in conjunction with
Tollison at George Mason University in the late 1980s and has continued
to pursue this subject to date. Meanwhile, Audrey Davidson enrolled in
the graduate program at Auburn University in 1990, where she chose to
do her doctoral research in the economics of the medieval Church under
the guidance of Ekelund. Her addition to the author team brought new
topical expertise to the group, the consequences of many hours of pains-
taking research, and two additional articles, "The Medieval Monastery as
Franchise Monopolist" and (with Ekelund), "The Medieval Church and
Rents from Marriage Market Regulations" in the *Journal of Economic Behavior
and Organization.*

Successful economic endeavors require an appropriate allocation of resources. The present work is no exception. Ekelund and Tollison conceived
the project, and Hébert served as production manager, taking the chief
responsibility for organizing, editing, and assembling a first draft of the
manuscript. Anderson's and Davidson's research efforts yielded several
specific chapters. Like most simple characterizations, however, this one,
too, obscures certain symbiotic consequences of collaboration that cannot be easily measured or represented. Important contributions to the organization, research, and expression of ideas were made at critical junc-
tures by each member of the team. What has emerged, therefore, is a
collective work that was executed according to the time-honored economic

principles of specialization and division of labor, even though this fact may not be self-evident in a list of five coauthors.

Inasmuch as collective efforts can be disaggregated, the following schedule more or less represents the allocation of major research and expository responsibilities: Chapter 1 (Anderson, Hébert, and Ekelund); Chapter 2 (Anderson, Ekelund, and Tollison); Chapter 3 (Davidson); Chapter 4 (Anderson and Ekelund); Chapter 5 (Davidson and Ekelund); Chapter 6 (Ekelund, Hébert, and Tollison); Chapter 7 (Ekelund, Anderson, Hébert, and Tollison); Chapter 8 (Hébert, Ekelund, and Tollison); Chapter 9 (Anderson, Ekelund, Hébert, and Tollison).

At the outset, it is important to describe the general contours of the present study and to specify its overall limitations. One limitation is that our analysis relies heavily on English-language, largely secondary, sources, and on translations, where they exist. Another is that we rely largely on anecdotal evidence—which, given the historical distance of our subject, is often the only kind extant. We have not set out to rewrite medieval history. This book is not an attempt to integrate economics and religion. Nor is it a comprehensive attempt to define *the* place of the Church in the history of Western civilization. Rather, it is a microeconomic inquiry of the medieval Church utilizing a stylized economic model that accords with standard economic theory.

We make no pretense that the particular subjects chosen for our study are exhaustive. Rather, we regard them as case studies—the beginning of a microanalytic investigation of facets of the medieval Church. We analyze medieval religious institutions surrounding the subjects of marriage, usury, heresy, the Crusades, and monasteries. Other topics are only touched on in this study and remain to be developed. Such topics include the issue of priestly celibacy, rent-seeking practices of the Roman vis-à-vis the Eastern Church, formal disputes surrounding the "investiture controversy," the position of the Church in the growth of towns and cathedral building, and the role of the Church in growing international trade (e.g., in the Hanseatic League).

Although the emphasis is on economic behavior, this research does not necessarily reject or impugn religious motives, as may be advanced by theologians or other historical researchers. Some of our conclusions may coincide with modern work on the economics of religion by contemporary historians or sociologists (such as Andrew Greeley), but we have made no attempt to use research on contemporary religions to enlighten the economics of the medieval Church. Clearly, other hypotheses (e.g., those embedded in the "public-interest" paradigm) may be observationally equivalent to our "rent-seeking" view. We recognize and are sympathetic to alternative approaches, but hold them outside the primary focus of this book.

We therefore apologize in advance to those researchers who become apo-
plectic when attempts—especially so-called unconventional ones—are
made to bring order to history. We do *not* believe that "history merely
happens."

In the final analysis, our aims are specific and limited: to provide a framework that may be used to analyze certain doctrines and policies of the
medieval Catholic Church. Toward this end, we push the private–interest
paradigm as far as we can in an attempt to devise meaningful insights into
Church behavior. Although our research stops short of the Protestant Reformation, we try to demonstrate that a microanalytic approach provides
fresh perspective on the role of the institutions of the medieval Church in
economic development (Chapter 9). Historiographers and assorted social
scientists may have other perspectives. We welcome them, and their evidence, to this dialogue.

We owe a debt of gratitude to both friendly and hostile readers of earlier
versions of this manuscript. Our colleagues at Auburn University and George
Mason University have been generous in their criticism. David Kaserman
(Auburn) and Don Boudreaux (Clemson) read and improved large portions
of this manuscript. Richard Ault (Auburn), Ed Price (Oklahoma State), Jim
Buchanan (George Mason), Andrew Greeley (Chicago), David Laband
(Auburn), David Gay (Arkansas), John Sophocleus (Auburn), Randy Beard
(Auburn), Paula Gant (Auburn), and Mark Thornton (Auburn) deserve
special thanks. Graduate assistant Frank Adams performed the tasks of copy
editing and reference checking with great efficiency and typist Cathy Kruse
was of her usual competence. Our project also owes an enormous debt to
the encouragement of Ken MacLeod of Oxford University Press whose
interest is deeply appreciated. In the end, however, this project is our own,
and so is the responsibility for the views expressed herein.

January 1996   R. B. E., Jr.
                                                        R. F. H.
                                                        R. D. T.
                                                        G. M. A.
                                                        A. B. D.

Contents

Sacred Trust

What Does an Economic Model of the Medieval Church Offer?

Introduction: The Economics of Religion

Religion in some form is as much a part of being human as food, sex, tool-making, or planning for the future. The enigma of existence has haunted us from the very beginning. Emotional and psychological shields from the vagaries of "rough nature" and assurances of life beyond physical death had and continue to have a hold on human societies. Particular forms of religion vary from culture to culture and age to age, but atheism—societies without "invisible" means of support—has not dominated any past society, as it does not our own.

One issue that has fascinated anthropologists, sociologists, historians, and scientists is the relation between religion, the material progress of society, and the range of human choice. A central goal in social science is to explain the course of Western civilization and the foundations of our own world in terms of the interactions between progress and one particular form of religious belief—Roman Christianity.[1] What was the nature and importance of the Roman Catholic Church in facilitating modern social, economic, and technological institutions? A brilliant and luxuriant literature, much of it particularized and episodic, has been channeled by scholars to elements of this overarching question. Economists seeking to provide order and organizing principles to the enterprise are latecomers.

Modern developments in the application of economic theory to the evolution of religious institutions comes on the heels of recent developments. On the eve of the twentieth century the great neoclassical economist Alfred Marshall (1890, 1) wrote that "the two great forming agencies

3

of the world's history have been the religious and the economic." Like most economists, however, Marshall tended to separate the two spheres, and eschewed opportunities to analyze religious institutions on economic grounds.[2] Two generations have elapsed since Marshall's death, and in the interim the domain of economics has continually expanded. Were he alive today, Marshall might be surprised at the breadth of modern economics, which runs the gamut of human actions—from "the ordinary business of making a living" (Marshall's own phrase), to lobbying activities in legislatures, to the form of contemporary music, to the sleep patterns of individuals, to the dynamics of family interactions. Even the human body itself has been modeled as a kind of market economy (Ghiselin 1974).[3] By ranging far afield, modern economics promises to increase our understanding of many interesting and varied aspects of human behavior.[4]

In its expanded form as "the science of choice," economics models the human decision nexus as a kind of economy, regardless of scientific domain. It matters little whether the problem is perceived as inherently economic or as anthropological, psychological, sociological, political, legal, or religious. For example, public choice theory applies economic principles to the study of political institutions. Following its lead, this book applies economic principles to the study of religious institutions.

The basic premise underlying these approaches is that economic elements come into play in all human decisions. Economists therefore have something to contribute to our understanding of such decisions. Whether or not economic elements *dominate* each decision is another question, one that cannot be resolved a priori, or in a generalized way.[5] Nevertheless, uncovering the economic elements in a decision nexus and applying economic analysis to the interpretation of the decision process should improve our understanding of observed behaviors at the margin.

This study lies outside the long-standing tradition that asserts that religious organizations are principally motivated by "other-worldly" interests (e.g., salvation). In this older intellectual tradition, the internal workings of religious organizations are treated as "epiphenomena," or outside the domain of self-interested maximization, primarily because religious belief is defined as a fundamental, faith-driven commitment to a system of ideas, norms, and values that lie beyond the calculus of rational choice. We employ the alternative approach that treats religious behavior as the product of rational choice. Spiritual considerations notwithstanding, decisions within religious organizations are made by human beings living in a worldly environment. Economists have long recognized that even actions ostensibly based on noneconomic criteria may be economically motivated because the decision makers may be satisfying several objectives, noneconomic and economic, simultaneously. Here we seek to uncover the purely economic aspects of decisions made by agents who, outwardly at least, were trying to satisfy economic and noneconomic goals simultaneously.

This work fits within a small but growing body of literature on the economics of religion. Some of the landmark contributions to this literature include Azzi and Ehrenberg (1975), who developed a model of religious participation based on Gary Becker's theory of household consumption; Redman (1980), who examined the economic grounds of religious choice; Iannaccone (1988), who explored the nature of cost-minimizing rules within religious organizations; and Hull and Bold (1989), who applied the economic theory of the firm to church behavior.[6] Heretofore this burgeoning literature has remained fairly isolated from economic history. This work is an exception since we focus our attention on the institution of the Roman Catholic Church of the Middle Ages. We choose this narrow focus because the historical facts lend themselves to a stylized model that is familiar to economists, one that allows wide use of the analytical tools of contemporary microeconomics.

The Stylized Facts of Medieval Life

Imagine a world where religion dominates everyday life. The priesthood plays a large role in the functioning of the ordinary economy. Ecclesiastical officials enact and enforce laws governing everyday transactions. Kings, princes, and dukes owe at least part of their power by grace of the religious authorities, who also arbitrate international disputes, maintain armies, and fight wars to promote their organizational ends. The dominant religious organization (*the* Christian Church) is immensely rich and controls most of the landed property in society. Most of the revenues of the Church flow from voluntary contributions of the faithful, who receive in return both spiritual and secular services. This thumbnail sketch approximately describes medieval Europe wherein the Roman Catholic Church exerted more power than any single monarch and wielded such authority that historians commonly refer to the West during the Middle Ages as "Christendom."

This kind of historical epoch lends itself to economic investigation. Our study analyzes the actions of the medieval Roman Catholic Church as it would any *economic* actor. Whereas previous economic studies of the medieval Church have treated only isolated parts of the Church economy, implicitly relegating the bulk of its operations to a kind of "black box" beyond the grasp of economic methodology, we attempt to develop a more comprehensive economic model of the medieval Church. Clearly, the medieval Church was a complex institution that pursued multiple, simultaneous goals. But whatever else it was, our research shows that it behaved as a rational, maximizing institution within which individual decision makers cooperated according to a stipulated set of constitutional constraints in order to promote certain collective ends. In this book, therefore, we model the Church as a corporation that marketed and "sold" a set of identifiable "products" in a rational, cost-conscious, "profit"-maximizing manner. We hope to show that such a model of the medieval Church is rich in explanatory meaning and that it improves our understanding of many complex (and seemingly irrational) historical events.

This effort is necessarily conscripted by a particular paradigm. It was suggested earlier that theories of religious behavior may be categorized as either spiritual or economic. Spiritual hypotheses might account for the fact that some religions are proselytizing (e.g., Catholicism), while others are not (e.g., Judaism), an issue that is not central to our present concerns. From an economic perspective, the chief drawback to models constructed on spiritual principles is that they require extraeconomic assumptions that stretch the credibility of economic analysis. One way to overcome this shortcoming is to reformulate the spiritual hypothesis in economic terms.[7]

The analogue of the spiritual hypothesis in economic analysis is the "public-interest" theory of government, in which spiritual goals become a collective expression of the common good. If religious organizations are motivated by considerations of "public interest," we would expect to observe them behaving like a "good" government: providing more information to the faithful; producing spiritual goods and services at competitive rates (i.e., marginal cost); internalizing externalities; and enforcing property rights for the common good. In examining the behavior of the medieval Church, our reading of the historical record does not provide overwhelming support for this approach. Nevertheless, pending a full-scale examination, we cannot reject this line of analysis outright and must await more complete historical analysis. In this book we choose to advance the self-interest approach over the public-interest approach because we believe the former stands in closer accord with the historical record and wields more potential explanatory power. Those who feel the case is compelling for the public-interest approach are invited to bring forth their evidence.[8]

Even within the self-interest paradigm, choice must be exercised among competing economic models. The two competing economic hypotheses relevant to this study are the profit-maximization and revenue (sales)-maximization theses. The former is "static," whereas the latter is "dynamic." We have chosen to apply the static model because we find it a more useful frame for the historical facts. We concede that both spiritual models and revenue-maximization models may yield the same predictions as the static, profit-maximization model. Our efforts are not aimed at a comprehensive comparative study of competing paradigms. Nevertheless, we have tried to remain sensitive to contrasting or complementary economic interpretations at appropriate places within the argument. Ultimately, the purpose of this book is not to advance *the* definitive model of Church behavior, but to break down existing entry barriers in a field of intellectual enterprise that economists traditionally have been reluctant to enter.

This study is far from exhaustive, even within the methodological constraints imposed. Our limited objective is to illustrate the fruitfulness of a certain line of contemporary economic inquiry for historical analysis. We attempt to sketch a basic economic theory of institutional behavior and follow the theory with a series of limited case studies of "economics in action," whereby the determination of Church policies and doctrines are interpreted in light of the basic theory. The plan of action is as follows. Chapters 2 to 4 explain the industrial organization of the medieval Church and its enforcement mechanisms. Chapters 5 to 8 constitute case studies of various market manipulations and regulations that affected the fortunes of the medieval Church. The final chapter summarizes the preceding exposition and tenders some conclusions about the impact of the medieval Church on the economic development of the Western world. Furthermore, we evaluate the dominant theories pertaining to the role of the Church in the birth and encouragement of capitalism.

The Medieval Church as a Problem in Economic Organization

Contributors to the vast historical literature on the medieval Roman Catholic Church can be classified into one of two categories. The first category is composed of historians who have taken the Church at face value and have analyzed it as an organizational manifestation of an elaborate system of theological beliefs. Many writers in this group have been practicing Catholics who have served as apologists for, or defenders of, Catholicism. Others have scrupulously avoided taking sides by trying to adopt a neutral, allegedly value-free approach to the study of the Church.

In the second category are mainly critics of the Church's official doctrine and policies, writers who have emphasized the opportunistic behavior of priests and clerics, especially the pope. Many Protestant opponents of Catholicism are in this group, such as the nineteenth-century historians, Henry C. Lea and Andrew D. White. Probably the best-known writer in this category is Karl Marx, whose infamous phrase "religion is the opiate of the masses," still rings through the ages. Marx's claim implies that the Church has acted throughout its history as a kind of protection racket, whereby clerics enrich themselves by exacting tribute from the faithful. A more recent adherent of this point of view, the French historian LeGoff (1988), provocatively named one of his books on the medieval Church *Your Money or Your Life*.

Despite conflicting views on the underlying motivation of priests and clerics in the operation of the Church, there is universal agreement that the Church was an institution of primary importance for understanding the history of medieval Europe. Over the course of at least five centuries, beginning at the end of the first millennium A.D., virtually all Europeans living west of a line running between the Gulf of Taranto in the south to the Gulf of Danzig in the north professed to accept the Roman Catholic Church as the One True Church, the sole representative of the Holy Trinity on earth.[9]

In addition to its dominance in the spiritual realm, the medieval Church played a key role in the European economy. Before the year A.D. 900, the Church directly owned approximately one-third of all cultivated land in western Europe, including 31 percent of such land in Italy, 35 percent in Germany, and 44 percent in northern France.[10] At the time, cultivated land represented that part of Europe that was economically developed. It is unclear how much uncultivated land was owned by the Church, but the proportion was likely considerable.

After 1300, England alone had over 50,000 priests, deacons and subdeacons (which constituted about 1% of its population), a number which excludes a large number of monastics and other clerics. According to Mundy (1973, 284), the situation in England was representative of Catholic countries on the Continent as well. On the Continent there were over 700 episcopal sees, or bishoprics, not to mention the large number of monasteries that were completely independent of the bishoprics. Southern (1970, 254) indicates that the Cistercians alone operated 525 separate abbeys. The building of churches and cloisters was the largest single investment of money and effort during the Middle Ages, with the possible exception of the construction of castle fortifications. According to Gilchrist (1969, 3), the medieval Church was a "richly endowed corporation whose income made it the wealthiest of societies. Through their revenues churchmen disposed of a great part of the liquid capital of the Western world."

The characterization of the medieval Church as a corporation is appropriate in many ways, not the least of which involves its wealth and economic influence. In terms of its economic organization, the medieval Church functioned as a franchise monopoly that enjoyed certain economies of scale but that continually faced the dual problems of enforcement and entry control. Consider its hierarchic structure. The Church was directed from the top (the Vatican) by a chief executive officer (the pope) and a board of directors (the College of Cardinals and an administrative toady called the Curia).[11] Its franchisees (bishoprics and monasteries) were themselves multitiered hierarchies with distinct lines of authority.

Bishops controlled amalgamations of individual parishes (dioceses); abbots controlled individual monasteries or collections of monasteries. Policy radiated from the top down to the parish or final level of "consumption." Interruptions of "profits" could occur from within (e.g., cheaters, shirkers, interlopers) or without (e.g., competition from competing religions). Under these circumstances, it is not far-fetched to model the medieval Church on a firm, that is, a nexus of long-term contracts designed to achieve various cooperative goals for its "owners." In fact, as we shall argue more forcefully later, the medieval Church surpassed many modern-day corporations in its size, complexity, and sophistication. Its chief difference lay in the absence of stockholder–owner control.

The Medieval Church as a Problem in Public Choice

Just as there exists a large body of historical literature on the politico-socioeconomic impact of the medieval Church, there also exists a formidable body of literature examining the internal workings of the complex medieval organization that composed the Church. What remains inadequately addressed by this vast literature is the question of economic motivation driving the design and implementation of Church policy. Why did the medieval Church make the particular choices it did instead of others that were also available?

We seek to fill this gap by explicitly addressing the broad issues concerning the economics of policy choice within the medieval Church. Toward this end, we offer a public-choice model of the medieval Church. As a branch of modern economics, public choice tries to open the black box of public decisionmaking, applying neoclassical microeconomics to rationalize individual maximizing behavior within the public institution under investigation. Whereas contemporary practice applies the principles of public choice to the operation of governments, we seek herein to apply its principles to the operation of the medieval Church, which, in many respects, superseded weak medieval governments.

Many writers have explicitly compared the medieval Church to a government, even suggesting that the massive and far-flung ecclesiastic bureaucracy actually served as a kind of role-model that was emulated by emerging nation-states. But while the Church resembled a government in some important ways, it was decidedly not a government in the most basic economic sense: although practices in individual countries varied, globally it did not appropriate the bulk of its revenue through coercive taxation.[12] This elemental difference notwithstanding, we consider our approach an application of public-choice principles because we attempt to extend neo-classical price theory to the behavior of a "public" institution that did not function in the usual market context. The Church produced "output" that it "sold" to consumers, but it did not engage in commercial exchange at publically posted prices.[13]

An economic model of any real-world process or behavior is based on a simplifying assumption—that it is possible to establish a relatively simple predictive framework capable of accommodating the behavior to be observed, however superficially complex that behavior might appear. A public-choice model of an enormous, complex organization like the medieval Church assumes that the relevant decision makers and resource allocators are rational, self-interested individuals who seek to maximize individual or group utility subject to available, known constraints. The goal is to explain how and why specific actions within the organization are taken in conformance with the axioms of the public-choice paradigm.

The Present Approach in Historical Perspective

Over the years, the medieval, corporate Church has been a subject of continual fascination to economic historians throughout the world. The economic history of the Church, like its counterpart, the general medieval history of the Church, is contained in a rich and varied literature that defies easy summary. Nevertheless, at the risk of oversimplification, it is useful to distinguish two alternate approaches.

The first approach may be called "Weberian," taking its name from Max Weber, who elaborated his basic argument in *The Protestant Ethic and the Spirit of Capitalism* (1930). A highly stylized version of Weber's thesis runs as follows. The medieval Catholic Church exerted a persistently negative influence on economic development in western Europe by persecuting scientists and free thinkers, stifling technology, constraining commerce and trade, and rechanneling investment from productive (material) to wasteful (spiritual) expenditures. Above all else, in Weber's view the Church discouraged the development of an individualist ethic that promoted commerce and trade.[14] Although Weber was primarily interested in the role of the Reformation in changing the relevant constraints on capitalist development, he nevertheless held the Church culpable for retarding European economic development. Weber did not place much emphasis on the opportunism of Church leaders, but writers in the tradition he inspired have argued that the corruption of popes and prelates was an ultimate and significant cause of many of the Church policies that restrained European economic development.

An alternative to the Weberian thesis was advanced by Werner Sombart (1915) who developed the notion that not only were Calvinism and Puritanism not conducive to implanting the capitalist ethos but were detrimental to it. Catholicism, and especially Aquinas's emphasis on the life of Right Reason and the living of life without surrender to the passions, was the prerequisite for developing the temper of capitalism. Joseph Schumpeter, a professed admirer of Weber, further developed the Sombart argument in his magisterial *History of Economic Analysis* (1954). Schumpeter contended that the medieval Church fostered the rise of modern capitalism in many ways, both directly and indirectly. The "Schumpeterian" thesis stresses the role of the medieval Church as a promoter and defender of learning and scholarship, drawing a connection between the hegemony of the Church in western Europe and that region's era of rapid economic development.[15] Schumpeter attributes numerous inventions and innovations to the educational policies of the medieval Church, and argues that less salutary Church doctrines, such as the infamous prohibition against usury, were not as harmful in practice as the rigid post-Reformation codes enacted by the new Protestant churches. In sum, Schumpeter argues that the medieval Church exerted a net *positive* influence on the economic development of western Europe.

After a long period of adherence to the Weberian view, many modern historians have swung to the Schumpeterian view. It is now recognized that the medieval period was actually one of persistent and robust economic growth, even if relatively slow by contemporary standards. The Schumpeterians argue that medieval economic development was spurred and accelerated by the invention and diffusion of new technology; that population and agricultural production expanded enormously; seafaring grew; and private capital markets evolved systematically. These opposing hypotheses, and others similarly motivated, have been constructed along macroeconomic rather than microeconomic lines. This book is decidedly microeconomic in its orientation. We wish to show that a complete and accurate judgment about the effects of the medieval Church on the macroeconomy of western Europe cannot be rendered without anchoring that judgment to the microeconomics of the institutional Church.

The latter is the task that we set for ourselves in this study. At the end of the day, of course, the proof is in the pudding. It will be apparent if a microeconomic approach contains the seeds of a richer understanding of Church behavior and its input on medieval society and economic development. If this is so, and our argument is persuasive, there is much work to be done to fill out and elaborate a microeconomic model of the medieval Church, and we point the reader in some of these directions in the final chapter.

NOTES

1. Here we completely ignore the issue of the meaning of "progress." Some modern "moral philosophers" urge the abandonment of the rationality ethos and "secular Enlightenment liberalism" and argue that the moral code of the medieval Church and, especially, Thomas Aquinas's interpretation of Aristotle's natural law, should serve as the imprint for modern politics and social behavior. In this world there are no *positive rights* of the individual, only the "authority of tradition," i.e., the Roman Catholic Church's moral tradition. We would not view progress as a return to commutarian principles, or medieval values and culture (in contrast to indoor plumbing and individual freedom), but we respect the rights of those who do.

2. Adam Smith, author of the *Wealth of Nations* (1776) and acknowledged founder of economics as a social science, first integrated the study of religious behavior with economics. In a far broader view than that of Marshall and his neoclassical contemporaries—appropriately called political economy—Smith studied the economic problems associated with the provision of religious services. Smith's analysis, while not providing a formal theory of monopoly supply of these services, revolved around incentive failures as characteristic of state-sponsored religious instruction. We develop these arguments at some length in Chapter 2.

3. Application of modern economics has even extended beyond the realm of human behavior to include the behavior of other animals, even insects (Battalio et al. 1985, 1986, 1991). Biology and economics increasingly tend to address similar problems. Modern biologists utilize "rationalistic" models of optimizing behavior in their studies of subhuman behaviors (for a seminal work in this vein, see Dawkins 1976). These studies suggest that the economic paradigm is a powerful tool for understanding many different levels of life and life forms.

4. At the same time, a number of economists remain critical of these far-flung applications, charging that economics has gone "too far" in its march. Oddly enough, one rarely hears the same criticism of modern physics or biology.

5. Over a hundred years ago Marshall (1890, 1) offered the view that "religious and economic influences have nowhere been displaced from the front rank even for a time; and they have nearly always been more important than all others put together. Religious motives are more intense than economic, but their direct action seldom extends over so large a part of life."

6. For more on this subject, see the excellent survey of recent work in the economics of religion by Iannaccone and Hull (1990).

7. We do not, of course, argue that the sole orientation of the Church was "economic." In fact the Church experienced a number of internal critics, including St. Francis, St. Dominic, St. Catherine of Siena, and a number of popes, who decried the "profit-taking," nonbiblical emphasis on wealth espoused at times by the Church. Such activity appears to indicate that some in the Church did adopt a "good government" or spiritual model. The reaction of the Church to some of these developments—for example, the legitimizing of Dominican and Franciscan Orders—may well have been an attempt to defend its doctrinal monopoly against entrants and potential entrants (see Chapter 4 for additional discussion).

8. Some historians, especially those economic historians positioned in the English tradition, label any application of a private-interest argument as a nineteenth-century backdrop to the "imperialism" of accepted economic theory. Thus, acceptance of the self-interest axiom constitutes an "ideology" or an "unscientific" method of interpreting events. However, most of these historiographers are themselves using an obsolete historical approach where all categories—ideas, customs, tradition, religion, and so on—have equal and *autonomous* weight along with self-interest. The economist, on the other hand, looks for explanations of institutional change in which ideas and other factors are only interrelated elements in an ongoing process driven by the self-interested behavior of economic actors and coalitions. Within this framework it is possible to pose hypotheses, such as private- or public-interest explanations for change, and to observe which theory best and most consistently fits the facts. As such, we use a positive approach to particular historical events surrounding the medieval Church.

9. For the millions of inhabitants of western Europe, their Church was administered from Rome. For many millions more in eastern Europe and the Near East, their faith was administered by the Eastern (Byzantine) Church. We discuss this independent entity and its relationship to the Church of Rome in Chapter 2.

10. These figures are from Herlihy (1961, 86), who notes that the ownership of arable land by the Church in southern France was somewhat lower (at 31 percent), and that the Church even owned 5 percent of the cultivated land in Spain, which was largely controlled by the Muslim Moors.

11. "Vatican" is used here to indicate the Pope's residence in Rome. The Vatican was a shrine until 1378 and used by the popes after 1418. Prior to this time, the popes usually lived at the Lateran, their Church as Bishops of Rome.

12. There are some exceptions to this statement, as we shall discuss later. Tithing, a tenth of every Christian's yearly income, was "required" in the Middle Ages. The Church collected substantial amounts, although collection was imperfect. Routine collection improved as the person lay on his death bed and left money for "tithings forgotten." In the main, the Church did employ various taxes, but not to the extent, nor with the same force of law, as contemporary governments.

13. The nature of the Church's chief product—assurances of eternal salvation—was a credence good and is discussed in Chapter 2. A credence good is one for which "quality" is not easily determined before or after purchase. Reputation of the supplier is the primary assurance of quality (see Darby and Karni 1973).

14. Henry C. Lea (1825–1909), a prominent church historian, advanced a similar argument in the nineteenth century, independently of Weber.

15. It is important to note, in fairness to Weber and Sombart, that they were both writing in the neoidealist tradition of social analysis where primary interest rests in the shaping of the individual and social consciousness—the Geist or the ethos of an era or a community—rather than on the impact of religious institutions on existing practices or economic institutions. As we will argue in Chapter 9, institutional progress or retardation of capitalism may be compatible with ideational repression by the Church.

PART ONE

The Industrial Organization
of the Medieval Church

CHAPTER TWO

The Medieval Church as a Multidivisional Firm

Introduction:
The Christian Church in the Middle Ages

For the first three centuries of its corporate existence, Christianity thrived as a kind of underground movement, loosely organized and highly decentralized. The formal character of the Catholic Church, the single institution that came to embody Christianity in its official capacity, emerged as a result of the Edict of Milan in A.D. 313.[1] In its early organizational structure, the primary authorities within the Church were bishops, who appointed and supervised priests at the parish level. By the time of Charlemagne, bishops were normally selected, or "invested," by monarchs of the countries in which their dioceses were located.

The pope was merely the Bishop of Rome over this early period and did not possess the central authority that has since come to be vested in the Vatican. Although he exercised limited authority, the Bishop of Rome was considered "first among equals," and was commonly selected by the emperor himself. Secular rulers sometimes intervened in the formulation of theological doctrine and ecclesiastical law in this fledgling Church (Berman 1983, 91). The majority of papal letters during this period merely approved what had already been decided at the local level. The pope did not have a bureaucratic organization that would have allowed him to monitor and control lower officials, nor did he have the power to enforce his decisions (Southern 1970, 96). In short, the early Church was closely controlled by secular governments.

The "investiture controversy"—the (sometimes acrimonious) debate over who had the right to appoint local or regional prelates—had its foundation in feudalism itself. Income-earning properties, most often land, were granted by lords in return for an oath of fealty by the vassal in an "investiture ceremony." This promise included some specific service or services in addition to loyalty to the lord. As in modern contracts, the transaction was based on reciprocity. Over time the fief became heritable and the subject of many disputes. These fundamental relationships along with feudal duties and appointment privileges demanded of the centralized Church set the stage for ongoing controversies between the Church and aristocratic and monarchical interests.

Secular and ecclesiastic governments actively competed for the right to appoint and oversee clerics and Church administrators between the ninth and twelfth centuries.[2] Despite attempts by some early popes, such as Nicholas I (856–867), to overturn the practice of lay or secular investiture, the papacy was unable to enforce its "independence" until the twelfth century, when Pope Gregory VII successfully wrested from the secular monarchs the authority to appoint bishops.[3] Following this "papal revolution" the pope emerged as the supreme judicial and legislative authority in western Europe. From the twelfth century on, all matters pertaining to the ownership, use, and disposal of Church properties came under his authority. All testamentary cases were adjudicable in Rome, meaning that in the long run, the pope determined the allocation of most property rights in Europe. Henceforth, bishops (who served as heads of regional franchises) were subject to papal approval before assuming their duties, and all monastic orders and new monasteries likewise required papal approval.

By granting vast new organizational powers to the pope, the Concordat of Worms (1122) marked a watershed in the economic history of the medieval Church. Although most historians attribute this development to the persistent reforming efforts of Hildebrand—a monk who later became Pope Gregory VII and provoked the confrontation with Henry IV that led to the Concordat—it is worthwhile to note that economic factors played a contributing role in the eventual resolution of competition between the papacy and the empire. Despite the fact that popes, bishops, and clerics had chafed under the overt authority of secular rulers for many centuries, previous attempts at securing papal independence were unsuccessful until certain significant constraints affecting the Church changed in its favor.

The first important change was steady improvement in communications within Europe. With the passage of time, roads became more numerous and better maintained. Vast parts of northern Europe were brought into direct communication through settlement. River and coastal shipping rapidly improved and travel time within Europe decreased. Large parts of the Low Countries and Germany came into the Christian orbit that were not part of the Roman sphere of influence. Scandinavian influences were not all violent and much contact was trade related. Consequently, the cost of controlling a unified hierarchical church from a central location dropped substantially.

The second factor is that European governments became progressively weaker and less able to protect Church assets and personnel during the tenth century. New military technologies (most notably the armored knight and the stone castle) strengthened the hands of local warlords and raised the cost of monarchical control. These local warlords often preyed on Church property rather than protect it. To the extent that the Church allowed lay investiture in exchange for protection by the monarch, the decline in quality of protective services caused the papacy to try to "renegotiate" the bargain. In addition, the diminished power of central governments made them more vulnerable to rebellion by clerics and other interest groups. Another factor that weakened European central governments was the rapid rise of towns and the expansion of trade that began in the middle of the eleventh century. As thousands of new towns emerged and trade rapidly expanded, central governments found themselves without the bureaucracy, technology, and resources necessary to exert effective authority over the growing commercial sector.

A third element that encouraged papal independence is that by the time of Gregory VII the Church and particular Church locales had acquired considerable economic muscle. Over the many centuries of its existence, the Church steadily accumulated property, so that by the eleventh century it owned, directly or indirectly, between 30 and 40 percent of the cultivated land in western Europe. Predatory attempts to gain control or possession of this property by local and central governments increased during the tenth and eleventh centuries (Herlihy 1961, 93). Thus the papal revolution was in large measure an attempt to establish once and for all the security of Church property. By the twelfth century, considerable movable wealth had also accumulated in Church coffers, mainly due to Church-encouraged bequests made by the faithful who believed that transfers of wealth to the Church upon their death would ease their way to heaven. In sum, the Church that confronted Henry IV in its fight for institutional autonomy was very rich, and this wealth permitted it to purchase political influence, if necessary, in order to secure its independence from secular authority.

Finally, the Church reacted to an increasingly chaotic political situation in Italy, which by this time had come to be the seat of its organizational control. Creeping anarchy in the Italian peninsula further threatened to weaken the Church's tenuous hold on its property and wealth, making a strong centralized papacy a better bulwark against attempts at political predation by local governments.[4]

The Corporate Structure of the Medieval Church

As the Church became increasingly centralized after the eleventh century, its internal organization began to assume many of the aspects of the modern corporation. There were, however, certain technical limits to its ability to centralize. Though improved, communications, even between the largest cities, were slow and unreliable by later standards. For example, transit time between Rome and London was, on average, about three weeks, and was both dangerous and expensive (Leighton 1972). Population was widely dispersed, making effective communication even more difficult. Under these conditions, a high degree of decentralization in decision-making was necessary.

These limitations imply that the medieval Church was not, and could not have been, a cohesive, monolithic corporate entity of the sort one finds in contemporary society. Nevertheless, the medieval Church was remarkably similar in other respects. Even today, many large corporations are organized in a manner that permits a high degree of decentralization in decisionmaking. The type of contemporary organization that the medieval Church resembled most is the multidivisional or "M-form" firm. According to Williamson (1975), this kind of firm is characterized by a central office that controls overall financial allocations and conducts strategic, long-range planning, but allows divisions (usually regional) a high degree of autonomy in day-to-day operations.[5] General Motors is a familiar example of this type of corporation, one that combines the advantages associated with centralization of planning and organization with the greater efficiency associated with local, decentralized operational management of corporate resources. Even though General Motors allows its Chevrolet, Pontiac, and Oldsmobile divisions a high degree of operational autonomy (presumably eliciting significant increases in internal efficiency as a result), it nevertheless retains a single, distinct corporate identity. So it was with the medieval Church.

Williamson (1975, 137) lists five characteristics and advantages of the M-form corporation:

1. The responsibility for operating decisions is assigned to operating divisions or (essentially self-contained) quasi-firms.
2. An elite staff is attached to the general office and performs both advisory and auditing functions. Both have the effect of securing greater control over operating division behavior.
3. The general office is principally concerned with strategic decisions involving planning, appraisal, and control, including the allocation of resources among the (competing) operating divisions.

4. The separation of the general office from operations provides general-office executives with the psychological commitment to be concerned with the overall performance of the organization, rather than become absorbed in the affairs of its functional parts.
5. The resulting structure displays both rationality and synergy; the whole is greater than the sum of its parts (i.e., more effective, more efficient).

Most important, the M-form firm functions as a "miniature capital market," assigning cash flows to high-yield uses (Williamson 1975, 143–48). The general office receives a portion of the revenues from each division's operations and redirects these resources for strategic purposes among the divisions, rewarding superior performance within the firm.

The medieval Catholic Church approximately followed this general pattern, establishing an organizational form that appears to have operated successfully for many centuries in a difficult political and technological environment. The Church assigned operating decisions to essentially self-contained operating divisions, or "quasi-firms," consisting of monastic orders, dioceses, and other subentities. The general office maintained an elite staff, the Curia (papal bureaucracy), that advised the pope in his role as chief executive officer (CEO) and also monitored the behavior of the clergy who were attached to the operating divisions (much in the manner of franchisees). The general office (Vatican) was the strategic director of Church policy. It planned, evaluated, and controlled Church functions and Church doctrines, without being directly "absorbed in the affairs of the functional parts." Finally, the Vatican allocated resources among competing divisions: for example, it could direct funding to special projects or grant tax exemptions to favored units, such as monasteries or specific "national" churches.

Unlike General Motors, the medieval Church did not separate its divisions in terms of physically differentiated products. Rather than producing Chevrolets, Pontiacs, and Oldsmobiles, the Church produced services that were all ostensibly aimed at the same religious goal—namely, spiritual salvation. Despite the lack of overt physical differentiation, however, the products generated by separate divisions of the Church were distinguishable. Monasteries catered to the spiritual needs of the more intellectually inclined and to higher-income individuals. At the same time, some monks also ministered to the poor, and some served as evangelists on the pagan frontiers of Europe. The cathedral chapters served inhabitants of larger urban areas and attracted pilgrims and other travelers who made monetary contributions to the cathedral.

The organizational Church also respected national boundaries to a considerable extent: the English Church offered religious services that were distinct from those offered by the French and Italian Churches, even though the basic liturgy and dogma were the same. Within national boundaries, moreover, individual dioceses acted quite independently in representing the One True Church.

Despite the fact that the internal structure of the medieval Church was less technocratic than the modern M-form firm, the lines of demarcation were effective and well understood by contemporaries. This was particularly true with respect to the monastic orders. Three of the most prominent orders of the day—the Benedictine, Cistercian, and Clunaic Orders—were each highly independent in their operations, each oriented toward different "missions."

Minor differences between the medieval Church and modern multidivisional corporations notwithstanding, the medieval Church definitely mirrored its contemporary counterparts in the complexity and sophistication of its diverse and geographically extensive operations. The Church had a transnational advantage at a time when governments and businesses were almost exclusively local in their planning and execution. Moreover, whereas governments and businesses planned along mainly short-run agendas, the Church had a distinctively long-run agenda. This difference is important because unlike medieval governments, the Church had strong incentives to pursue policies that were likely to have a positive effect on European economic development—and ultimately on its own revenues. The basic corporate structure of the medieval Church has been commonly overlooked in contemporary studies of firm structure. Williamson cites many government agencies (e.g., the U.S. Army) as early models of M-form organizations, whereas in reality the medieval Church was probably the first multidivisional enterprise that was not a government.

Powers of the Papacy and Its Chairman of the Board

Two generations before the Concordat of Worms (1122), which allowed the medieval Church to become a corporation independent of the state, Pope Nicholas II decreed that future popes should be selected by the College of Cardinals from among their own number. The College of Cardinals consists of high prelates who are appointed by the current or previous popes and who serve for life. In effect, this group served as the Board of Directors of the medieval Church, with full voting authority to elect a "Chairman of the Board."[6] The College of Cardinals was strongly insulated from outside political pressures and acted independently of lay rulers. Although secular rulers (especially the emperor) continued to exert intermittent pressures on papal selection, after 1059 the Church and the papacy rapidly gained autonomy.

Since the eleventh century, the pope of the Catholic Church has been elected to a lifetime tenure and installed according to Catholic dogma as the heir to St. Peter and the representative of Christ on earth. The "infallibility" provision, formalized only in the nineteenth century, is far less sweeping than the term implies, but it does lend an aura of "supreme" authority to the office.[7] Insofar as there is no official, established mechanism for removing a pope for malfeasance or other cause, the nature of the position might suggest that the pope is less a CEO in the modern sense than an absolute monarch. By the standards of conventional business practice this arrangement would be relatively inefficient because it places the corporate CEO beyond effective accountability to shareholders. But there is reason to believe that the stable security of tenure given to the pope was a reasonable adaptation to medieval circumstances, one that lowered certain transaction costs and provided limited incentives for efficient papal behavior.

The pope's stable security of tenure contributed to the efficiency of the medieval Church in several ways. First, it helped to insulate the Holy Office from secular political pressure (e.g., having to face reelection). Prior to the Concordat of Worms, secular rulers often appointed, and terminated, popes at will, for openly political reasons. Restricting the access of temporal rulers to such blatant "papal patronage" not only served to protect Church assets from governmental confiscation, it also raised the costs of rent seeking to potential "replacement" popes and their supporters. Lifetime tenure also reduced potential conflicts of interest on the part of popes, who felt no compulsion to transfer Church wealth to their own account in anticipation of providing for their retirement years. Likewise, lifetime tenure greatly reduced the pope's incentive to take bribes or yield to intimidation by outside forces. Finally, lifetime tenure also meant that the pope had an incentive to promote the long-run over the short-run interests of the Church—the Church itself was a permanent institution that did not have to yield to short-run expediency.[8]

Despite certain advantages, lifetime tenure was not absolute in the Middle Ages. Although tenure was normally quite secure, papal behavior was subject to an informal but effective constraint: the possibility of competition for the position by pretenders who were able to enlist the support of cardinals and bishops. In other words, the pope could technically, albeit unofficially, be fired and replaced. In the period between A.D. 1000 and 1450 twenty different "anti-popes" actively claimed the papal office. Most were elected by rebellious cardinals, and many with the support of various secular rulers. Some of the pretenders were actually more powerful than those legitimately elected. For instance, at the time of the First Crusade, anti-pope Clement III occupied the Vatican and commanded the support of most bishops in Germany and Italy. Partly for this reason, Pope Urban II called the First Crusade from Clermont in southern France. Furthermore, in an era when many officially elected popes held their office for less than a year, several anti-popes maintained power for extended periods. Elected as an anti-pope in 1080, Clement III remained in power until his death in 1100.

The process of competition between popes and anti-popes in the Middle Ages was, in many respects, analogous to proxy fights that take place today between various shareholder groups of a limited-liability corporation. Bishops, who held effective property rights in Church assets (with various limits on transferability), might elect an anti-pope to replace an existing pope if and when they felt their interests were threatened by papal policies, or when they became dissatisfied with the performance of a sitting pope. But only when the general clergy (those with grassroots control of Church assets) supported the usurper could the anti-pope hope to succeed in wresting away control. Failing such support, the pretender had no more prospect of deposing the "legitimate" pope than dissident stockholders who lack a voting majority have of replacing an unpopular CEO. Thus, even with lifetime tenure as official Church policy, a pope (theoretically at least) could not engage in significant malfeasance without running the risk of encouraging an outside challenger.

Another constraint against papal malfeasance came from canon law. Although the pope was ostensibly above the judgment of other prelates, the canonist Gratian maintained that he could be judged and potentially sanctioned by other Church officials "if he is caught deviating from the faith." This early wedge in canon law eventually led in the twelfth and thirteenth centuries to a full-blown theory of the deposition of popes on grounds of heresy. According to Berman (1983, 214), canonists of the period went so far as to conclude that the pope might be deposed if he acts contrary to the character, general welfare, or public order of the whole Church. Although no precise venue was specified by the Conciliar writers in such cases, it was presumed that adjudicatory authority was vested in the General Council of Bishops. Practically speaking, the canon law constraint did not become effective until the fifteenth century, when the Council of Constance deposed two rival popes and accepted the resignation of another (Berman 1983, 91).

Aside from the threat of competitive entry, the pope was subject to other constraints that impinged on his decisions. He could not legally sell off Church property nor commit heresy, for example, nor could he introduce new dogma at will (Berman 1983, 214). In other words, the principal "capital stock" of the church—its body of basic theological precepts—was protected against dissipation by certain rules that were the rough equivalents of constitutional guarantees. Also, the various subentities of the Church possessed legal rights of their own, and hence were not subject to the unconstrained whim of a pope. According to Tierney (1955), bishoprics, abbeys, colleges, chantries, guilds, religious orders, congregations, and confraternities all exercised substantial rights of self-government.

Ultimately, of course, the tenure of a pope was limited by his mortality. Although elected for life, the average age at election was high and the typical period of office brief. Among the sixty-three legitimate popes who held office between A.D. 1000 and 1400, the average term in office was about six years. Eighteen of the sixty-three popes served one year or less. During this same interval, two reigning popes resigned, and three were deposed (albeit by political maneuvers of the emperor rather than by internal censure and removal).

Although the powers of the pope as corporate CEO were sweeping, a word of caution is warranted about the notion of papal infallibility. This doctrine is sometimes mistakenly interpreted to mean that the pope was incapable of error. In reality, however, the intent was to establish the pope firmly as the preeminent head of the Church, rather than as a "second source" of divine revelation. As an organizational leader, the pope could personally err, but the real intent of the infallibility doctrine was that Divine Providence would always prevent the whole Church from being led astray. In his great compendium of canonical texts, Gratian listed several instances of popes who had sinned and erred in matters of faith, concluding that the pope's immunity from human judgment did not extend to matters involving the actual practice of religion. An individual pope was merely an imperfect symbol of the Church. According to Tierney (1972, 31–53), he did not possess unerring teaching power that would necessarily command unconditional obedience from the faithful.

In sum, the pope was not the absolute monarch of the medieval Church but rather the central decision maker, exalted by office, but subject to a variety of institutional and competitive constraints. His position was not unlike that of the modern CEO of a large corporation, whose authority is delimited by various constraints dictated by the peculiar economic environment in which the CEO operates.

Nature of Output in the Multidivisional Church

Given the complex and extensive nature of the medieval Church, it is necessary to distinguish between the institutional Church as a provider of public goods on the one hand and a supplier of private goods on the other. As a kind of surrogate government, the Church provided a number of social and public goods to medieval society. An entire system of law and courts

emerged under Church auspices that supplemented the ramshackle structure of governmental and legal institutions that existed during the Middle
Ages. At a time when governmental social welfare programs were virtually
nonexistent, the Church maintained an elaborate system of voluntary institutions and practices designed to aid the poor. The Church also organized and supported educational institutions, which provided the bulk of
human capital investment during the Middle Ages. Long before the emergence of strong nation-states, the Church used its transnational influence
to limit armed conflict among petty warlords who dominated the political
landscape of western Europe.

As important as these contributions were, it is not our intention to examine in detail the public-goods aspect of the medieval Church. Our focus
in this book is on the Church as a provider of private goods—that is, goods
and services that were "purchased" in something resembling a market context. In this market context, religion is by its nature a service industry. The
primary service supplied by the medieval Church to its customers was
information about and guidance toward the attainment of eternal salvation.
At issue here is not the veracity of the Church's theological claims, nor its
ability to guarantee the end-product, but rather the fact that whatever
knowledge consumers possessed in this regard was provided entirely and
exclusively by the Church. An important aspect of this service concerned
the afterlife: the idea that the soul continues to exist for all eternity after
the death of the body. To a medieval Christian, one's existence on earth
was a tiny part of "life"—while the average person might live a mere forty
or fifty years in the earthly realm, the soul's existence in heaven or hell would
be forever. Each Christian therefore looked to the Church for advice and
guidance on actions required to get to heaven. In this connection, the clergy
provided a vital kind of "brokerage" service for the faithful.

Most people in medieval Christendom accepted the fact that the Church
of Rome had a major influence over the disposition of their immortal souls—
in other words, whether they went to heaven or hell. This belief is crucial
to understanding the medieval Church as an economic organization. By
virtue of this fact the Church was the monopoly provider of a pure credence good. The credibility of Church courts, the validity of canon law,
the acceptance of the Church as divinely sanctioned arbiter of earthly disputes, and the ultimate trust in the Church's various commercial commit-
ments, all derived from the credibility of the religious doctrines promul-
gated by the Church of Rome.

Some characteristics of this credence good are unique, but many others
share the traits of ordinary, commonly marketed services. For example,
medicine is a credence good insofar as the average patient lacks the spe-
cialized knowledge required for expert evaluation of the quality of medical

care received. The credibility of the physician (usually based on reputation, training, or possession of a professional license) is the patient's primary indicator of quality. Likewise, many automobile purchasers lack the expertise to ably evaluate the mechanical reliability of their proposed purchase, so they rely on the reputation of the manufacturer or dealer in making their decision. So, too, the medieval Church relied on its reputation to assure the quality of its services. Insofar as it dealt in the afterlife, however, it could not elicit the usual testimonials on its behalf from satisfied customers. Nevertheless, by most other criteria, it dealt with an extreme case of a rather common economic problem.

Despite some rather obvious limitations—the customer could not take salvation for a test drive, nor get a sneak preview of heaven (or hell) and return to tell about it—some facts of medieval life make a compelling argument for treatment of the Church's product as a credence good. During medieval times (and earlier) the distinction between the worldly and the spiritual was often blurred. For example, the belief in miracles was very widespread. In the minds of the faithful, miracles constituted credible evidence of divine intervention. Likewise, the intercession of saints in the daily affairs of men was regarded as a way in which God directly affected the lives of believers. In other words, to the extent that theology was a kind of "technology" through which affairs in the physical world were manipulable, interpretations of phenomena without otherwise apparent explanation were regarded as "evidence" for the efficacy of the divine.

Just as today's consumer can evaluate the quality-related claims of an automobile by driving it or by hiring a mechanic to inspect it, a medieval Christian could evaluate claims by a parish priest about the powers of God and the saints by monitoring for "miracles" and other manifestations of the efficacy of religion. In contrast to ordinary consumer decisions about tangible goods and services made in the modern economy, the evaluation of quality claims in the case of medieval religion involved a process of mutual determination. The basis of acceptable evidence for divine intervention was founded partially on preexisting theological beliefs.

In expounding the philosophy of communism, Marx and Engels denounced religion as an implicit conspiracy by the ruling class to defuse potential revolutionary awareness among the masses. Marx's characterization of religion as "the opiate of the masses" presents, like much of his writings, a glimmer of insight beneath a mound of purple prose. Karl Popper and others have dismissed as unworkable the idea that organized religion is a massive conspiracy directed by some nebulous ruling class. But the suggestion that religious beliefs affect the subjective perceptions of believing individuals, thereby providing them with a utility-enhancing experience, has merit. In a narrow sense, religious belief is indeed analo-

gous to the use of certain drugs: it generates an altered state of consciousness that has net pleasurable consequences.[9] Adherents of religious beliefs
usually insist precisely on this point: an individual's acceptance of religious
doctrines concerning the nature of the divine or the supernatural modifies
that individual's experience of the world. Thus, the analogy to using drugs
is telling in a certain sense.

When economists observe rational individuals voluntarily engaging in
some activity or consuming some good, they assume that those individuals expect to achieve a higher level of utility by their actions or else they
would behave otherwise. It also seems self-evident that if said individuals
continue to behave in like manner—that is, engage in repeat transactions
aimed at consuming the same good—it can be concluded that those persons found their *ex post* gratifications to have met their *ex ante* expectations.
If this economic rationale applies to the consumption of ice cream, auto-
mobiles, and television programs, it logically should also apply to the consumption of religion. Axiomatically, people engage in religious pursuits
because such actions increase their net utility.

There would be no need to belabor this seemingly obvious principle
except for the fact that some modern historians and commentators have
often insinuated that the Church reduced net social welfare by impeding
the advance of science, encouraging superstition, and dissipating surplus
productive resources through wasteful expenditures on cathedrals, shrines,
and so forth.[10] This view overlooks the utility-enhancing nature of religious
practice and Church membership. It is as if we were to criticize spending
by modern consumers at Disneyland by bemoaning the lost opportunities
for utilizing the same funds to repair roads or advance new medical cures.
Even granting the dubious anti-clerical assumptions often made by critics
of the Church (e.g., the inhibition of science), Roman Catholicism more
than likely generated huge increases in the utility of many religious consumers, and, in all likelihood, corresponding gains in consumers' surplus.

As an extensive and pervasive monopolist in medieval society, the
Church held a major advantage as producer of the credence good of salvation, which included intercession with God. The monopoly status of the
Church, coupled with its great temporal power, reinforced the credibility
of its claims concerning the quality of its nontestable product. The Church
could convincingly maintain that its temporal position was testament to
the veracity of its religious claims. Thus, aspiring entrants to the medieval
religious market faced a daunting task: convincing their potential customers that the alternative product they offered was more reliable than that
already available from an institution endorsed by an Omnipotent God.
Obviously, as the Protestant Reformation eventually revealed, this obstacle
was not insurmountable. But before losing market share to new entrants,

the Church had persistently and successfully erected and maintained "barriers to entry" for centuries.

Market Structure of the Medieval Religion "Industry"

The medieval Church solidified its monopoly position by defining competing entrants (heretics) as criminals to be either imprisoned or executed. If successful in its "prosecution," the personal wealth of a dissenting member or a heathen challenger was subject to confiscation by the Church. Often the Church enlisted the authority of secular officials in this regard, and sometimes shared the spoils. The Church even orchestrated massive military expeditions (Chapter 7) in order to prevent the spread of Islam, a competing religion. Clearly, the One True Church strove for monopoly power in the theological marketplace, but it also enlisted the aid of secular governments to systematically exclude competitors.[11]

The medieval Church was not monolithic in the strictest sense. It consisted of a confederated group of cooperating branches that shared common theological premises and goals. The various branches often behaved in a highly autonomous manner. On the macro level, historians refer to the English Church and the Church of Rome as the "Two Churches" as though to underscore the extreme independence of the former. On the micro level, the relatively high mobility of peasants in medieval Europe implies a substantial amount of migration across parishes, with the resulting "Tiebout effects" restraining the ability of priests and other clerics to act as pure monopolists.

To assert a high degree of mobility in medieval society is in many respects to go against conventional wisdom. Yet, despite a common perception that the Middle Ages were stagnant and resources immobile, recent scholarship asserts that geographic mobility—as opposed to social mobility—was substantial. Peasants often left their native domain to move elsewhere. It was possible to escape a particular serf relationship with one lord for a better deal with another. Such movements were often across parish boundaries. After the Black Death of the mid-fourteenth century, the degree of peasant mobility increased markedly, leading secular governments to enact legislation aimed at protecting wealthy landowners against the upward pressure on wages induced by greater labor mobility (e.g., the 1363 Statute of Labourers in England). The Church itself tried to limit mobility by a ruling of the Third Lateran Council that prohibited cross-parish movement. These attempts were mostly unsuccessful, however, thereby leaving intact an effective constraint to monopoly power at the parish level.

Conditions among local church parishes provided another kind of restraint against abuse of monopoly power. Tithes paid by parishioners constituted a small fraction of corporate Church revenue but represented the major portion of a local priest's income. Inasmuch as the parish priest had essentially no enforcement power against nonpayers (priests were forbidden to withhold sacraments for nonpayment), they had to resort to satisfying the parishioners in order to encourage voluntary compliance. Although in theory a priest could sue for unpaid tithes in ecclesiastical court, in practice this remedy was rarely effective.

In sum, the medieval Church was not an unbridled monopoly in the market for religion, nor did its market power come directly or indirectly from government, as is most often the case with contemporary monopolies. Medieval governments were generally weak, disorganized, and largely unable to provide monopoly rents to special interest groups. The effective monopoly power of the Church came mainly from its unique position in a rather unique market. Even so, it faced a number of practical constraints. These institutional constraints limited the economic power of the medieval Church somewhat, but the fact remains that the "owner-operators" of the medieval Church clearly benefited from a host of effective restrictions on competitive entry. As a result, the Church was able to consolidate its wealth and power over many centuries, reaching its peak during the late Middle Ages.

A common explanation for increasing concentration in an industry is the superior efficiency of whichever firm occupies the dominant position. Contemporary firms that operate efficiently attract consumers from other firms, and thereby tend to expand operations and market share. The medieval Church achieved its position of market leadership, and the accompanying confidence of its customers in the reliability of its "product," in part by efficiently satisfying the demands of its consumers. By the same token, once it became less responsive and efficient, it began to lose market share to upstart rivals, such as the Protestant sects.

Residual Claimancy and Clerical Opportunism

Given the make-up of the medieval Church, there were ample opportunities for managerial rent seeking and X-inefficiency. Successful monitoring and control of managerial employees to prevent malfeasance involves detecting and punishing undesirable behavior. From the perspective of the Vatican, an example of rent seeking would include cases where a Church official failed to report income accurately to Rome, thereby "cheating" on the payment of taxes. An example of X-inefficiency would include cases where a bishop shirked his ecclesiastic duties or responsibilities, thereby damaging the reputation of the institutional Church. The papacy utilized a variety of mechanisms to minimize intraorganizational malfeasance, including "farming" the collection of clerical taxes to private contractors. However, the primary monitoring and control mechanisms of the medieval Church involved the use of residual-claimancy arrangements. The Church attempted to structure property rights to residual streams of income within the organization in a manner that would provide incentives to its agents to behave efficiently in conformance with the organization's goals.[12]

These internally structured property rights were, however, highly attenuated. Although monks, priests, and bishops acted as stewards of certain assets, they did not formally "own" the resources under their supervision. These resources officially belonged to the corporate Church. Church officials charged with the responsibility of managing Church assets were prohibited from selling or otherwise transfering ownership of those assets. This restriction meant that Church property was, in effect, common property. Thus, the internal property-rights assignment did not provide incentives for officials to act efficiently in the management of those assets. The situation regarding the medieval Church was roughly comparable to that involving the bureaucratic management of federal lands in the United States.

The problem of management of "common-pool" assets within the medieval Church was nevertheless amenable to certain corrective measures. Consider the modern corporate analogue to the transnational medieval Church. Contemporary firms hire managers to monitor and operate their productive assets without assigning formal ownership rights to those managers, and the subsequent arrangements can operate quite efficiently. The mere fact that a medieval bishop could not legally transfer ownership of assets under his supervision without papal approval did not necessarily preclude the possibility of an efficient structure of internal decisionmaking. Modern firms utilize similarly structured residual-claimancy arrangements to provide efficient incentives that otherwise would be absent. For example, managers are often remunerated in the form of stock options that provide them with a partial claim on the residual value that they add to the firm. These and other perquisites are designed to reward managerial employees, whose executive behavior increases the value of the firm, and to discourage shirking and other forms of malfeasance. Although stock options, as such, were obviously unavailable to the medieval Church, other residual-claimancy arrangements were employed that functioned in the same manner.

In particular, rather than place its cleric-managers on salary, the medieval Church assigned them temporary rights to portions of revenue flows from common-pool assets under their supervision. This was the case with practically all clerics outside the papal bureaucracy. Such residuals were termed "benefices," in the vernacular of the medieval Church, and they constituted a major element of internal control against malfeasance. As with all ecclesiastic administration, the system operated along divisional lines. Bishops, who controlled the finances of their dioceses, granted benefices to the priests under their supervision, and in turn were granted benefices by the pope. The auditing function was supplied by the papal bank (*camera*), which routinely hired bankers and other private parties as monitors.

A specific form of malfeasance that became increasingly troublesome to the papal bureaucracy during the Middle Ages was the practice of simony, that is, the outright sale of Church offices. Following the terminology proposed by Rodes (1977, 46), there were basically two different kinds of simony. Payment for clerical services—as one would pay for professional services today—constituted *professional* simony. Although many writers have persisted in labeling this practice simony and declaiming it as mortal sin, the practice of priests accepting fees was both common and long-standing (from the earliest days of the Church). Indeed, this form of compensation had much to recommend it, insofar as it gave customers the wherewithal to reward efficient, and discourage inferior, clerical services. Moreover, the practice did not require the papal bureaucracy to erect a costly, centralized financial apparatus. Although the Church hierarchy periodically railed against the practice, it eventually settled for regulation (tacit approval) rather than prohibition (condemnation) of professional simony. The Fourth Lateran Council (1215) imposed limits on the amount of fees that could be collected and simultaneously outlawed priestly "boycotts." (It forbade priests from withholding services in order to exact payment.) Under the regulations imposed, priests were to perform services as required and seek legal remedies (i.e., sue in ecclesiastic courts) in the event of nonpayment. The Church's regulatory response was akin to that employed by contemporary state public service commissions invoking the common carrier argument, whereby customers have a right to be served at a certain price. Insofar as suits of this nature were common occurrences in the Middle Ages, it might also be noted that the described regulatory response may have inflated the demand for the services (and fees) of the ecclesiastic courts.

By contrast, *proprietary* simony was unambiguously denounced by Church officials as mortal sin and made the target of persistent reforms. This practice involved the purchase and sale of all manner of Church assets, including land, offices, relics, and consecrated vessels. Beginning with the papacy of Gregory VII, the Church waged a vigorous campaign against proprietary simony, albeit with mixed results. Unlike professional simony, proprietary simony did not reward efficient behavior. Rather, it was a pure drain on Church resources, in short, theft of Church property. Some cases involved simple theft, such as the sale of a blessed relic on the open market. Other cases were more complicated, such as the sale by a presiding bishop of his holy office to a noncleric. In medieval society, proprietary simony was difficult to detect and even more difficult to prove. Due to the high cost of monitoring, reformers sought a total prohibition of the practice as the most cost-effective way to reduce this kind of malfeasance. If a cleric was caught selling an office (or if the holder of an office was determined to have purchased it), the Church imposed heavy penalties, including excommunication, which carried serious legal consequences in the Middle Ages.

Other controls against employee malfeasance imposed by the medieval Church were more subtle, but on closer examination can be seen to have economic consequences. For example, the requirement of clerical celibacy reduced the tendency to appropriate assets that could be transferred to one's heirs. During the early Middle Ages, benefices were often hereditary and came to be "owned" by families for long periods of time. In the legal environment of medieval Europe, Church sanctions against this practice were difficult and costly to enforce, so the Church found it expedient to legislate mandatory celibacy as a means to minimize the loss of its assets through inheritance.[13]

The Financial Economy of the Medieval Church

As an M-form firm, the medieval Church was characterized by a central office that makes strategic financial and product planning decisions but allows considerable degree of autonomy to its regional divisions in everyday affairs. The medieval fiscal documents of the Vatican, many of which have become available only in this century, as well as the circumstances of its elaborate financial administration and collection apparatus (Lunt 1934, 1939) are broadly consistent with this view. As the medieval Church's spiritual and temporal power grew, so did its financial clout. This gave rise to new financial institutions within the M-form church that were capable of collecting revenues, enforcing franchise restrictions, and underwriting expansion.

As a corporate entity in the medieval economy, the Church controlled enormous wealth. Its sources of revenue included tithes, land rents, donations, bequests, fees charged for judicial services, proceeds from the sale of indulgences, and income derived from the monastic production and marketing of agricultural produce. Bishops themselves often owned large estates. The pope was the ruler of a major portion of Italy known as the Papal States, deriving revenue from his subjects in the same fashion as other secular rulers. Periodically, the Church succeeded in securing direct transfers of (secular) governmental tax revenues, particularly for the ostensible purpose of funding the Crusades (Chapter 7). The Church also controlled most of the liquid capital in the West, and with the exception of Byzantium in the early Middle Ages, its annual income greatly exceeded the annual revenues of any government in Europe.

The collection of revenues by the papacy was centralized in the office of the *camera*, an office that originally administered the pope's personal household but took on more sophisticated functions as the Church's wealth increased. From the latter part of the twelfth century through the end of the Middle Ages, the *camera* administered papal finances. The director of this office (the *camerarius*) was appointed by the pope and advised by a College of Clerks. The *camera* functioned both as a bank and as a court of law—with civil and criminal jurisdiction over papal debtors and all matters affecting papal finance. Jurisdiction of the *camera* over clerical usurers, for example, is clearly established by documents in the Vatican archives (Lunt 1934, 1:179–80). To administer its twofold mission as bank and court, the *camera* enlisted all manner of functionaries, including scribes, notaries, tax collectors, and lawyers. As a court, it was empowered to enforce its decisions by use of excommunication and imprisonment.

Since the majority of debtors subject to cameral court jurisdiction were clerics delinquent in their payments of fees to the Vatican, excommunication was a particularly effective enforcement mechanism. An excommunicated cleric was shut off from any and all service-related income until absolved. The relative efficiency of cameral courts led them to acquire jurisdiction gradually over ordinary civil suits involving contracts outside the papacy as well as within. This expanded jurisdiction of papal courts is analogous to the evolution of the English Court of Exchequer during the same period. As a bank, the *camera* received and disbursed funds, and negotiated loans. Sometimes the papacy was a lender and sometimes a borrower (despite clear cut prohibitions against usury). Figure 1 presents a schematic of the fiscal network of the medieval papacy.

The annual sums collected by the *camera* rivaled those received by the larger contemporaneous governments, such as Byzantium. During the pontificate of John XXII, for example, the *camera* collected about 228,000 florins per year. These revenues fluctuated up and down, but near the end of the fifteenth century, on the eve of the Protestant Reformation, the *camera* took in 390,000 florins per annum. Like every large bureaucracy, over time the Church developed an insatiable appetite for revenue. In response, it developed a complex fiscal system consisting of all manner of voluntary and involuntary payments. Given the nature of its organizational framework, revenues collected by the Church were designated for certain divisional levels. At the local level, the primary source of income for clerics was donations by the faithful, which represented an explicit exchange of money for clerical services rendered.

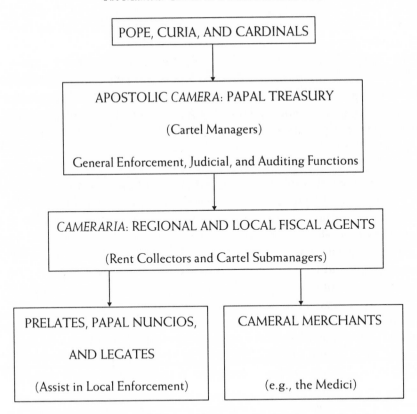

Figure 1 An organizational diagram depicting the fiscal network of the medieval church.

The two major forms of donation were bequests and tithes. Of these, the bequest was the largest source of income. Through testamentary means the Church became the single largest landowner in western Europe during the Middle Ages. The importance of bequests to the Church is affirmed by the explicit allocation of Church resources to administering testamentary law, as such testamentary cases constituted the bulk of litigation administered by ecclesiastic courts. Whether conceived on one's deathbed or planned long in advance, such transfers of assets to the medieval Church were inherently insulated from suspicion of coercion. Therefore, a bequest constituted prima facie evidence of the donor's reliance on the veracity of the Church's teaching.

The second largest source of income to local clerics was the tithe. But as noted earlier, collection of tithes was problematic because local priests had no enforcement mechanisms to force compliance. Nonpayers were not easily coerced in this world, but since failure to contribute was a sin, they were subject to sanctions in the afterlife. How effective these sanctions were in forcing compliance depended in large part on the individual's elasticity of demand for heaven. Thus, the parochial tithe amounted to a kind of monopoly price for consolation in this world and guidance to the next. Originally considered "spontaneous and voluntary" (Boyd 1952, 35), tithes became increasingly associated with the seignorial regime after the eighth century. Under lay control, tithes became taxes, the payment of which was diligently enforced. Eventually, lay tithes lost their connection to religious obligation and service. During the period of Gregorian Reforms, the Church tried to recapture the revenues and property transfers associated with the tithe, but had only limited success. Thus, throughout the remainder of the Middle Ages, a large proportion of what were called tithes continued to represent a kind of tax payment to feudal authorities.

Although tithes were earmarked as local income for the parish priests, each parish was expected to pay fees to the Vatican based on its income. In effect, the Church levied franchise fees on its local parishes. Monasteries were also treated as franchisees and were expected to pay fees in relation to their tithe income. Many monasteries negotiated elaborate tithe exemptions from the papacy in exchange for their support of papal policy. It appears from (incomplete) papal financial records that popes carefully calculated the elasticity of monastic income with respect to tax rates and pursued a policy of revenue maximization from this source. They were not averse to monastic competition for papal favor in the pursuit of tax exemptions because such rivalry was viewed as an efficient means to generate fervor for papal directives. In the context of the M-form Church, the papacy's willingness to grant differential tax exemptions demonstrates the strategic transfer of resources to different divisions or subunits of control.

Like its general operations, the finances of the Church were highly decentralized. Only a relatively small portion of the total revenues that flowed to the parish, monastery, or diocese was transferred to the pope, and the pope himself, as combination CEO and chairman of the board, exerted little control over day-to-day financial operations. Profits from local or divisional operations were mostly retained at that level. Still, the pope had great directorial powers and made strategic decisions to reward superior performance on the part of particular divisions.

The apostolic *camera* employed regional and local fiscal agents—papal legates and nuncios—as enforcers to collect rents and revenues and to repatriate taxes and tithes to the home office in Rome. These agents were loosely analogous in duties and responsibilities to Colbert's *intendants* in mercantilist France (Ekelund and Tollison 1981, 87–90). They transferred papal revenues through a network of cameral merchants, or papal bankers, such as the Medici (De Roover 1948b). These merchant bankers, in turn, allowed the *camera* overdraft privileges in anticipation of revenues. According to cameral records in the Vatican archives, the Medici were creditors of the *camera* in 1473 to the extent of 62,918 florins (Muntz 1878–1882, 63–64), a sum that represented about 20 percent of that year's papal revenues, equivalent to almost $3.3 million in today's money.[14] Jordan (1909, 119–27) reports that the cameral banking firms were so closely associated with the papacy that their welfare was intrinsically tied to that of the Church.

An interesting example of this nexus was the Societas Aluminum, a cartel arrangement between the Holy See and the Medici Bank. Although this incident does not conclusively prove that the medieval Church acted in monopoly fashion regarding salvation, it presents yet another instance of the clash of economic interests with spiritual (i.e., public) interests within the Church's sphere of influence. The Church owned the Tolfa alum mines near Civitavecchia in the papal states. In the Middle Ages alum was an essential ingredient used to fix the dyes in textiles. Before the discovery of rich deposits at Tolfa, high-quality alum was produced mainly by the Turks, who exacted high prices. Within a decade of the new discovery in 1459 (only the third such high-grade mine in Christendom), the apostolic *camera* made the Medici its exclusive agent to oversee the production and distribution of alum.[15]

From the time it entered the papal cartel in 1466, the Medici set out systematically to eliminate all competition. They first suppressed production at Volterra, which was under Florentine rule. When the citizens of that region objected to the loss of income and threatened to break away from Florentine authority, Lorenzo de Medici used his political influence to quell the revolt, which was accomplished by military siege. Next, the papacy joined the Medici's attempt to eliminate Turkish competition. The pope earmarked income from the Tolfa mines for the crusade against the Turks and the Hussite heretics. He also forbade, under threat of ecclesiastic censure, the importation of Turkish alum into Christian territory. Meanwhile, the Curia sought to establish territorial rights among the main alum vendors and to restrict output. In 1469 the Curia reached an accord with Bartolomeo Giorgio, the most important dealer, that gave him the exclusive right to sell papal alum in Venetia, Lombardy, Romagna, southern Germany, and Austria. In return for this concession, Giorgio agreed to take an annual quota of 6,000 *cantari* of papal alum and to exclude Turkish alum from the Venetian market. The final step was to abolish competition from the Ischia mines in the kingdom of Naples. The Medici accomplished this through a long-term contract with the mine owners that set prices, established quotas, and divided the profits between the two remaining producers.

The medieval Church's exploitation of its alum cartel affords merely one glimpse of how the apostolic *camera* collected rents directly and indirectly, including "cartel farming."[16] Given the fiscal requirements of the medieval Church, the evolution of the *camera* was both necessary and predictable, but it eventually became the focal point for institutional practices that resemble rent seeking.

Conclusion

The medieval Catholic Church resembled a modern firm in several key aspects.

- It produced and sold a product in the form of a service valued by a large segment of the world's population.
- It established effective spans of control by organizing along divisional lines.
- It adopted an internal structure that established incentives for efficient behavior on the part of the clergy and maintained control through legal and financial means.
- It was organized in a complex, sophisticated manner whereby long-term, strategic policy was centralized but authority over day-to-day decisionmaking was decentralized.
- Within this structure a highly organized revenue-collecting mechanism—the *camera*—facilitated downstream financial collections.

In many respects, the medieval Church fit the pattern of a modern M-form corporation. The problem of controlling the behavior of far-flung agents so that firm revenues are maximized is not new, and the organizational structure of the medieval Church is an example of how an institution dealt with this problem. This conclusion should not surprise anyone, least of all the proponents of the idea that the M-form firm is a modern concept.

NOTES

1. The Edict of Milan was a formal act of toleration issued by the coemperors Constantine and Licinius, each sympathetic to monotheism. The imperial ordinance read, in part, that "we decided to establish rules by which respect and reverence for the Deity would be secured, i.e., to give the Christians and all others liberty to follow whatever form of worship they chose, so that whatsoever divine and heavenly powers exist might be enabled to show favor to us and to all who live under our authority" (quoted in Eusebius 1984, 402). Although the two emperors did not exactly follow their own adjurations to tolerance, the notion of a state religion ended with the Edict and the Church became the recognized legal holder of property.

2. The details of the investiture controversy are not analyzed here in an economic perspective, but the struggles between the papacy and German, English, and French monarchs (especially the critical disputes between King Henry IV and Pope Gregory VII) are given excellent treatment in Blumenthal (1988).

3. This power was established in England and Normandy by the Concordat of Beck (1107), but not recognized by the Emperor until the Concordat of Worms in 1122 (see Berman 1983, 97).

4. We do not wish to minimize the impact of the "spiritual revival" of the Church in the eleventh century, as emphasized in much medieval literature. The Cluniac reform movement led to renewal of monastic institutions which, indirectly at least, led to new Church investments. Monastic reform meant a revision of liturgy and, among other things, Church building and a flowering of Romanesque architecture. Medievalists also credit the popular enthusiasm for the First Crusade to the spiritual revival of the Cluniac movement. While spiritual values undoubtedly played a role, we emphasize the economic interests of the Church in providing a monastic movement. The monastic movement itself had enormous economic implications (see Chapter 3 for a "case study" of the Cistercian development). In addition, the movement was a practical and doctrinal defense against heresy (Chapter 4). We, of course, do not deny that spiritual motivations were intertwined with economic goals.

5. Prior to Williamson, Chandler (1966, 1977) argued that the invention of the multidivisional firm in the early 1920s in the United States was a major organizational innovation. More recent research (Anderson et al. 1983) has shown that from its founding in 1600, the English East India Company employed the principles underlying the multidivisional M-form firm. As is obvious from the discussion in this chapter, the medieval Roman Catholic Church was organized along these lines even earlier than the East India Company.

6. A clear distinction must be made between the Curia, a papally appointed administrative body located in Rome, and the College of Cardinals. The College of Cardinals, also appointed by the pope, is composed of bishops who have been honored as "Princes of the Church"—a high honor carrying duties to the papacy, including the election of popes (The rank of bishop is the highest administrative rank of church prelates—the pope is the "Bishop of Rome.") Cardinals are geographically disbursed in sees located throughout the world. The Curia is the administrative arm of the papacy tending to the worldwide administration of Church rules, holy orders, doctrine, censorship, and many other matters relating to day-to-day Church regulation. Some but not all members of the Curial staff are also cardinals. However, both the College of Cardinals (meeting in synods or other tribunals such as Vatican Councils along with other bishops) and the Curia have immense power over the many elements of Church policy. Until it was abolished by Pope Paul VI in this century, for example, an office in the Curia dealt with direct censorship of books and other materials, including an "Index" of works forbidden to members under threat of serious sin.

7. The doctrine of papal infallibility as to matters of faith and morals was formally established by the First Vatican Council of 1870. Prior to that time, how-

ever, considerable power was claimed through the doctrine of the Petrine Succession, that is, the pope as the successor to St. Peter, who was charged, according to Scripture, to establish Christ's Church on earth. The *idea* of infallibility and great moral authority was attached to the pope long before the formal doctrine was pronounced. It remains so attached, although the only official invocation of the doctrine of papal infallibility occurred in 1950, when Pius XII proclaimed that the Virgin Mary was "assumed" bodily into heaven—the doctrine of the assumption.

8. Other factors contribute to the plausibility of a long-run agenda for the Church in addition to lifetime tenure of the pope. Although the Church was not a publicly traded corporation (and appears not to have residual claimants), certain institutional features contributed, in all likelihood, to a long-run agenda. The nature of the product sold—assurances of eternal salvation—required the maintenance of the Church as a bond for credence. Furthermore, over certain periods at least, a de facto inheritability of high office (e.g., positions of prominent families, such as the Medici, distributed through Church hierarchy) might have achieved effective residual claimancy.

9. By this statement we merely mean to advance a useful analogy, not to demean religion in any way.

10. Many medievalists appear to believe, however, that the Church-supported culture was enriching to the period. Some concentrate on how society disposes of "surplus profits" and argue that the dearth of scientific and technological outlets for funds resulted in other productions, e.g., cathedral building. In Chapter 9 we evaluate the effects of Church institutions and institutional change on the development of capitalism, finding some of them to be clearly positive.

11. The one major exception was Judaism. Despite many forms of persecution leveled at Jews throughout the Middle Ages, the Catholic Church neither labeled them as heretics or refused to accept Jews as fellow "People of the Book" (i.e., the Bible). The key consideration allowing for religious tolerance in this case seems to have been that Judaism was not evangelical. Since it did not actively seek converts, the Roman Catholic Church did not consider Judaism a competitor intent on poaching its members.

12. Adam Smith's contribution to the economics of religion proceeds precisely to this point. In a sustained discussion "Of the Expense of the Institutions for the Instruction of People of All Ages," Smith (1776, 740–68) analyzes the implications of the structure of the religious marketplace on the incentives faced by clerics relevant to their diligence as providers of religious services. Even in the case of clerics, he argues, material rewards for effective industry tend to bring forth more vigorous effort. Clerics in the employ of religious organizations holding state monopoly franchises tend to be rewarded less for their effective instructional efforts and more for their success in the game of bureaucratic politics. For Smith, monopoly religion tended to mean state-sponsored monopoly religion. Free competition in the supply of religious services led to a much improved level of service quality provided by clergy simply because those preachers constantly needed to persuade their members to stay within their congregation.

The Church of Rome was not the worst example to Smith of the incentive failures characteristic of state-sponsored religious monopoly. The medieval Church *did* benefit from the support of secular governments (e.g., in supporting Church efforts to sanction heretics). But, according to Smith, in the Church of Rome "the industry and zeal of the inferior clergy are kept more alive by the powerful motive of self-interest than perhaps any established [that is, state-sponsored] Protestant church." This was due to the fact that a considerable proportion of the Catholic clergy depended for much of its income on "voluntary oblations," by which Smith meant the free contributions from parishioners. Given this connection between reward and performance, the incentive problem Smith associated with religious monopoly was reduced in severity, if not actually eliminated, by the organization of the Catholic Church.

13. We do not focus on the issue of priestly celibacy in this book, but we do discuss a possible motive for the transition from married priests to a celibate clergy in Chapter 5 on marriage regulation.

14. In 1471, Pope Paul II (1464–1471) estimated that his annual revenues were not more than 200,000 florins. The alum cartel brought in an additional 100,000 florins (Pastor 1949, 4:261–63; 4:498). This was a typical year for papal revenues, so it may be inferred that revenues in 1473 were about 300,000 florins, more or less. In 1252, the precious metal content of the Florentine gold florentine was set at 3.55 grams or 0.114135 ounces of pure gold (Lane and Mueller 1985, 54).

15. The terms of the papal contract, executed in 1466, were as follows: (1) the Medici became partners in the Societas Aluminum; (2) they took over operation of the mines and the sale of its entire output; (3) the Medici agreed to pay a royalty of two ducats to the apostolic *camera* for each *cantaro* of alum taken from the papal warehouses at Civitavecchia; (4) all the alum mined at Tolfa was to be stored in those warehouses in order to prevent any leakage to the detriment of the papal treasury; (5) nothing could be taken from the warehouses except in the presence of a papal official; (6) in addition to the royalty, the apostolic *camera* was to receive two-thirds of all extra profits (Zippel 1907; De Roover 1948b, 47).

16. De Roover (1948b, 49) concluded:

It is difficult to deny that the formation of the alum cartel was inconsistent with the teachings of the Church. The canonist writers [especially San Antonino, San Bernadino, and Cardinal Cajetan] were outspoken in their condemnation of monopoly. They knew very well that a monopolist restricts output and raises price "for his own private gain and benefit" and "in prejudice of the public." The papacy was not unaware of the discrepancy between its policy in the matter of the alum cartel and the doctrines professed by the church in the matter of social ethics. The curia condoned its policy with regard to the alum cartel on the questionable principle that the end justifies the means.

Monasteries as Agents of the Corporate Church

Introduction: The Nature of the Medieval Monastery

The medieval monastery was a complex organization of production and distribution set within the more elaborate corporate structure of the institutional Christian Church. Monasteries were conspicuous in the local economies where they played a dual role as retail distributors of the assurance of eternal salvation and as producers of agricultural products. In the corporate structure of Christendom the medieval monastery operated as a (downstream) franchised firm, receiving quality assurance and name-brand recognition from the Church of Rome in return for certain payments (upstream).

In keeping with the original concept of the monastery as a refuge from worldly concerns and a place where spiritual matters dominated daily life, medieval monasteries were regulated by a constitution or set of internal rules. One of the most widespread constitutions was the Rule of St. Benedict that applied to both the Benedictine and Cistercian Orders. It entailed specific guidelines that controlled the organization and operation of monasteries and regulated the daily activities of the monks.[1]

We focus in this chapter on one particular type of monastic "firm": the Cistercian Order.[2] The Cistercians were a "reformed" offshoot of the Benedictine Order and were championed by a group of "purists" who advocated strict adherence to the Rule. The first Cistercian monastery was established at Molesme in 1075 and was led by St. Robert, formerly the abbot of St. Michel de Tonnerre (Knowles 1963, 198). Even with the establishment of the monastery at Molesme, some monks felt observance of the Rule was still lacking. In response twenty monks moved and established another monastery at Cîteaux in 1098. A strict observance of the Rule was followed at Cîteaux, and as the monastery dwindled in size, St. Bernard arrived in 1112 with 30 men to lead and spread the new order.

Following St. Bernard's leadership, the Cistercian Order grew rapidly, aided by an unending tide of endowments. In time the Order was drawn away from its original intention of a life of solitude and poverty and moved into the public life of the Church. Only one year after his arrival, a new colony was founded at La Ferté and another at Pontigny in 1114. In 1115, St. Bernard was sent to found Clairvaux where he remained as abbot until his death. During his lifetime 500 Cistercian abbeys flourished, and 3,000 existed a century later. The Cistercians arrived in England in 1128, founding a monastery at Waverly in Hampshire, while only four years later Rievaulx was founded in Yorkshire by St. Bernard. The Cistercians quickly grew to be the largest monastic order in Great Britain as well as France, and soon held a privileged position within the Church that entailed status, involvement in Church business, and extra privileges, all of which contributed to jealousy among the clergy and other religious orders. As its prestige grew, the Cistercian Order tested its independence. In order to pursue their goals of solitude and isolation more freely, the Cistercians rejected ecclesiastic and manorial support, using their ensuing "economic vulnerability" to lobby the Vatican (successfully) for an exemption from taxes and tithes. The largely unregulated status of the Cistercians, as compared with other monastic orders, provided them with opportunities to engage in profit-maximizing activities that they readily pursued. The tax exemption, for example, accelerated the Cistercians' move into sheep farming by making grazing more profitable on lands of marginal agricultural value.[3] Perhaps because of its success in securing differential advantages, the Cistercian Order earned a reputation "for avarice and group acquisitiveness" early in their history (Lawrence 1984,161). From its ranks came a number of bishops and cardinals, and a pope, Eugenius III, who reigned from 1145 to 1153.

Cistercian monasteries were intended to be self-sufficient entities, focusing on spiritual purity as manifest in strict adherence to the Rule. Like other institutions, monasteries went through stages of development, moving from economic self-sufficiency to a state of production characterized by persistent agricultural surpluses. Market participation, in turn, led to increased agricultural innovation, and agricultural prosperity by the monasteries created more opportunities for local employment. As the prominence and visibility of the local monastery increased through its market participation, its benefactors were increasingly willing to "donate" land to the monasteries in exchange for the spiritual output (i.e., prayers and divine intercession) of the local monastery.

With expansion of its real estate holdings the monasteries began to operate like agricultural firms in a more explicit fashion. In France the development of commercial viticulture in the Côte d'Or was the specific legacy of the Cistercian monks who, despite their concern for spiritual matters, displayed great temporal sophistication in winemaking. Recognizing the value of wine as both bargaining chip and diplomatic tool, they began the lengthy process of classifying land in order to ascertain the market value of wine from one vineyard to the next—a practice that continues to this very day under the various *appelation* rules established by the Institut National des Appellations d'Origine. Sheep farming and other forms of husbandry were introduced to increase the return from land that was of marginal agricultural value. This change brought about a new lifestyle for the monks and concomitant structural changes within the monastery. A new class of monks, the *conversi* (or lay brotherhood), was established as an additional source of labor to work the land. While the *conversi* took the monastic vows and wore the habit, these monks were typically recruited from the lower class and served the monastic community primarily as a permanent workforce. With their main focus on agricultural endeavors, the work of the lay brothers enabled the choir monks more time for liturgical devotions and private prayer.

Conversi were recruited to such an extent that in most Cistercian monasteries they were the largest component of the community. At Rievaulx in 1167, for example, there were approximately 500 lay brothers as compared with 140 monks, whereas Pontigny had 300 lay brothers and only one-third as many choir monks (Lawrence 1992, 178–79). This practice continued into the next century, where at Himmerod in 1224 there were 200 lay brothers and only 60 choir monks. Not only did these monks have separate duties, they were also housed separately, and they were set apart from the choir monks by a screen at services. While part of the increase in the number of lay brothers is attributable to the lengthy period of population expansion that increased land values, making it more difficult for peasants to manage their subsistence, for this class of society it was the first opportunity to pursue a religious vocation with the same fervor as they had fought the crusades. Prior to the establishment of the *conversi* class of monks, the monastic vocation was reserved mostly for literate aristocrats.

The development and recruitment of lay brothers greatly benefited the monastic economy by facilitating the utilization of distant lands known as granges. Granges were monastic farm settlements, and as these land acquisitions became increasingly scattered and distant, monks were unable to journey back and forth each day from monastery to farm. Hence, the lay brethren were dispatched to the granges to work. The output from these off-premise monastic farm units further increased the wealth and influence of the Cistercian monasteries.

With this enhanced wealth and influence came a decline in the spiritual purity of the monasteries. Spiritual corruption accompanied the inherent trade-off (as defined in the Rule) between spiritual purity and worldly concerns. In the initial stages of economic self-sufficiency the opportunity cost of spiritual purity of the monasteries was low, but as the monastic economy expanded, the maintenance of spiritual purity became increasingly costly since greater economic benefits had to be sacrificed in order to maintain it. In effect, the price of worldly concerns fell relative to the price of spiritual purity, and spiritual corruption increased alongside economic profit.

As the prosperity of the Cistercian monasteries grew, their agricultural capital (farm structures and implements) increased on a par, or nearly so, with their religious capital (i.e., abbeys and churches). Many of the granges had sheep folds, fueling mills, general storehouses, dormitories for the lay brothers, and an oratory (Donkin 1964, 99–100). In fact, many granges became small-scale replicas of monasteries, and some Cistercian monasteries established dairy farms and facilities for cattle breeding as well (Donkin 1962, 31). It was this commercial growth, attracting as it did monks who were not truly contemplatives, but oftentimes only seeking food and shelter or salvation by joining a monastery, that may have contributed to the corruption and monastic decay of later times.

Toward the end of the thirteenth century the growth of monasticism was curtailed by a confluence of events: economic recession, stagnant population, plague, and the development of apostolic (noncloistered) religious orders. Following the Fourth Lateran Council of 1215, the immediate face of monasticism was changed by the emergence of the first orders of friars, led by Francis of Assisi and Dominic the Spaniard (founders of the Franciscan and Dominican Orders, respectively). With this influx of apostolic orders the followers of St. Benedict lost their dominant-firm position. The new orders of friars, combining religious zeal with the intellectual support of theologians at many respected universities, attracted larger numbers of gifted men, leaving the older orders to recruit predominantly from the lower classes or from the surrounding community (Knowles 1969, 112–13).

Like most firms and institutions, the Cistercian Order experienced a life cycle consisting of birth, expansion, and eventual decline. This chapter concentrates on the Cistercian Order during the height of its influence within the corporate Church. As long as the Order was small, many Cistercian monasteries were able to achieve their goal of a contemplative life. Over time, these monasteries changed in response to environmental and economic events that altered the relative prices of behavior. To all outward appearances these changes occurred in a way that would be predicted by modern economic theory and history (e.g., North and Thomas 1973; North 1981).

The Individual Monastery as a Franchise Monopolist

From the standpoint of economic organization, the relationship of the monasteries to the corporate Church parallels the experience of contemporary franchised firms in several fundamental respects: the relationship between downstream firms and the upstream monopolist was constantly strained by problems of successive monopoly, vertical integration, time inconsistency, and retail price maintenance.

Property Rights Assignments

The Vatican was the sole supplier of the intangible inputs and the assets that made the monasteries profitable franchisees within the industrial organization of the Latin Church. The intangibles provided by the Church included guarantees of salvation, doctrinal purity, and a brand name that reduced search costs and (theoretically) was an advertisement for the Church. At the local level the abbot held attenuated property rights to the resources of the monastery. In principle monastic property was communally owned, as defined by its constitution, but in practice the abbot controlled the distribution and use of monastic property. In fact, the abbot's hold on economic property rights was stronger than his hold on spiritual property rights. This situation provided the abbot with an incentive to act more like an economic entrepreneur than a spiritual entrepreneur. By entering into a franchise agreement with the Church, the monastery could "buy" guarantees of the quality of its product in exchange for a lump-sum fee paid to the Church. For its part the Vatican could more easily control the acquisitiveness of the monasteries by granting them franchises. Thus, given property rights assignments, the monasteries and the Church had mutual incentives to enter franchise agreements.

The Successive Monopoly Problem

In keeping with their mission of increasing spirituality through solitude and isolation, the Cistercian monasteries were granted exclusive territories. The Vatican routinely barred new monasteries from locating in close proximity to existing Cistercian monasteries. As monastic behavior became increasingly worldly, however, their local monopoly interests (which resulted from exclusive territories) inevitably began to conflict with the global monopoly of the Church. As a retail seller of assurances of salvation, the monastery was poised to increase its rents at the expense of the Vatican by altering the quality of its product or by restricting output at the local (retail) level. The familiar market response to this type of problem is vertical integration and franchising. Long before the formal theory of vertical integration had been worked out, the medieval Church was experimenting with such measures of organizational control. In such circumstances, exclusive territories—where only one retailer has the right to sell the franchised good in a specific geographic locale—are important for maintaining the solvency of franchised firms because they significantly reduce *intra*brand competition, and they help to resolve the so-called time-inconsistency problem.

Blair and Kaserman (1983, 31) have demonstrated that the retail distribution of a good carried out by firms possessing some degree of local monopoly power often gives rise to the successive monopoly problem. Medieval monasteries were no exception. Within the organizational structure of the medieval Church, the monasteries operated as downstream successive monopolists.[4] The Church was unable to avoid the successive monopoly problem due to the presence of high transaction costs embedded in the medieval agrarian economy (e.g., widely dispersed monastic land holdings and primitive means of communication).

When successive monopoly exists, the retailer will attempt to maximize profit by equating downstream marginal cost (which is equal to the retailer's marginal cost of transforming the monopolized input into a unit of output plus the price paid to the manufacturer) to net marginal revenue. The retailer then benefits from being a successive monopolist by earning monopoly profits. However, the successive monopolist also has the ability to restrict output and increase profit, thereby causing a diminution in the manufacturer's profits. By contrast, competition among downstream retail firms assures that more of the manufacturer's output will be sold at a retail price between the successive monopoly price and the competitive price. Absent the discipline of competition, the existence of successive monopoly reduces the manufacturer's profits and increases the monopoly profits of the retailer. This potential transfer of income from the upstream firm to downstream firms provides an incentive for the manufacturer to integrate forward and use vertical contractual restraints to prevent erosion of output and quality at the retail level.

During the Middle Ages, monasteries carried out a major share of the retail distribution of salvation. Furthermore, each monastery possessed some degree of local monopoly power due to the assignment of exclusive territories and a general absence of competing firms (i.e., alternative religious organizations). Because salvation is a credence good (i.e., the quality of the good is uncertain both before and after its purchase), quality had to be authenticated (or warranted) by the (upstream) Church. The quality of its salvation services was upheld by the manufacturer–Church through its teachings and doctrine, thereby validating the local monopoly power of the monasteries. As the principal manufacturer in the salvation industry, the Church had a profit incentive to integrate with the monasteries in order to expand its influence and to increase total industry profits. This was accomplished by developing franchise arrangements with the monasteries.

Vertical Integration

A forward-integrated firm absorbs or controls downstream firms (i.e., wholesalers and retailers) through contractual restraints. In the standard franchise arrangement the upstream firm typically provides some intangible input or asset, such as a trademark or brand name, to the downstream firm in exchange for some form of compensation, such as a fixed fee, a sales revenue royalty payment, or some combination of the two. In addition, a "tying" arrangement may be used to transfer rents to the upstream firm by means of lump-sum franchise fees (Blair and Kaserman 1983, 69). Other potential contractual restraints include resale price maintenance whereby the manufacturer sets maximum prices at the retail level to prevent output restriction by the downstream firms, and minimum prices at the retail level to maintain quality standards. Over time, the medieval Church and the monasteries engaged in one or more of these kinds of vertical arrangements.[5] The global Church was a (loose) vertically integrated monopoly that enforced franchise contracts under conditions of fixed proportions (i.e., a soul saved by the downstream monastery equals a soul saved by the upstream Church).

The Cistercian monasteries typically paid a sales revenue royalty of up to 5 percent of their annual gross income to the bishop who collected the franchise fee on his annual visitation (Snape 1926, 97–98). In an effort to maintain local autonomy, many Cistercian monasteries sought papal exemption from visitation, which was, technologically, the only means by which the Church could oversee the state of affairs within the monastery, financial or otherwise. Visitations were relatively expensive obligations for the monastery since beyond the annual fee, they entailed room and board for the visiting bishop and his extensive entourage during the visit. One monastery in Bolton, for example, spent 20 percent of its income (in 1321) on the annual visitation (Snape 1926, 97–98). These visitations were profitable for the bishops who were able to save their own income throughout their travels as well as exact the visitation fees from their reluctant hosts.

In lieu of the annual fee, monasteries that were not under a bishop's direct jurisdiction were required to obtain papal confirmation for all new abbots (a costly process involving travel to Rome). Such confirmations entailed the payment of substantial fees known as *servitia*—which consisted of a lump-sum entry fee payable directly to the pope by the abbots of exempt monasteries. The exemptions were expensive undertakings, sometimes requiring monasteries to contract a loan (usually with the papal *camera*, at relatively high interest rates). Snape (1926, 104) computed the average cost of installment of eleven English abbots during the thirteenth and fourteenth centuries to be in excess of £958, the current equivalent of $52,000.[6]

Over time, papal confirmation became a relatively small fixed component of downstream production costs, but early on many monasteries struggled financially to repay debts they had undertaken in order to be enfranchised. Seeking an exemption was a long-run strategy: though it entailed high front-end costs, elimination of the sales revenue royalty lowered the total production costs to the monastery and increased its net rents at the downstream stage. The upstream Church's decision to grant exemptions was equally problematic. On the one hand, lump-sum fees provided an alternative method of generating rents for the pope.[7] On the other hand, such a payment system has two major drawbacks. Lump-sum fee payments typically enhance downstream monopoly power. Also, the determination of an optimal fee depends on imperfect knowledge of the demand curve at the retail level in each locale over the time that the fee is extracted (Blair and Kaserman 1983, 81). Moreover, the primitive communications technology that existed in the Middle Ages made acquisition of information regarding demand conditions both uncertain and costly, even as it raised the cost to the upstream firm of policing downstream firms.

Time-Inconsistency Problems

A time-inconsistency problem exists when a franchise is granted and a franchise fee is collected without guarantee that other franchises will be prohibited in the same geographic market. Because the monasteries had to estimate their profitability to enter into a franchise arrangement, it was a common practice for the Church to support their economic viability with territorial restrictions. Thus, monasteries were geographically dispersed to reduce *intra*brand competition, and their territories were circumscribed to enable each monastery to develop and maintain a local monopoly.

Another way the medieval Church avoided the time-inconsistency problem was to rely on its own reputation. The Church was not the franchiser of a single monopoly-monastery; rather, it entered into franchise arrangements with many monasteries, each with local monopoly power. Consequently, if the time-inconsistency problem arose in one locale, other monasteries would likely have been unwilling to enter into subsequent franchise arrangements with the Church.

Although exclusive territories decreased the costs of collection and enforcement, problems remained for the upstream Church because bishops could be bribed by wealthy monasteries. The degree of local monopoly power retained by the monasteries as a by-product of holding exclusive territories provided some residual incentive for opportunistic behavior and successive monopoly output restriction. In the face of contractual restraints the downstream franchisees sought to maximize their profit subject to the lump-sum franchise fee. The monasteries took advantage of relevant uncertainties when setting the franchise fee and sought "insurance" through diversification, such as the acquisition of land, expansion of sheep farming, and the establishment of different classes of monks (Hill 1968; Wardrop 1987). In addition, the monasteries diversified through technological innovation, implementing water-mills, windmills, and fulling mills to augment the productive efficiency of their diversified endeavors (Williams 1990).

Resale Price Maintenance

The medieval Church also set minimum and maximum resale prices. Faced with the successive monopoly problem, manufacturers often set maximum resale prices in order to prevent output restriction at the retail level. Likewise, manufacturers often impose minimum resale prices in order to maintain the quality of the product or service offered at the retail level. Of course, if a manufacturer sets the exact price of a good or service, he effectively establishes both a minimum and a maximum resale price—which effectively resolves the two distinct incentive–incompatibility problems regarding output and quality simultaneously.

The medieval Church attempted to resolve both incentive–incompatibility problems (output and quality control) in the same fashion, through the development of confession manuals. Similar to the detailed operations manuals provided to modern-day franchisees in response to the incentive–incompatibility problem, confession manuals established minimum and maximum prices (penances) associated with various sins. Telser (1960) has shown that providing product-specific services at the retail level, such as confession manuals by monasteries, is a means of increasing demand for a product. In this vein an "unregulated" medieval monastery could have raised the price (penance) of absolution and simultaneously restricted output, reducing the affordability for many consumers. The prices (penances) employed at the monastery level were established by the Church in the confession manuals, thereby solving the problem of output restriction at the retail level. Alternatively, an unregulated monastery could have lowered the price of absolution to the point that consumers' perception of the quality of the service would have been diminished, causing a decline in the value of the Church's trademark. The development of confession manuals provided an effective resolution to an incentive–incompatibility problem faced by the Church and its monasteries.

Monastic Granges as Agricultural Firms

The preceding discussion focused on elements of vertical integration between the global Church and its monastic franchisees, a major component of the economic organization of the medieval Church. There were also important elements of intrafirm organization that affected the behavior of the monastic farm. Medieval monastic farms were organized into granges that were consolidated land holdings devoted to multiple agricultural pursuits. The land controlled by medieval monasteries was often widely dispersed although its control was consolidated in the hands of a single manager. The Cistercian constitution dictated that land acquisition was to be by donations of wasteland only. Hill (1968) and Wardrop (1987), however, present evidence that the Cistercians actively purchased, leased, and traded lands in order to augment and consolidate their holdings.[8]

Vertical Integration in the Wool Market

Monastic farm managers faced decisions regarding the allocation of labor and capital to the production of each particular product, as well as decisions regarding alternative land uses. As the woolen trade became an ever more important aspect of the medieval European economy, the monasteries responded by devoting more of their economic resources to sheep farming.

The technology of medieval sheep farming was such that it required variable quantities of land, labor, and sheep to produce wool. As producers of wool in a competitive final good industry, the granges were likely to integrate vertically because some of the required inputs were competitively supplied while others were monopolistically supplied.[9] In the medieval economy most monasteries were the primary source of employment at the local level. Most Cistercian monasteries developed an abundant internal supply of labor through the creation of the *conversi*, a class of monks set apart from the choir monks in several ways, including the fact that they received wages for their labor services. Once the monastic labor supply was intact, the monastery could integrate into the downstream production of wool without having to pay higher wages to lay workers. This labor-cost advantage allowed the monasteries to employ more labor per unit of land, thereby augmenting the quantity and quality of the final-good output. Without interference this kind of forward vertical integration would persist until the input monopolist (the monasteries) eventually monopolized the final good industry, which appears to have occurred in the medieval wool market.

Several historical accounts indicate that monastic expansion into the wool trade was substantial, and that the monasteries generated enormous demand for their wool because of its high quality. One such account is contained in the commercial list of English monasteries collected by Pegolotti, an Italian businessman. The list records that the finest wool was produced by Tintern Abbey, Abbey Dore, and Stanfield Abbey. Their wool commanded a price of 28 marks per sack compared with a price of 7 marks per sack of low-quality wool (Power 1941, 23). The reputation of the quality of the monastic wool tended to drive up the monastic prices relative to the smaller farmers in the vicinity, and thereby enabled the monks to extract economic rents. One piece of evidence suggests that the Cistercians accumulated large stockpiles of high-quality wool: it was Cistercian wool that was used to pay the ransom for Richard I in 1193 and 1194 (Power 1941, 33–35).

The founding of new monastic orders and the rapid growth of the Cistercians throughout the twelfth century effectively show how expansion meets economic opportunity. The Cistercians were regulated by their constitution to acquire donations of remote wasteland only—which actually facilitated their expansion into sheep farming because such land was more suitable for grazing than for planting (Power 1941, 33). As the wool market expanded, the Cistercians became more sophisticated in their dealings, entering into advance contracts with wool exporters (Power 1941, 42–43). It became common practice for exporters to enter into futures contracts with monasteries for their wool crops two to three years in advance. Some contracts ranged up to twenty years. Such futures contracts increased the monasteries' risk, for when output did not reach expectations, they found themselves in debt to their exporters. For some monasteries the practice of seeking cash advances through futures contracts eventually led to financial difficulty because, in effect, these monasteries had overencumbered their future resources.

The case of Fountains Abbey provides a telling example. From its records it appears that Fountains actively pursued expansion and grange development. Within twenty years of its foundation in 1130, Fountains held land close to the abbey, had six granges, and had founded eight new monasteries (Wardrop 1987, 16). To finance its expansion Fountains entered into advance contracts, receiving cash advances in exchange for its forthcoming wool crop (Wardrop 1987, 22–24). When the sheep flock was halved as a result of a pestilence in the 1280s, Fountains found itself in financial difficulty due to its inability to provide the promised wool that had secured its cash advances.

Team Production and Efficiency Considerations

The monastic grange and its sheep-farming operations relied on team production, as defined by Alchian and Demsetz (1972, 779). A firm achieves a comparative advantage in its coordination of inputs in production only to the extent that the firm assigns payments to inputs in proportion to their productivity. If the reward system is random, there is little or no incentive for input owners to behave efficiently. But measuring productivity of inputs in a team context can only be achieved by observing behavior which entails monitoring costs. In the presence of monitoring costs, moreover, an input supplier will have greater incentive to shirk because the probability of detection on a team is lower. Consequently, economic theory dictates that team production techniques will be adopted only if productivity increases net of monitoring and production costs. The presence of competition lowers monitoring costs, but insofar as medieval monastic labor markets were monopolistic and farm operations were decentralized, the incentive to shirk on the part of workers was high. Moreover, the monks were not rewarded in accord with their individual marginal products, further increasing the incentive to shirk.

In general, the incentive to shirk was proportionate to the number of monks employed and the size of the grange. One common means to reduce shirking is to hire a foreman and make him a residual claimant to team production. In other words, the foreman is allowed to keep the earnings remaining after payments to other input suppliers. This option was not open to the medieval monasteries as long as the abbot was the sole residual claimant. So while the development of the grange permitted some cost reductions associated with efficient management, the customary assignment of property rights to the abbot prevented the achievement of a higher level of efficiency.[10]

Technology and Monastic Profitability

Insofar as the medieval monastery was ruled by a religious constitution, the amount of time the monks could spend on economic pursuits was constrained. A great part of each monk's day was spent in prayer, contemplation, and worship. The monastic emphasis on self-sufficiency, combined with time constraints on productive activity, motivated medieval monasteries to develop more efficient farm-production techniques, providing an incentive to embrace technological advance. The Cistercians, for example, invariably located near running water so that they could utilize the productive power of water mills. Reynolds (1984, 123) notes that by 1300 nearly all Cistercian monasteries had at least one water mill, while some monasteries had several. Likewise, Williams's (1990, 36–68) inventory of eighteen Cistercian monasteries in Wales shows that sixteen had water mills (sometimes more than one), four had windmills, and thirteen had fulling mills. In addition to the early and frequent use of mills, the Cistercians experimented widely with plants, soils, and breeding stock. Their expertise in stock-breeding has been credited with the development of a select breed of sheep in England that provided the original impetus to extensive sheep farming.

Price Discrimination and Entry Restrictions

Price discrimination is commonly understood as the practice of setting different prices for the same good produced at the same cost to different demanders, and is frequently used by a producer with monopoly power in order to maximize profit. Some medieval monasteries employed this pricing strategy in attempts to control entry of members into their ranks. Entry payments were frequently in the form of donations of land which represented yet another way that monasteries could acquire wealth.

There were three main types of monastic entrants: (1) at large, adult members of a parish who were either converts or long-standing members of the "faithful," (2) the old, infirm, or diseased (entrants *ad succurrendum*), and (3) child oblates, who were children offered by their parents to the monastery in an effort to secure the parents' salvation (Lynch 1976, 26). Those with the most inelastic demand for entry had the highest willingness to pay and were therefore charged the highest entry price.

Although every class was accepted, those in the first category were considered to have the "truest" vocation. Those who entered *ad succurrendum* believed that by taking the monastic habit, they would avoid eternal damnation. The largest of the three groups of entrants, however, was the child oblate. The donation of a child was perceived as a supreme act of piety, the greatest test of one's faith. In actuality, donations of children were motivated by economic concerns on many occasions. Donations were more likely if there were several children in the home already, or if the child being offered was handicapped in some manner. In addition, the law of primogeniture dictated that only the first born, male child could inherit property, so other sons were "freely" offered by parents as a religious sacrifice.

All three classes of entrants faced varying income and time constraints. Those seeking entry *ad succurrendum* had the highest opportunity cost and therefore were most willing to sacrifice worldly possessions in exchange for entry. Parents who offered their child as a living sacrifice also had a relatively high willingness to pay. The economic burden of a large family, as well as the piety of the "penitential" act of offering a child to God, often combined to raise the price of entry for child oblates. The entry price was lowest for converts and the faithful, who had the most elastic demands. Because of the monopoly power held by the monastery, however, it could still maintain a price above the competitive level, even for the most elastic class of entrants.

Cost considerations may also have intervened. Having purer motives for entry, converts and the faithful made more productive and contented monks. Children often became restless as they matured, eventually choosing to move to other monasteries or to leave the monastery completely. Entrants *ad succurrendum* sometimes sought to leave the monastery after recovering from their illnesses. The membership pricing schedule adopted by the monasteries weighed different elasticities and costs, making it possible to extract rents by charging each entrant a price above the level of competitive marginal cost.

Rent Seeking in the Monastic Labor Market

Price discrimination was also evident in the monastic labor market. As the Cistercians' land holdings grew apace, so did their demand for labor. To meet the higher demand for farm labor, the monasteries devised the aforementioned *conversi* class of monks. The *conversi* quickly became important cogs in the commercial success of the monasteries, enabling the monasteries to gain a competitive edge in the all important wool industry. The creation of the *conversi* created a second labor market that facilitated payment of different wages to each class of monks. Since the *conversi* were relieved of several spiritual obligations that might be considered onerous, yet received the monastic habit on profession of the traditional monastic vows, the abbot was able to hire this new class of labor at lower wages than in a secular market.[11]

Successful price discrimination requires not only a degree of monopoly power but also the ability to segment markets and to prevent recontracting in separate markets. Accordingly, medieval monasteries preserved the separability of their two-tiered labor market by establishing strict lines of demarcation between choir monks and the *conversi*. For example, whereas literacy was a requirement for choir monks, the *conversi* were denied the opportunity to read or learn anything beyond the few prayers that were required to maintain their "monkness."[12] While the cost to the monastery of providing the assurance of salvation was the same for each monk, and since prayer and manual labor were the two mainstays of the Rule, both choir monks and *conversi* were glorifying God according to the Rule (Fry 1981). Hence, since cost conditions were the same and the labor markets were separate, the abbot was able to price discriminate between the two classes of monks.

Societal Changes and Monastic Decline

North and Thomas (1973) argue that societal changes, institutional or otherwise, typically affect the relative prices of economic resources, which in turn, explain economic transformations. During the Middle Ages, the ebb and flow of disease and monarchic power led to changes in the relative price of labor and the ultimate control of important property rights. Specifically, the rising power of the English monarchy and the onset of the Black Death brought about increases in the relative prices of land and labor that eventually led to monastic decline.

Near the middle of the twelfth century, monastic expansion came to an abrupt halt. One force for expansion was dissipated by the deaths of the two foremost champions of Cistercian monasticism, Bernard of Clairvaux and Pope Eugenius III (himself a Cistercian). But more fundamental changes were ushered in during the reign of Henry II of England (1154–1189). Henry developed a strong monarchy based on the fealty of his knights, whose swift rise to power was accompanied by a shift in land distribution from the older nobility to the warrior-knights. This shift of ownership meant that the knights began to supplant the nobility as chief patrons of the monasteries, which might have had minimal impact, except for the fact that the new class of landowners were burdened by more obligations than the former class. The knight-landowners were bound to the crown not only by military service but by more complicated financial responsibilities. Because monasteries were exempt from military service, knight-landowners could not escape this obligation when they leased land to monasteries (Hill 1968, 63). To compensate for these nontransferable responsibilities, the knights began to require annual payments for the use of their lands. Donations without annual payment became increasingly scarce, and explicit rental agreements between knights and monasteries became increasingly common. The result was a rise in the relative price of landleases due to the increased obligations tied to the land.[13]

Simultaneously, the relative price of labor rose in medieval society because the Black Death caused a massive reduction in the aggregate supply of labor. The *conversi*, as a class, eventually disappeared from the monasteries, a phenomenon that can be explained by rising opportunity costs: in the face of large reductions in the aggregate supply of labor, wages outside the monastery rose relative to monastic wages. Faced with labor shortages and higher labor costs, the profitability of the monasteries eroded, eventually leaving many monasteries to become lessors of the lands they owned. Under the circumstances monasteries were forced to settle for smaller rents on their lands, or let the land remain idle for lack of hands to work it. Ironically, many monasteries wound up leasing land to the people who had previously comprised their own inexpensive labor force.

As long as medieval monasteries enjoyed above-normal profits, they had an incentive to raise and maintain barriers to entry. As franchisees of the corporate Church, they could invoke certain competitive advantages. However, in the face of structural change that systematically lowered profits, the monasteries found it increasingly difficult to maintain barriers against competitive entry. In the end they found themselves fighting a rearguard action against economic decline.

Conclusion

Even though the Cistercian Order remains active within the Church today, insolvency beset some medieval Cistercian monasteries. This development was coincidental with the ascendancy of the mendicant orders, such as the Franciscans and Dominicans. These orders focused on evangelical interaction with the community rather than withdrawal and seclusion from it and offered the laity a more accessible religious ideal than the cloistered Cistercian monasteries. Although the Cistercian Order originated as a reform movement, railing against laxity and material wealth, it soon adopted an acquisitive nature that made it the wealthiest religious order in the Church.

While individual monasteries with financial difficulties survived by leasing their land, the spiritual reputation of the Cistercians suffered as a consequence of their history of acquiring wealth and exemptions, sometimes at the expense of other clergy and laity. As a result, the renewed emphasis on poverty by the mendicant orders met with a resounding chord of welcome among Church followers. Thus, the combined impact of the diminished reputation of the Cistercians, the financial difficulties of some monasteries, and the new presence of the mendicant orders all contributed to the decline of monasticism. This decline was later buttressed by the Protestant Reformation that effectively eliminated the monopoly position of the Church and its religious orders.

NOTES

1. Monastic orders such as the Cistercian and Benedictines are in contrast to the medicant or apostolic orders of the Church (such as the Dominicans or Franciscans). The latter were "traveling" orders dedicated to support of the sick and poor, whereas the former were typically housed in monasteries and focused on liturgy and prayer.

2. Many aspects of the Cistercian economy will be addressed later in the chapter, including its policies with respect to land acquisition, development of an internal labor supply, product differentiation, and technological innovation, as well as the use of price discrimination by the monasteries.

3. In general, firms or institutions that receive tax exemptions have an advantage over other firms without such exemptions since costs are lower.

4. On the subject of successive monopoly, see Spengler (1950) and Machlup and Taber (1960).

5. The literature on medieval monasticism illustrating these arrangements is abundant. See, for example, the comprehensive works of Knowles (1948; 1955; 1963), as well as Hill (1968), Lekai (1977), Power (1941), Snape (1926), Wardrop (1987), and Williams (1990).

6. The modern equivalent of medieval monies is somewhat problematic. The method used here is based on the current market value of the precious metal content known to exist in medieval coins. In the thirteenth and fourteenth centuries, the British pound sterling contained 10.3 ounces of pure silver (Rogers 1963, 173). The "spot" price of silver at this writing was $5.27 per ounce.

7. As Caves and Murphy (1976, 577) explain, the franchiser who owns an intangible asset has to determine a method of capturing rent from franchisees with differing inputs and local conditions. Papal exemption from visitations on the condition of papal confirmation can be viewed as a means of capturing these rents. The monasteries that sought exemptions were generally those who were heavily engaged in rent-seeking activity.

8. Evidence of leasing arrangements is sizable and includes Fountains Abbey, where 15 of 38 land grants required an annual payment. Kirkstall had 16 of 31 requiring payment, Byland had 12 of 36, Kirkstead had 13 of 18, and Meaux had 6 of 11 (Hill 1968, 72). For these five monasteries alone, 46 percent of their land "donations" were, in fact, from leasing arrangements.

9. Cf. Vernon and Graham (1971, 924–25) and Blair and Kaserman (1983, 48–52), who develop a theory of production whereby a competitive input is combined with a monopolistic input. Because the monopolist will attempt to maximize profit by setting a high input price, the competitive producers of the final good will substitute away from the monopolized input in favor of the competitive input, creating an incentive for the monopolist to integrate forward into a competitive final-good industry.

10. Monastic granges often employed a foreman, known as the "reeve of the single manor" (Knowles 1948, 42), but did not endow him with residual claimant status.

11. Choir monks were the more "traditional" monks who were bound by the vows of poverty, chastity, and obedience. They were expected to attend all community liturgical observances (Mass and eight hours of the Divine Office), as well as engaging in *Lectio Divina,* a form of private spiritual reading and prayer. For a more complete understanding of the Divine Office, see Fry (1981, chaps. 8–19).

12. A passage from the Observances of the Augustinian Priory of Barnwell (England) reveals the "official" policy of separability: "Lay brethren are not to be

admitted to the habit unless they are instructed in some craft which is useful to the monastery; for as regular canons ought to be occupied day and night in things spiritual, so lay brethren ought to labor for the profit of the Church in things corporeal" (Snape 1926, 7).

13. Hill (1968, 70) notes that by the close of the twelfth century nearly every English Cistercian monastery was obligated for annual payments to their land donors. However, payments were not always pecuniary. One donor, for example, required burial in the monastery's cemetery; others secured promise of entrance to the monastery at a later date if they so wished; and some extracted an agreement that their families be hospitably received at the monastery whenever they wished (Hill 1968, 65–72).

Attempts to Maintain Market Dominance

Introduction: Entry Control and Enforcement Mechanisms

As a monopolist, the Church had to protect its "market" against entry by competitive firms. The product—assurances of eternal salvation—was surrounded by doctrinal characteristics and conditions that had to be met in order to attain the final good. The power to interpret the Bible and to establish *dogma*, a set of principles that defined the product, was therefore of necessity accompanied by forms of entry control to protect the Church's monopoly position. Those who challenged the medieval Church's authority in this regard were considered to be transgressors, and the medieval Church wielded two major threats of punishment. Both involved exclusion, or expulsion, from the ranks of the "saved." The first, excommunication, was fearsome and broadbased. The second, sanctions against heresy and witchcraft, was narrower in scope and more violent in practice.

Excommunication could take place immediately on committing certain transgressions (ipso facto) or could take place through ecclesiastic decree. Heresy was different in kind and degree. In some literal sense heresy was any transgression against the dogma of the Latin Church, but that meaning is too broad. Heresy was a *fundamental* difference on matters of faith, most often represented by a belief in an alternative system of dogma.[1] Witchcraft was, of course, also "heresy" of a particular kind—the denial of Christ as God and the worship of the devil.[2] All of these sanctions, it is important to note, were used to maintain the Church's monopoly on doctrine and codes of behavior. Let us consider a more detailed distinction between excommunication and heresy before we proceed to analyze these controls as entry-limiting devices.

The influence of the Church derived mainly from the perception among Christians that it had the authority to directly or indirectly affect the quality of every individual's life-after-death. Exclusion from the Church was equivalent to a huge fine, equal to the "present discounted value" of the eternal "income stream" that such exclusion implied—exclusion from heaven—to persons with this belief.[3]

Excommunication is the exclusion of an individual from participation in the sacraments of the Church (Holy Communion, Last Rites, and so on). In medieval times excommunication was a widely used and harsh penalty. The soul of an excommunicate who died before he or she had successfully achieved absolution served a weighty sentence in purgatory. A contumacious excommunicate (one who failed to seek absolution) faced the ultimate sanction, confinement in hell for all *eternity*. Social ostracism of varying degrees of severity was an additional cost to excommunicates in this life. Some excommunicates were legally restricted in their ability to enter into contracts and others could actually be murdered with impunity. Moreover, excommunication was not a sanction whose imposition was restricted to heresy or doctrinal misdeeds, which of course had little effect without recantation of the heretic. Rather, excommunication could be meted out as punishment for various crimes, including murder, theft, and failure to appear in court. In fact, excommunication was largely a secular punishment even though it was administrated by the Church.

We interpret excommunication as an attempt to keep members within the doctrinal and behaviorial ranges sanctioned by the Church. This mechanism facilitated the monopoly hold that the Church had on its members. Furthermore, we argue that the excommunication power of the Church— established through the elaborate canon law court system—may have been an economically efficient form of law enforcement for *particular* kinds of behavior. Church law enforcement may have compensated for the absence of effective government, police, and courts in *particular times and places* and for *particular offenses* during the Middle Ages. In some cases the Church courts served to reduce transaction costs for market participants, helping to define and protect property rights. In other cases such as those involving usury (Chapter 6), the Church courts might have thwarted commercial exchange. In matters such as elaborate regulations regarding marriage, the courts administered and enforced openly monopolistic charges for its services (Chapter 5), although here as elsewhere the Church provided utility as well. On balance, however, we characterize excommunication and the Church court system as complimentary devices to aid in the collection of rents.

The suppression of heresy was fundamentally different from that of witchcraft. While excommunication was an effective sanction for believers only, the suppression of heresy was an active policy of the Church to eradicate competing sects whose dogma openly challenged Roman Catholic doctrines concerning the means to salvation.

The Church, as we will see, attempted to suppress heretical beliefs on two fronts: (1) by redefining its product or the *institutional structures* surrounding the supply of its product, and (2) by forceful suppression of dissidents, a tactic that included rampant executions and confiscation of property (as in the frequent "inquisitions" held in France, Italy, and Spain) over the medieval period. The military suppression of heresy was initially a tool used in *extremis*—when excommunication and other means failed—but military and other violent forms of suppression (often imposed by secular authority) became the tools of choice to enforce entry control in the later Middle Ages. Due to sparse and inadequate records, the empirical magnitude of total prosecutions and executions for heresy, witchcraft, and the practice of magic is difficult to assess. The charge that millions of Europeans were executed is a likely exaggeration, since deaths in the hundreds of thousands for all "heresies" are most likely.[4] Nevertheless the horror and terror wrought by these Church practices, especially when one considers the often false and hysterical charges against many individuals, were the ultimate tools of entry control which, of course, failed in the end.[5]

Ecclesiastic Jurisprudence

Throughout this work we argue that the route to paradise was a toll-road, and the Church's spiritual activities provided it with a source of tangible revenue. Thus, the medieval Church behaved like an M-form firm, as we argued in Chapter 2. But the Church was also a "stockholder" in the macro-economy of medieval Europe—it benefited directly from the improvement in public order and the security of transactions that its courts provided. In other words, there was a public-goods aspect to peace and security and to some extent the medieval Church was a producer of these public goods. Nevertheless, economic development, increases in literacy, and advances in knowledge and technology were a double-edged sword for the Church. On the one hand, economic development led to increased donations to the Church because ultimately the Church was a "residual claimant" that profited from activities which enhanced general economic development. On the other hand, a society energized by new wealth, new markets, and new technology tended increasingly to challenge the Church's spiritual and temporal hegemony over individual behavior. The English aristocracy, for example, was more constrained in its dealings with the Church because of a longer history of democratic institutions and practices in civil society, and the severity of Church punishments there (e.g., excommunication) was far less stringent.

Canon Law

In the course of its "business" operations the medieval Church developed and enforced a complex set of rules that proscribed the actions of both clerics and laypersons. During the Dark Ages, when emergent nation-states were weak and a generally enforced, consistent code of law was nonexistent, the Church developed its own legal structure and rules. Called "canon law," this internally consistent set of guidelines detailed adjudication procedures for a wide array of cases and disputes. Canon law was administered by a separate system of ecclesiastic courts, under the jurisdiction of bishops.

In substance canon law represented the accumulated body of decisions issued by the popes in the form of decretal letters, as well as written directives pertaining to matters of Church policy and doctrine. This body of rules was both supplemented, and constrained, by a mass of interpretation and exegesis. Over the course of the Middle Ages the study of canon law became a major scholarly discipline, and by a continual process of elaboration and interpretation a complex body of law was refined into an internally consistent code (cf. Gilchrist 1969, 12–13).

Throughout Europe generally, and in twelfth-century England particularly, ecclesiastic courts claimed jurisdiction over (1) all civil and criminal cases involving clerics, including disputes over Church property; (2) all matrimonial cases; (3) all testamentary issues; (4) certain infringements of doctrine perpetrated by nonclerics (e.g., heresy, sacrilege, sorcery, usury, defamation, fornication, homosexuality, adultery, defacement or destruction of religious property, assault against clerics); and (5) issues involving contracts, property, and perjury (violation of a sacred oath) (Berman 1983, 261).

One function of canon law and the ecclesiastic courts was to prevent national and local governments from interfering in Church business. Another function was the improved *internal* coordination and organization within the medieval Church. In this way canon law tended to reduce opportunistic behavior on the part of downstream suppliers of the Church's main product. On the one hand, the Church sheltered its priests from the jurisdiction of the civil courts; on the other hand, it carefully monitored its internal staff. Surviving evidence suggests that ecclesiastic courts dealt harshly with clerics found guilty of serious crimes (especially downstream opportunism such as theft of Church property). But the Church also protected its servants from external violence. The ecclesiastic courts invariably pursued such cases more vigorously, and prosecuted them more diligently, than secular authorities were wont to do. By thus imposing a high cost on those who would assault its internal staff, the medieval Church established a strong deterrent. Indeed, until the late Middle Ages, violence against the clergy was quite rare despite the fact that the age itself was a violent one.

The most tangible and direct benefit of the ecclesiastic court system was, of course, the revenues generated by legal fees that flowed to the bishops under whose jurisdictions the courts operated. It is difficult, if not impossible, to gauge the full measure of these revenues because quantitative evidence is scattered and fragmentary. Also, a variety of fines and fees were described euphemistically as "alms to the poor" that further obscured the magnitude of the revenues.[6] But it seems clear that court fees and fines were a major source of revenue at the local (diocesan) level.

Ecclesiastic courts in the Middle Ages enjoyed a clear advantage over their secular counterparts. In an age when belief in an omniscient and omnipresent Supreme Being was practically universal, the cost of "enforcing" the decisions of the ecclesiastic courts was very low.[7] Conviction (or faith) was, in effect, a substitute for a police force. Secular law did not have the same advantage although sometimes the Church would add the force of its authority to secular laws. As a result, in medieval Europe canon law was essentially self-enforcing. This fact was extremely important as certain secular entities in particular places were unable to generate the fiscal means required to provide effective temporal law enforcement.

Church Sanctions Against Malfeasance

It might be supposed that the medieval Church's legal sanctions were all ultimately based on that institution's rather unique deterrent, the threat of hell. But while the quality of the afterlife was critically important in defining many of the economically valuable "services" the Church offered to medieval believers (e.g., Bold and Hull 1994), the threat of eternal damnation was not a major sanction employed by the ecclesiastic courts. Rather, penalties for infractions of canon law were precisely graduated in relation to the seriousness of the transgression.

The most frequently used device for coping with crimes was the sacrament of penance. Penance is a complicated practice with multifold purposes. The Church insisted that its primary purpose was remedial—to make amends for sin and cleanse the soul of the sinner—but it was also a form of punishment. The penitent was required to perform certain ritualistic acts, on the completion of which he or she received absolution for the sins committed. Penance was imposed as a rather mild punishment for sin, but many of the sins punishable by penance were also secular crimes.[8]

Penances administered in the Middle Ages could be public (the most common form) or private (between the priest and the penitent). Until the tenth century penance in Europe was imposed by the bishop. Afterward it was ordinarily imposed by the parish priest. Penances were usually given for terms of three, five, ten, twelve, or fifteen years. It was up to the bishop to allow reconciliation, which depended on the successful completion of the penance and demonstrated penitence. According to canon law, sinners who failed to accept and perform assigned penances were subject to excommunication.

In the early Middle Ages, public penance was required throughout western Europe for sins that included homicide, rape, usury, fornication, adultery, perjury, arson, robbery, soothsaying, magic, incest, and marriage within the prohibited degrees (Oakley 1932, 45).[9] The punishment of perjury was particularly significant. In the ancient Church, and prior to the period of Gregorian reforms, perjury was defined almost exclusively in terms of dishonest dealings with the Church. Over time, perjury became increasingly used as a term that implied breach of contract, the most common breach being failure to pay a debt. This change of emphasis had to do with a technicality, albeit an important one, associated with medieval contracts. In the Middle Ages a contract was almost always based on a mutual oath between the participants, sworn on some sacred object (e.g., the Scriptures or a sacred relic). Thus, the typical contract included a sacred oath that was sinful to break (Oakley 1932, 186). Perjury *per cupiditatem* (from greed) therefore, which was frequently mentioned in the Penitentials, referred to theft and nonpayment of valid debts (Oakley 1932, 191).

All things being equal, public penance imposes higher costs on the penitent than private penance because public penance involves humiliation of the penitent.[10] The usual procedure in the Middle Ages was for penance to be assigned before the assembled congregation, in a manner calculated to emphasize the heinous nature of the transgression. Throughout the penitential period, the penitent was required to perform various rituals at worship services, which added further to his or her humiliation. Miscreants were often forced to wear somber clothing (e.g., "sackcloth and ashes"), to submit themselves to scourging by the congregation, to be exiled to a monastery, or to be prohibited from carrying arms. This last penalty often exposed the penitent to serious danger, given the violence of the times. In the extreme some miscreants were imprisoned for the duration of their penitential period (Oakley 1932, 49).

Private penance was usually reserved for lesser transgressions, although it was sometimes required of those assigned a public penalty as well. The forms of private penance were less severe. They included prayer and fasting, with the latter being the most frequently assigned penance. Penances differed both in regard to the particular offense, the motivation of the sinner, and the means of the sinner. Richer penitents usually bore a heavier penalty than poorer ones, so that the variation in practice was akin to a discriminatory tax.[11]

Penance was designed not only to offer the offender a chance to consider the seriousness of his misbehavior, but also to allow restitution to victims.[12] The imposition of penance was not itself a judicial process. Punishment was left to the discretion of the bishop. Once penance was assigned, however, the accused had no right of appeal. Although this discretion gave the bishops great power in theory, in practice their actions were closely monitored by higher administrators, namely, archbishops, the Curia, and the papacy. Abuses of ecclesiastic power were held in check by the threat of excommunication.

In instances where the performance of penance was impractical due to age, occupation, or disability, provisions were made for the expiation of sins through the payment of fines, which were referred to as "commutation and redemption." Penitential codes gave precise instructions as to the amount of money required to purchase equivalent periods of a fast, for example (Oakley 1932, 52). In this manner penance was gradually transformed into a tax that transferred wealth (directly or indirectly) to the Church. The practice of substituting fines for nonpecuniary penance grew rapidly after the end of the ninth century (Oakley 1937, 494).

Offenses Punishable by Excommunication. In a sense excommunication was the punishment of last resort. It could only be imposed by a pope, a bishop, or an ecclesiastic court. Viner (1978, 47) called it "the most formidable sanction in the Church's arsenal," and Tentler (1977, 303) refers to it as an "awesome weapon." In an age when the protection of the Holy Church was considered the only defense against eternal damnation available to many mortals, the withdrawal of that protection was itself a severe threat. Excommunication meant expulsion from the community of saints, literally cutting one off from participating in the Eucharist. The consequences for the sinner were both social and economic.

Excommunication must be viewed in the context of Christian beliefs about life-after-death. The source of the Church's influence, and most of its revenues, derived from its exclusive control over the afterlife. Salvation could only be obtained through the agency of the Church. However, the Church did not claim to have jurisdiction over souls once they had left their bodies. Thus, excommunication was *not* a condemnation of the excommunicant to hell. Technically, the Church could neither condemn a soul to hell nor have any direct effect on a soul already consigned there. Indeed, Church doctrine maintained that excommunication did not prejudice one's chances in the afterlife, provided the excommunicant repented and gained absolution.[13] Of course, the decision to grant absolution was made by the Church. In most instances, however, absolution was granted automatically to excommunicants who sincerely sought it. Only "contumacious excommunicates," those who refused to seek absolution, were destined for hell, although even in these cases, the Church stopped short of actually pronouncing sentence.[14]

Over time, Church doctrine about the afterlife evolved to a point where a third place (between heaven and hell) became part of the creed. Like hell, purgatory was an unpleasant place, but unlike hell, "sentences" in purgatory were finite, and souls in purgatory were subject to the jurisdiction of the Church. The Church could assign sentences to purgatory as well as reduce sentences for souls already consigned there. These were, in other words, contingent punishments for excommunicants, so that if an excommunicant failed in his or her effort to have the sanction removed, he or she could be delivered to purgatory after death.[15]

An excommunicant could obtain absolution in one of two ways. First, she might perform the penance assigned by the ecclesiastic court, whereupon the excommunication would be lifted. Alternatively, the court could suspend the penalty, on condition that the sinner make restitution. Restitution might consist of victim compensation; donations to the poor; or pilgrimages to a sacred shrine (Berman 1983, 193). Second, a pope or bishop might lift an excommunication decree for other reasons that did not involve direct court participation.

Excommunication is commonly regarded as a punishment for heresy or as a tool of the Inquisition. However, canon lawyers carefully distinguished excommunication as a form of punishment for heresy from other forms of excommunication. In reality, few excommunicants were heretics. Moreover, excommunication as a form of punishment existed long before the various inquisitions and was only one form of punishment available to the inquisitors. Historically, the original major function of excommunication was to shield Church property from various forms of depredation. In early times it was invoked as censure against clergymen; against rulers who imposed "unauthorized" taxes against the Church; against forgerers of papal documents; against those who aided the Saracens (during the Crusades); and against various other acts of malfeasance against the papacy (Vodola 1986, 34). By far the most common transgression leading to excommunication, however, was for nonpayment of debt—and not even debt owed to the Church. Lay debt cases usually came into the ecclesiastic courts because debt contracts were commonly sealed by oath, so that failure to perform according to the terms of the contract was treated as "perjury" (Hill 1951, 2; Vodola 1986, 38). The idea became so entrenched that in fifteenth-century England, the simple failure to pay a debt was interpreted as a breach of contract involving perjury whether or not an oath had actually been sworn to on a holy object.

Social and Economic Consequences of Excommunication. Excommunication was not merely a spiritual punishment; it also exacted substantial social and economic costs. Except for family members, excommunicants were cut off from almost all social contacts. Christians were obligated by law and custom to avoid dealings with excommunicants. Surviving documents reveal that "pollution" from association with excommunicants was a major concern. In an anecdote told by Peter the Chanter, Bishop Gilbert Foliet, under excommunication by Thomas Becket, is said to have destroyed his own eating utensils after concluding a meal (Vodola 1986, 53). Giving gifts to excommunicants, or even remote contact, such as written correspondence, was believed to cause "contagion" in much the same way that diseases are transmitted. Providing employment to an excommunicant was strictly forbidden, and lawsuits were occasionally brought in ecclesiastic court to prevent such action (Hair 1972, 172). Ties were severed between excommunicated lords and their vassals, and the latter quickly abandoned a lord in such unfortunate circumstances (Vodola 1986, 67–69). In the culture of feudal Europe this constituted an enormous fine on the excommunicated lord. Legal procedures, moreover, discriminated against excommunicants (Vodola 1986, 88). Under a common legal device known as "exception," the plaintiff in a court proceeding was required to prove that he was *not* an excommunicant, if called on by the defendant to do so (Vodola 1986, 97).

Excommunicants were also constrained in their access to legal remedies. They could *not* testify in court, although, ironically, the threat of excommunication was sometimes used to make witnesses testify (Vodola 1986, 122–23). This meant that excommunicants could not sue, regardless of the merits of their case. Thus, excommunication placed its victims beyond the protection of the courts. Indeed, twelfth-century canonists tended to regard litigation against excommunicants as harmless fun. The Council of Tribur (895) decreed even that contumacious excommunicants could be killed without secular or ecclesiastic penalty. Those who owed money to an excommunicated creditor could ignore such debts with impunity. Moreover, canon law held that because contracts entered into by an excommunicant were "born dead," they had no legal standing (Vodola 1986, 151).

Because of its effectiveness as a sanction against undesirable activity, secular institutions tried to "capture" the regulation of excommunication for their own use. Thus, the secular courts frequently cooperated with the ecclesiastic courts in enforcing the provisions of excommunication. Rodes (1977, 90) maintains that the "most important [deterrent] effect of excommunication was provided by the civil processes that could be invoked in support of it." As a consequence, the link between the punishment and "sin" became more distant over time. With the passage of time and the conflation of judicial practice, excommunication became a fairly common punishment for "secular" offenses, such as failure to appear in court when summoned (Berman 1983, 266) and other forms of common criminal behavior. Secular authorities often profited handsomely from cooperation with the Church. In France, for example, secular authorities were especially vigorous in their confiscation of the property of "contumacious" excommunicants according to the provisions of canon law (Vodola 1986, 78–79).

Finally, the earthly penalties of excommunication did not end at the grave. In the early thirteenth century a decretal of Pope Innocent III declared that heirs of an excommunicant, who died "contrite" but "unabsolved," were compelled to satisfy the court, *post mortem*. Hence, the heirs of a convicted perjurer were responsible for the outstanding debts following his death. Additionally, the body of the deceased could not be buried in consecrated ground, a prohibition that had important consequences for the soul of the departed, since it could not enter heaven until the situation was rectified. A further consequence of this unresolved situation is that the reputation of the survivors was also damaged.[16] In this manner the Church often confiscated property from those who had fallen out of its favor.[17]

Crime, Punishment, and Rent Seeking

The effect of medieval Church institutions—including the ecclesiastic courts—on the development of western Europe has been examined by many historians, but the Church's secular interests in providing such a legal system has received far less attention. The orthodox assumption among Church historians is that the Church provided an elaborate system of law and jurisprudence in support of its religious doctrine, that is, to offer salutary guidance toward the goal of eternal salvation. While the ecclesiastic legal system in the Middle Ages was an obvious integument of its doctrinal framework, our research underscores the fact that the Church generated huge material benefits for itself and its agents through the provision of penitential and legal sanctions. In other words, penance was profitable.

Reliable quantitative information concerning the amount of revenue received by local clergy from commutations of penance and fines is relatively sparse,[18] but it is clear that payments for the commutation of punishments was a major source of revenue for the Church in western Europe. Papal documents provide a clearer picture than parish records, many of which have not survived. From about the tenth century on, the payment of pecuniary fines became increasingly significant. For example, penitents making restitution for stolen property were required to pay a fee called "composition," a kind of excise tax, to the Holy See (Lunt 1934, 1:130). But until the thirteenth century, the proportion of monetary commutations transferred directly from the localities to Rome was a minor source of papal revenue. It should be noted, however, that although most commutation revenue remained at the parish level prior to the thirteenth century, the papacy received a portion of these revenues indirectly through a number of taxes imposed on the local clergy.[19]

Beginning in the thirteenth century, the papacy began to centralize revenue collections by systematically eliminating its "middlemen" clergy as revenue agents. Papal action in this regard seems to have been motivated by rising (internal) enforcement costs. As the clergy expanded, it became increasingly difficult for the papacy to monitor shirking and malfeasance at the local level. Given the primitive transportation and communications system of Europe in the Middle Ages, it was relatively easy for a parish priest or a local bishop to appropriate an "excessive" proportion of revenues from parish or diocesan operations, and, in fact, many local prelates became extremely wealthy from this source of revenue. The papacy attacked the problem of malfeasance at the local level by expanding the sale of indulgences, which required penitents to purchase commutations directly from the pontiff.[20] Rather than pay a certain sum of money to the local priest or bishop, the penitent paid a sum directly to the pope in return for a papal guarantee of remission. The widespread use of indulgences began following the First Crusade and became a universal practice by the early fourteenth century. As the practice grew, it provoked trenchant criticism from anti-clerical writers, but, in fact, there was little practical difference between the sale of indulgences by the "home office" and the practice of commutation at the local level (which had been an established practice in Europe since at least the ninth century).

Both the absolute and relative size of papal revenues from indulgences expanded rapidly after the fourteenth century. But the use of indulgences was merely one means by which the papacy sought to consolidate its power of administering punishments and fines in a jurisprudential system that generated vast amounts of wealth. As the "big stick" in its enforcement apparatus, excommunication played an important role in the generation of revenue. It was a legal sanction the pope could impose against the clergy for nonpayment of taxes. Not even abbots and bishops were exempt. Default in payment of the *census*, a tax levied against monastic property, could result in excommunication of all members. And archbishops who failed to pay their assigned visitation tax or service tax (*servitia*) on time could be excommunicated. Excommunication prevented clerics under sentence from exercising their spiritual functions, thereby cutting off most of their revenue.

Excommunication was used as a tool to generate revenues from the laity as well. A major source of the donations of land to the medieval Church derived from excommunicants seeking absolution at death. Partly from such gifts the Church became the largest single landowner in Europe by the thirteenth century, owning as much as one-third of all land in the West. Finally, excommunication, and the related sentence of interdict (the prohibition of trade with excommunicants), were also used by the medieval Church to sanction entire towns or regions.[21] Used in tandem, excommunication and interdict represented a powerful political tool, and as its political clout increased, the use of this sanction became an increasingly important source of profit to the Church. Towns under interdict were occasionally subject to the total confiscation of its inhabitants' goods by the apostolic treasury. In the later Middle Ages, however, this sanction lost force as town inhabitants managed to ignore the sanction.

Heresy as Entry Control

The condemnation of and punishment for heresy was known from the earliest days of the Church as was the penalty of excommunication.[22] But, as we have noted, the suppression of heresy was a particular form of entry control wherein excommunication lost its force. While heresy might be perceived as "any unorthodox belief," a workable definition should probably include any religious teaching that strongly deviates from officially accepted dogma and forms of worship put forward by the Roman Catholic Church.[23] As such, heresy existed alongside Christianity from the very beginning, although the heresy we are concerned with here is the rejection of Catholic orthodoxy encapsulated within large mass movements between the seventh and fifteenth centuries. These heresies confronted Catholic teachings with alternative and fundamentally different interpretations of categories such as existence, death, and spirituality.

Our view is economic in nature. The Church monopoly faced dual problems in the kind of entry control represented by active heretical beliefs. First, heresy presented a doctrinal alternative to the characteristics, philosophical and practical, that the Church attached to the attainment of the final product the Church was selling. Second, loss of members meant loss of revenues and the temporal power that the Church sought in medieval society. The monopoly pursuits of the Church may have actually stimulated heretical developments through arbitrary and capricious repressions, especially in the twelfth and thirteenth centuries.

The Philosophical and Economic Bases of Heresy

Heresy was based on both philosophical and popular (i.e., grassroots) movements. The philosophical basis for heresy was ancient religions, especially those of the late Greek and Roman eras. Gnosticism, literally "religious knowledge," was a non-Christian sect that was regarded as a major threat to the Church from the second century.[24] Philosophically, Gnosticism and most medieval heresy was based on an ancient view of the spiritual world called dualism. According to Lambert (1977, 7), this dualism, a perennial belief spanning two thousand years, is fundamentally inimical to orthodox Christianity: the dualist exaggerates and distorts the ascetic, world-renouncing texts of Scripture and postulates an evil material creation. What can be seen is evil: flesh itself is the creation of an evil God or of a fallen creature, given over to evil. What is unseen is spiritual. The ultimate purpose of existence is to escape from the evil material world. The effects of this set of beliefs on orthodox Christian doctrine are profound: the incarnation of Christ is made void; Christ cannot truly have taken on man's nature since human flesh is a part of the evil creation. With the denial of the incarnation, the orthodox doctrine of redemption is void; the sacraments of the Church, in so far as they use evil matter—water in baptism, bread and wine in the Eucharist—must also be repudiated. Attitudes to sin and free will are changed. Meat-eating is rejected. Logically, marriage must be eschewed, for it perpetuates the human body that is part of the evil creation.

There were of course many variants of this dualism with some significant differences between Eastern and Western thought.[25] But the basic philosophy spanned the entire history of heresy from the Gnostics to the Cathars and the Waldenses, a heresy still extant on the eve of the Protestant revolt against Catholicism.

Yet another foundation of medieval heresy was blatantly economic since it was the very foundation of "popular" heretical rebellions. The foundation of alternative theologies on often arcane and complex philosophies would probably not have gone very far in a period of widespread illiteracy. One great impetus for medieval heresy was the belief that a poor church should supersede the rich and powerful feudal Roman Catholic Church. The opulence of the Church was proof positive that it had lost touch with the poverty and simplicity espoused by Jesus and early Christians. In this view the Church had become an institution in which the privileged clergy jealously guarded their monopoly on the key to salvation. The attributes of the Church were power, glory, and wealth, and although over the centuries individuals and, subsequently, whole orders, such as the Franciscans, came to the fore aspiring to emulate the poverty and asceticism of the Early Church, these were only partial solutions that had little effect in changing the fundamental nature of the medieval Church (Erbstösser 1984, 9). Again and again during the Middle Ages, the sentiment of "poverty and service as a means to salvation" was advanced as a source of popular heresy to counter the image of the increasingly wealthy, property- and power-driven Church.

The Church was also faced with secular power struggles in which particular heresies and particular heretics played large roles. Investiture disputes regarding who—the papacy or local secular authorities—had the power to appoint bishops and monastery heads was of course one source of conflict (Chapter 2).[26] But there were other struggles of a secular nature linked to heretical developments. In particular, the emergence of medieval towns and the emergence and establishment of the medieval bourgeoisie as a social, economic, and political power became a serious threat to Church dominance. Town burghers coalesced to overthrow feudal lords (many of them bishops and archbishops) who sought to place restrictions on their activities, including trade and artisan manufacture. The somewhat natural "libertarian" attitudes of traders and artisans and the desire for "self-rule" of town dwellers helped foster the protection of heretics and particular heresies within towns. Dualistic teachings became part of a new, town-based ideology extolling principles of merit and achievement through asceticism, poverty, and inner piety and rejecting the pomp and external forms of Church worship. Peasants were attracted to the new teachings and their interest was "based on rejection of the clergy with a very specific abolition of tithing" (Erbstösser 1984, 75). These twin themes of "poverty as the way to salvation" and "rejection of a corrupt monopoly Church that taxed even the poor" permeated the major heretical episodes of the early and later medieval Church. Many of these movements, especially the Waldensian heretics active from the twelfth to the sixteenth centuries and the Cathari from the eleventh to the thirteenth, adopted a milder form of dualism that simply espoused a life of poverty and chastity to achieve ultimate salvation. It is important to note that the local clergy, especially in southern France and northern Italy, were much attracted to the popular ideals espoused by heretics and were, in many cases, themselves spearheads of heretical movements.[27]

Patterns of Repression and Accommodation of Heresy

The Church's response to these philosophical and economic developments was twofold. Early in the period the Church attempted to put down heresy using Crusades and other devices as a means of entry control. Later, the Church attempted to mold particular institutions through product differentiation to accommodate "aesthetics" within the Church. Here the Church attempted to counter heresy with the foundation of mendicant and supplicant orders. When this kind of differentiation failed to stem the tide of heretical developments in western Europe, the Church moved toward severe repression in order to assert doctrinal hegemony and maintain the Church's monopoly hold on society.

Heretical movements quickened in western Europe around the year 1000. Early on the Church engaged in repression. The center of the movement until the middle of the eleventh century was northeastern France and the German territories. Only later did heretical developments emerge in northern Italy. These popular heresies rejected the worship of the cross, denounced the sacraments, condemned "intercession" on behalf of the dead, and refused to pay tithes. Along positive lines they stressed chastity and asceticism as exercises in piety and espoused poverty as the Christian ideal. Repression followed. In Orleans, 13 heretics, including clergy, were burned at the stake in 1022. In Monteforte, near Turin in Italy, 30 were convicted by the Archbishop of Milan and burned about the same time (Erbstösser 1984, 62–64).

Despite drastic measures the punishment of heretics was spasmodic and under the jurisdiction of the bishops until the twelfth century. Afterward, in common with the transaction-costs Church policy associated with excommunication, the secular authority was brought into the suppression of heresy. In the 1120s French synods came down hard on heretics who were to be excommunicated and shunned by the faithful. More important, if they did not repent, the *state* or secular authority was to implement further punishments—exile, expropriation, and imprisonment. Here again, however, the anti-clerical views of the princes and leaders of emerging towns prevented them from carrying out such sentences. Such was certainly true in Italy where many Italian towns correctly surmised that more power to the Church meant less power to them. Economic interests, throughout the medieval period, figured significantly in the success and perpetuation of popular heresies such as Catharism and Waldensianism.

The grudging success of popular heresy, especially in southern France and northern Italy, produced a marked change in Church policy. Pope Innocent III launched a two-prong offensive. More moderate groups of Waldenses were making inroads in the Catholic clergy. Innocent accommodated and gave credence to the poverty movement *within* the Church. He did this by granting legitimacy to mendicant orders such as the Dominicans and Franciscans. These two groups adopted the lifestyle of the heretics—wearing sackcloth, traveling on foot and begging, giving aid and comfort to the poor in France (Dominicans) and Italy (Franciscans). In 1217 Dominic was given papal permission to found his order and the Franciscans received their order regulations in 1223. Friars from these orders debated the Cathari in France and the Waldenses in Italy but failed to convince many heretics. In fact, the wealth- and power-accumulation of the Church continued apace. In regular Church circles, especially in the power base at Rome, these innovative Church orders were sometimes looked on with grave suspicion.[28]

The failure of this institutional innovation to stem the tide of heresy was met with much harsher repressions by the centralized Church monopoly after 1200. Even before the official recognition of the new Church orders, Innocent launched the Albigensian Crusade against the Cathari in southern France.[29] Between 1209 and 1229 an all-out assault took place with the monopoly Church attacking a Christian territory. Once more, however, the action must be viewed in terms of overall social and political struggle. The monopoly Church, represented by Innocent, was allied with the French monarchy in subduing the feudal Duke Raymond VI of Toulouse. Innocent wanted the monarch to force the secular powers in southern France to deal with heresy. When the town-based secular authorities refused to take action against heretics and Jews, Innocent launched the Albigensian Crusade with the aid of the French monarchy.[30]

The result was mass executions. The military leader of the Albigensian Crusade was Simon de Montfort, a northern French noble, whose armies attacked towns in southern France. While the aim was to crush the (non-violent) Cathari, whole populations were slain indiscriminately. In Béziers, "no one bothered to distinguish between Cathari and Catholics. Even those who had fled to the churches were not spared—the chronicles speak of 20,000 murdered, 2,000 of them in churches" (Erbstösser 1984, 112). Towns (including a famous siege on Carcassonne) were ruthlessly plundered and the towns of southern France were brought, at least temporarily, into submission by 1229.

The pattern of armed suppression continued in other locales. Widespread suppression by Catholics of the Bogomil heresy in the fifteenth century is another good example of the vicious repression of anti-Catholicism by the papacy and economic interests that clothed themselves in clerical garb.[31] At times, economic interests of Catholics and Bogomil Bosnians coincided in the region. When they did not and the economic interests of the Latin Church were threatened, threats of Crusades and armed repression followed. In the fifteenth century, according to Erbstösser (1984, 56),

Bosnian peasants were persecuted, captured and sold in droves into slavery by native Catholic nobles and foreign traders. Dubrovnik developed into a slave market, and young women and children were particularly sought after. The buyers were Venetians and traders from Crete, Bari, Marseilles and Majorca. As those being sold were heretics, the church had no objections to their mass-scale enslavement.

Formal trials and witch hunts—the inquisitions of the later Middle Ages—followed and interplayed with armed aggressions throughout Europe. Far from being the peacemakers who stemmed the tide of heresy in western

Europe, the Dominican and Franciscan orders were given the task of carrying out inquisitions against heretics in 1233 and 1237 respectively. The Treaty of Paris (1229) gave papal inquisitors unlimited powers of search and seizure. In southern France and Italy, despite reluctant compliance by secular authorities, the inquisitors proceeded ruthlessly to acquire wealth for the papacy, all in the cause of fighting heresy. The inquisitors answered only to the pope whose aims were total domination of dogma (an indirect aim) and the acquisition of as much wealth as possible for the coffers of the Church (a direct aim).[32] As the repression moved northward to central Europe (north of the Alps) in the fourteenth century to attack the Waldensians, the level of persecution and abuse grew. Tens of thousands of people were tried, condemned, relieved of property, or killed. Thousands of witches were murdered between 1300 and 1499 alone (Kieckhefer 1976, 108–47).[33] Since heretics were often difficult to identify, bona fide believers in the tenets of the Latin Church were often snared in the same net (in statistical terms, a Type II error). Nevertheless, the Church persisted in consolidating and preserving its power despite these individual consequences. Such actions are difficult to reconcile with a public-interest objective of Church policy.

Conclusion

The degree of the Church's success at controlling exit and entry over the Middle Ages is debatable, as are the economic effects of Church policy. One major inquisition followed another right up to the first part of the fifteenth century. The horror and terror caused by the "holy inquisitors" throughout the Middle Ages in France, Italy, Germany, and Spain created backlash reactions by many believing Catholics, but the competition was, at least for some points in time, suppressed.[34] As history and the success of the Protestant Reformation records, however, the Latin Church was ultimately unable to suppress entry.

Heretical developments, such as those represented by the Cathari and the Waldenses, did not represent competition *within orthodox or traditional* forms of Christianity. But they had the effect of offering alternative belief patterns to members and potential members of the Latin Church. The immediate deleterious effects on Church revenues is obvious, but the potential rise of theological alternatives, especially alternatives that coincided with secular competitors for Church power, most certainly motivated the centralized Church at Rome. The Church's suppression of heresy and its use of excommunication were clearly effective in achieving particular Church goals at particular times.

The question of the *long-term* economic effects of excommunication, the establishment of canon law, and heresy suppression are somewhat less tractable. If dualistic philosophies along with the enthronement of poverty had captured the day in medieval Europe, economic development would have most certainly suffered. But the Church's policy along these lines must be read in a broader political and social context. The economic alignment of towns with popular heretical movements may have encouraged economic development through the protection of nascent and developing markets, trade, exchange, and technologies. In the early Middle Ages the suppression of towns was in the Church's interest. As such, the suppression of heresy was as much a pretext for the suppression of towns and markets as it was an attempt to control theological, doctrinal, or institutional entry.

On other fronts the monopoly and rent-seeking aims of the Church might have accidentally promoted a Church role in the economic development of Europe: the provision of law and order by means of ecclesiastic courts enforcing canon law. Regardless of the motives of the Church, the actual operation of canon law *helped* provide a *consistent* system of property rights' enforcement at a time when governments were unable to supply similar public services in some areas. The Church was, of course, not the sole provider of services, and its move into certain areas of law—marriage law, for example—was a power-grabbing, rent-seeking strategy to supplant secular arrangements. Some of this legal incursion on the part of the Latin Church—Church laws respecting usury, for instance—may have positively thwarted market developments in western Europe. But while many of the Church's activities appear to have had other ends (monopoly, wealth, power), some contributed to an efficient legal framework producing a "public good." To this extent, the emergence of modern capitalism might have been an unintended by-product of rent seeking by the monopoly Church of Rome. Nevertheless, the horror inflicted on society by the bellicose policies of the Roman Catholic Church must stand in stark contrast to any benefits produced.

NOTES

1. This definition, as any definition of heresy, is unsatisfactory for some purposes. What, for example, is the difference between "heresy" and "reform?" Did Luther, for instance, want to change the system or reform the system? We sidestep such issues here, but they are of genuine importance to medievalists and to historiographic interpretations of some events over the period.

2. There are also important and sometimes subtle distinctions between witchcraft and heresy and between religion and magic. One distinction regarding the latter is that magic (often related to demonology and witchcraft) is goal oriented, immediate, worldly, or empirical (sacrifice brings good crops), whereas religion is

"other-worldly," organized, public, and nonempirical (supplication for eventual salvation). There are, of course, many gradations between these extreme definitions of magic and religion (see the fascinating discussion in Levack 1987, 1–24). Magic may use the power of gods or spirits and religion—it often did in received Greek and Roman forms from the early centuries A.D. The emergence of the Christian devil and the links of witchcraft with heretical demonology is chiefly a Western phenomenon. Witchcraft, devil worship, the practice of magic, and belief-systems contrary to those of the Roman Catholic Church all became forms of heresy. For some purposes distinctions are important (see the discussion of magic, science, and technology in Chapter 9), but they are all lumped together here as "heresy." It is useful to remember that one person's cult is another person's religion.

3. Note that for excommunication to be effective, individuals must have *self-selected* belief in the tenets of the faith. Moreover, they had to maintain that belief in order to work toward removal of the condition of excommunication. On this count excommunication is vastly different from heresy. Heretics were oblivious of excommunication because they *self-selected out* of the basic tenets and practices of the Roman Catholic faith.

4. Certainly, hundreds of thousands of individuals were brought before Inquisitorial tribunals in all of western Europe. Levack, who studied witchcraft in the late medieval period (roughly fifteenth through seventeenth centuries), gives figures approximating 110,000 prosecutions and 60,000 executions in Europe (more than half in Germany) (Levack 1987, 21).

5. Ultimately, the Church was unable to suppress the entry of Luther and other "heretical" reformers. The revolt of Henry VIII and the emergence of other Protestant religions was clearly presaged by earlier heretics such as John Wyclif (1330–1384).

6. As Lea (1971, 115) observed:

It was always "the poor" on whom charity could be most worthily and advantageously bestowed, and the success of [the Church's] teachings is seen in the immense growth of its possessions. . . . Even so high-minded a pontiff as Alexander II, in a case of voluntary fratricide, had no hesitation in imposing as penance the confiscation to "the poor" of the whole of the penitent's property, allowing him, however, the usufruct of one half of it during life.

7. Obviously, if everyone had been convinced with certainty that no crime could go undetected and unpunished by an all-knowing God, the enforcement costs would have been zero. We do not contend that enforcement costs were zero, but they were much lower than in secular circumstances. Allowing for changes in technology and institutions such as one finds in an Orwellian scheme, "Big Brother" served the same purpose as the Almighty in this respect.

8. The Penitentials (manuals that prescribe "tariffs" for various sins, used by priests in assigning penance) of the medieval Church dealt to a large extent with sexual sins (Payer 1984), but treated also sins involving violation of person and property (e.g., rape), and simple crimes such as assault and theft.

9. See Chapter 5 for a discussion of marriage regulations and fines levied against infractions of such laws.

10. Public penance may have had spillover benefits in the economy as well. For traders it lowered the transaction costs of distinguishing cheats from noncheats, and this may have generated more trade and greater economic growth.

11. As penance came more and more to be assigned at the local level, the degree of knowledge the priest had about the penitent's personal circumstances—including his wealth—increased, thus making "price discrimination" more efficient. Only in particularly serious cases, such as violence committed against a priest, was judgment reserved for the pope (Hill 1951, 216).

12. Hill (1951, 217) gives a number of representative cases taken from the Register of Bishop Oliver Sutton, who presided over the See of Lincoln from 1280 to 1299. These examples demonstrate that restitution was often required of those accused of theft or other harm. In one instance the bishop ordered the thieves who had stolen swans from the rector of Gosberton to either restore the birds or repay their value. In another, John Gile of Kidlington, who injured Nigel of Hargrave by dragging him out of the churchyard of St. Giles in Oxford (where the latter sought sanctuary), was required to pay Nigel's doctor bills, visit him in prison, and use all lawful means to secure his release. Finally, certain individuals who desecrated the church of Gosberton were ordered to sell their weapons and equipment and give the proceeds to the parish priest to pay for the damages.

13. The first Council of Lyon (1245) declared that excommunication did not jeopardize salvation unless it was ignored or refuted by the excommunicant (Tentler 1977, 42). A person might be excommunicated, seek and obtain absolution, and die as a respected member of the Church, fully expecting to secure a place in heaven.

14. An unusual measure, related to excommunication, yet different, was the declaration of "anathema" on a sinner. Anathema was reserved for excommunicants who refused God's merciful offer of salvation and therefore were destined for hell. It was sometimes treated like a "sentence" handed down by the Church. In the Middle Ages, anathema took the form of a solemn ritual, conducted in Church, during which the excommunicant was formally given over to Satan, the community allowing the devil to "rage inside the excommunicant" (Vodola 1986, 45–46). This not only meant that his soul was destined for hell, but also that various ills were likely to befall him in mortal life. For example, the Canonist Johannes Andreae (d. 1348) argued that excommunication "put the sinner into the hands of the devil, who could do with him as he wished"; and further, that excommunication hastened the onset of illness and death. Those subject to anathema typically regarded it as a "sentence" and attempted vigorously to have it removed.

15. See Chapter 8 for a treatment of purgatory as a form of product differentiation.

16. This *in negotio exhumationis* allowed the court to bypass the delays and uncertainties associated with probate, and at the same time circumvent the secular jurisdiction over immovables (Lea 1883, 246). Thus, the estate of an excommunicant was automatically brought within the jurisdiction of the ecclesiastic court.

17. See Chapter 6 for a discussion of how the Church engaged in similar confiscatory actions against usurers.

18. See, however, Chapter 5 on the Church's returns from marital regulations.

19. These taxes gave the papacy a way of appropriating profits collected by its downstream agents in the field. The local clergy (agents) were allowed to retain sufficient revenues to cover operating expenses, plus some small percentage of profits (i.e., a kind of "profit-sharing" plan was in effect).

20. Here an analogy with modern retailing is suggested: the Church avoided the successive monopoly problem created by local priests and bishops by moving to direct retailing akin to catalog sales. The direct retailing of Church services (more assurances of eternal salvation) increased Vatican profits, at least over some period of time. Profits of local parishes and bishoprics were reduced by avoiding this aspect of successive monopolization.

21. The Church even collected religious "tolls" from persons who passed through towns under sentence of interdict (Lunt 1934, 1:131).

22. Excommunication for "economic crimes" such as failure to pay a debt was known as far back as the fourth and fifth centuries and in the eighth century penitential heresy was strongly condemned along with most other serious matters. According to "An Old Irish Table of Commutations" "there are certain sins which do not deserve any remission of penance, however long the time that shall be asked for them, unless God Himself shortens it through death or a message of sickness . . . such as are parricides and manslaughters and man-stealings, and such as brigandage and druidism and satirizing [probably the making of defamatory verses], and such as adultery and lewdness and lying and heresy" (McNeill and Gamer 1938, 143).

23. An accurate definition of heresy might simply be "an opinion held by a minority of men which the majority declares unacceptable and is powerful enough to punish" (Christie-Murray 1976,1). Most definitions are narrower, however.

24. The threat and prosecution of heresy from the earliest days of the Church through the late Middle Ages are subject to a number of intriguing possible interpretations that we do not analyze here in depth. First, it appears that rival religions that proselytized were attacked more harshly than were rival religions that did not proselytize. Judaism, a nonproselytizing religion, managed to exist alongside the growing monopoly in *relative* peace. The Jews experienced serious repression from particular inquisitorial interests only in late medieval Spain (Peters 1988, 86–104). Such behavior, if convincingly demonstrated, would be evidence of worldly motives influencing the content of Church doctrine and practice. Yet another point is that the sure practice of entry control was absolutely prerequisite to the establishment of the Church monopoly. The "official" condemnation of heresy in the first millennium was attended by costly "enforcement." High transactions costs in the form of highly dispersed citizenry, high communications and transportation costs, and general illiteracy meant that magic, witchcraft, and heretical ideas could flourish, relatively unmolested, in the countryside. Later, as power began to be concentrated in the Roman Church and as transaction costs to prosecuting heresy fell, formal, active pursuit was initiated. Heresy and heresy control, according to this interpre-

tation, were important elements in the transition from a "competitive" to a monopoly environment.

25. A heretical assault on the Byzantine Church called Bogomilism, a ninth-through eleventh-century heresy, is a case in point. The Bogomils advocated a modern dualism wherein God banished one of the angels (Satanael) to earth. This "fall" occasioned the creation of the earth *by Satan*, who, in his creation of man, managed to imprison good angels in earthly bodies creating a conflict between "good" and "evil" within man himself. Christ was a messenger sent by God to acquaint man with his fate and to banish Satan to hell. Satan escaped, however, enlisting the support of the wealthy, the Church and Church theologians. The Bogomils emphasized personal spirituality (rather than that enforced by the orthodox Church) and were distinctly optimistic in their belief that "good" will ultimately triumph over "evil" (see Erbstösser 1984, 47–49). Catharism was also based on a variant of this philosophy (Christie-Murray 1976, 105–6).

26. Erbstösser (1984, 76) describes the "investiture struggle" over the latter half of the eleventh century through the early years of the twelfth century as a "huge offensive to elevate the Papacy to the ideological and political centre of Europe."

27. Illiteracy was rife among low-level Catholic clergy. Over the early medieval period, clerics were increasingly indoctrinated into the Church monopoly by requiring the learning of Latin—a literacy test. In part, this requirement might have been an attempt to strengthen the upstream part of the vertical monopoly and to help guard against opportunistic behavior and the attractions of popular heresy at the lowest levels of the sale of the Church's chief product.

28. The suspicions surrounding these orders, particularly the Franciscans, persisted. Later, in the fourteenth century, John XXII reigned in the Franciscans who espoused poverty as an ideal leading to perfection. According to Lambert (1977, 202), John left the clear impression that "heresy had come to consist in opposition to the orders of the pope," who did not believe that "perfection through poverty" was the Christian ideal. Neither, of course, did the monopoly apparatus of the Church. The extremist "Spiritual Franciscans" split from the Church over these matters.

29. The term "Albigensian" is a synonym for Cathari—the southern French town of Albi was the center of Catharism at the time.

30. The Albigensian campaign came on the heels of the recently concluded Fourth Crusade (1202–1204), which Erbstösser (1984, 112) correctly characterizes as having been "directed at Christian Byzantium" with the effect of destroying the empire. At its centers, "the Crusaders, avid for spoils, had set up the Latin Empire, demonstrating the value to them of the Crusades." (In this connection, see Chapter 7.)

31. Bogomilism was institutionalized as the "Bosnian Church "

32. Inquisitors dispatched wide ranges of punishment, from a "slap on the hand" for poor peasants, through property confiscations and death for serious (often aristocratic) heretics. Even for the poor, however, a "penance pilgrimage" (which profited area churches) was required (see Erbstösser 1984, 137).

33. Details of the witch trials reveal a wide variety of crimes as shown in the following reports. In France (1308–1313) a bishop, Guichard of Troyes, was tried

by secular and ecclesiastic authorities for sorcery (killing a queen and others by "image magic" and potions). Some witch trials reflect the desire of the papacy (allied with the monarchical interests) to put down towns and feudal lords. Between 1320 and 1326, the allies of Federico of Montefeltra (count of Urbino) were charged by John XXII with idolatry, heresy, and invocation. Some accounts clearly reveal the ignorance of the times. In Rome in 1420, a woman was burned to death by an inquisitor for changing herself into the form of a cat and killing children, with the devil's aid. (See Kieckhefer 1976, 108, 110, and 121 passim, for these and many other examples.)

34. Many victims of the Spanish Inquisition were Jews. For this reason, torture and confiscation of property were the preferred instruments of judicial investigation in connection with inquisitorial proceedings (see Lea 1883, chap. 7).

PART TWO

Rent Seeking Through Demand and Supply Manipulations

How the Church Preempted the Marriage Market

Introduction: Incursions into the Medieval Family

Everyone familiar with the infamous dispute between the Catholic Church and King Henry VIII of England, over who he could and could not marry, knows that the medieval Church wielded great power over the institution of marriage. But the fundamental questions of how and why the Church gained control over this basic contract have received far less attention. This chapter shows that over time the Church successfully captured the medieval marriage market by implementing a twofold strategy. First, it linked regulatory compliance with eternal salvation; second, it varied its interpretations of what constituted a "valid" marriage in accord with certain economic objectives.

In regard to the marriage market, the medieval Church was able to increase its rents by increasing the amount of litigation (brought before Church courts) occasioned by successive changes in marriage regulations. By restricting its members to valid marriages if they hoped to attain heaven, the medieval Church was able to increase its societal influence and to extract higher rents from its "customers." Moreover, regional variation in interpretations of canon law offered distinct opportunities for rent seeking by lawyers and Church officials, particularly when a marriage was found in discord with Church doctrine. Finally, by redefining a valid marriage to require a priest's blessing, local economic agents of the Church were given controlling roles in the Christian marriage market.

As noted earlier, the medieval Church supplied a "premium" product in the form of assurances of salvation for those who accepted its doctrine. But to be a Christian in good standing, loyal customers were required to "buy" a *package* of doctrines, whose makeup and market mix were determined by the Church hierarchy. In other words, customers were given an "all-or-nothing" offer in the sense that they could not pick and choose among the various, often interconnected, doctrines that comprised the overall package. By introducing more elements into the doctrinal mix, the Church could manipulate market variables in an effort to increase profits. Marriage rules were simply one component of the overall doctrinal package and should be interpreted in that light.

Economic theory holds that as a dominant-firm monopolist in the salvation industry, the medieval Church could be expected to pursue demand maintenance policies, including the establishment of rules and regulations governing the interpretation of Church doctrine. The application of economic theory to policy decisions of the medieval Church is therefore illuminating in several doctrinal areas, as this chapter and succeeding chapters attempt to show.

Marriage as a Medieval Institution

Inasmuch as medieval society considered marriage a precondition for establishing a family, the ideas of marriage and family were necessarily intertwined. Like its contemporary counterpart, the medieval family was a social and economic organization. As a social unit, the medieval family has been subjected to extensive study; however, its economic character has received less attention.

Economic Character of the Medieval Family

The medieval family, like its modern counterpart, was heavily influenced by the existing state of technology. The relatively primitive technology of the Middle Ages imposed high information and transaction costs on economic agents, thereby encouraging large kinship groups as a means to pool and verify information, reduce transaction costs, and "insure" against uncertainty. Uncertainty had many faces: variation in annual agricultural output, disease and poor health, abbreviated life expectancy, and insecurity of property rights. Without a strong government insurance markets were slow to develop because the necessary enforcement could not be assured. The family, and the kinship group which is its extended form, may therefore be seen as substitutes for the modern insurance company or certain social programs usually provided by modern governments (Posner 1980, 12).

Then as now the size and structure of the medieval family were shaped by the existing laws, customs, and institutions of society. The medieval family functioned as a self-serving unit that provided defense, education, justice, religion, and livelihood for its members. Kinship groups were of vital importance in facilitating activities such as arranging marriages, transferring property, and monitoring group members to prevent malfeasance. Theoretically speaking, the size of the kinship group in the Middle Ages depended on the nature and development of property rights. The less developed the system of property rights and its enforcement mechanisms, the greater the need for "insurance" and thus the larger the expected kinship group.

At a certain strata of society, therefore, medieval marriages were a natural device used by monarchs and the landed aristocracy to consolidate and enlarge kingdoms or estates. Consequently, there were clear economic benefits to be derived from the power to control marriages, and marriages at a certain social level were arranged in line with these economic benefits. The objective of increasing the utility of the conjugal parties to a marriage was, in these instances, secondary to the goal of acquiring land. Under these circumstances, marriage regulations could be invoked in a particular economic interest. One family, wishing to resist a family "merger," could fight off a competitor's "raid" by invoking existing prohibitions against "incestuous" marriages (Gies and Gies 1987, 52) or by lobbying for new prohibitions. Another family, eagerly pursuing a merger, could apply pressure to lift marriage restrictions that impeded consolidation. During the Middle Ages, therefore, there were clear opportunities for rent seeking on the part of those who made the rules concerning marriage eligibility and contractual validity.

Secular versus Church-Approved Marriages

Like all social institutions, marriage has evolved over time. Ideally, we would like to be able to track the "natural" evolution of marriage so as to be able to compare its "pure" nature with the form that has emerged as a result of cultural and institutional influences. In concrete terms, however, it is difficult to define a natural path of evolution or even to specify what constitutes a "traditional" marriage. Alternatively, we attempt to distinguish between "secular" and "religious" (Church-sanctioned) marriages by tracing the evolution of rules and regulations concerning marriage devised by the medieval Church and comparing them with their secular counterparts.

A secular, albeit modern, view of marriage is provided by Becker (1981, 27), who defines marriage as "a written, oral, or customary long-term contract between a man and a woman to produce children, food, and other commodities in a common household." This notion provides a starting point for Becker's economic analysis of the household. According to this economic schema, a market is said to exist wherein mutually beneficial exchange occurs whenever the value of the individual's share of the marital joint product exceeds the value that could be obtained by remaining single. In such a market the level of welfare of individuals and households is related to the kind and number of constraints placed on contracting parties.[1]

Becker's notion of marriage (minus its modern theoretical trappings) is easier to transplant to early history than the religious notion of marriage that eventually displaced the secular version after the medieval Church entered the picture. In the early Middle Ages secular marriages were used as a means of trade. Marriage contracts, like purchase contracts, were used by aristocratic families to pool resources and sustain economic growth. The contracting families gained from such arrangements both socially and economically. Recognizing this fact, secular law was designed to protect family inheritances and the economic status of the family. Church regulations, by contrast, were sometimes at odds with these goals.

After the Church became a dominant player in the marriage market, secular marriages came to mean simply those beyond the network of Church regulations. These marriages were engaged in by nonmembers of the medieval Christian Church, such as Jews, Muslims, and pagans. By custom, these marriages were arranged by parents, but in some cases they were contracted by mutual consent of the partners independently of parents' initiatives. Under secular law, cohabitation among partners of the same class was also recognized as a legal union (Brundage 1987, 436). In general, secular law considered marriage a private matter and required neither ceremony nor record. Moreover, secular marriages could be terminated at will, without court proceedings (Helmholz 1974, 4; Brundage 1987, 94).

As the medieval Church gained power, status, and influence, it used its position of moral authority to gain access to the marriage market. Gradually, marriage became less a private matter and more a public matter. At the height of its power the medieval Church faced only two rivals *within* Western Christendom: the monarchy and the nobility. Both rivals used marriage as a means of increasing their power, wealth, and influence, and their success in this regard was often perceived by the Church as a threat to its own power, wealth, and prestige. In the context of our analysis it is important to understand the *nature* of Church-imposed marriage regulations and the particular ways in which they changed. In other words, before we can draw tentative inferences about whether the public-interest or private-interest hypothesis better explains the historical record, we must investigate *how*, *where*, and *why* the Church imposed such constraints. Were these constraints simply responses to the utility-maximizing demands of customers in an era of poverty and distress (i.e., a public-interest response)? Or were the actions of the Church calculated to increase profits in the face of encroachment on its domain by elements of secular society or competing religions?

Although we cannot provide definitive answers to such historically distant questions, we can analyze the economic consequences of successive marriage regulations on the medieval marriage market and, in particular, their effects on the utility of the marriage partners. For prospective marriage partners with a low discount rate, the higher cost of a public, Church-approved marriage may have been offset by certain benefits: elimination of uncertainty about marital status, more security of existing property rights, and greater assurance of salvation. Those individuals with a high discount rate, however, faced higher costs due to binding regulations that restricted choice. Additional costs were imposed insofar as the Church's regulations subjected Christians who planned to marry to public scrutiny, greater parental influence, and more bureaucratic red tape.

For all Christians, moreover, the medieval Church's prohibition against divorce raised the cost of marriage. By removing prospects of recontracting, which was permissible under secular law, the Church increased the cost of correcting "errors" in mate selection, *ex post*. *Ex ante*, the divorce prohibition prompted individuals seeking marriage to spend greater amounts of time and money searching for a suitable spouse. Christians could avoid these costs only at the risk of losing the Church's chief product—the assurance of salvation. Although the net balance of utility resulting from these regulations is problematic, the changes in regulations over time clearly created opportunities for the medieval Church to extract rents from its members.

Before proceeding deeper into this question, a few caveats are in order. Our interpretation of the policy behavior of the medieval Church in regard to the marriage market necessarily rests on conditions in specific markets at specific times. In fact, enormous intertemporal variability existed in particular practices and even differed markedly between and within the different countries embraced by Christianity. Consequently, concrete generalizations in this domain are difficult, if not impossible. Our position is simply that a "comparative-statics test" of the Church's manipulation of marriage regulations is consistent with the expected behavior of a dominant firm that faces competitive challenges in its contested market. Whatever public benefits might be attributed to the marriage regulations enforced by the medieval Church, it should be pointed out that such rules established doctrinal barriers to entry for other prospective religions and served as a bulwark against intrusion by secular institutions vying for the same customers in certain service markets.

The Nature and Collection of Rents in a Medieval Marriage Market

By tying the prospect of salvation to the "blessedness" of marriage, the medieval Church could stimulate the demand for litigation and thereby increase its fee income. The fees established by the medieval Church in this regard amounted to "excise taxes" on the faithful. Given the extensive and complex doctrines that comprise a "faith," the medieval Church demonstrated a preference for this revenue strategy over other alternatives that might be considered more efficient from a contemporary perspective. For example, the question arises as to why Church finance in the Middle Ages did not rely on the simpler fiscal strategy of imposing "income" or "head" taxes?

In fact, attempts to raise revenue by such measures were not lacking. The medieval Church tried to implement the practice of "tithing" by the faithful, and it did levy an annual tax known as "Peter's Pence."[2] But historical circumstances made it costly and relatively inefficient for the medieval Church to engage heavily in income taxation. Primitive conditions of transportation and communication meant that information and transaction costs were high in the Middle Ages. The complexity of the Church's administrative structure, the distances over which revenues needed to travel, the available technology for repatriating such revenues, and the opportunities for evasion, all contributed to high collection costs for an income tax. Consequently, the medieval Church turned to user charges, or excise taxes, as a more practical (i.e., less costly) strategy of revenue enhancement.

Fees charged for blessing and dissolving marriages, granting exceptions to endogamy rules, and enforcing marriage contracts were collected at the local level by regional fiscal agents (the clergy) and subsequently transferred to the Vatican (Chapter 2). Inasmuch as the Vatican's fiscal agent, the papal *camera*, had the power to recover debts and excommunicate people for nonpayment, the entire ecclesiastic system is reminiscent of, and may have provided the model for, later secular financial administrations, such as Colbert's system of *intendants* in France or Elizabeth I's system of justices of the peace in England, both of which also used local and regional fiscal agents to collect rents and remit taxes to the central authority.

For the faithful, the demand for Church guidelines, expertise, and guarantees in various areas of human activity—of which marriage comprised merely one sphere of action—derived from the overall demand for salvation. Changes in relative prices of these particularized demands could be expected to induce changes in the price elasticity of a specific service, but the overall demand for assurances of salvation retained its price-inelasticity, despite elasticity variations among its component parts. Thus, user charges constituted a flexible, relatively efficient means of raising revenues.

Rents were available in religious markets because the price of the "product" was above marginal cost for *some*, but not all buyers. Inasmuch as some customers self-selected out of a wide assortment of salvation-related activities, the Church could engage in a crude form of second-degree, block-rate pricing. Differential pricing also allowed the inclusion of paupers and low-income customers into the market, although the emergence of the mendicant orders of friars suggests that the poor and indigent were not being ministered to in optimal amounts. All things considered, the poor typically consumed a smaller proportion of religious services than did the rich. For example, lacking property, the poor had few concerns about their heirs (whose legitimacy was determined by marriage regulations) and therefore were less likely than the rich to marry in a "proper" Church-approved ceremony (Lynch 1992, 292).

Economic theory holds that under usual circumstances monopoly profits can be collected only once, and that it is futile to attempt to levy monopoly charges on a wide range of services (Posner 1976; Bork 1978). But the power to price discriminate among buyers of services in a local, diffuse market, coupled with the inability to exact *full* monopoly charges through a poll tax or income tax, meant that it was economically rational for the upstream monopolist to continue to devise new rules and regulations for the attainment of ultimate salvation.[3] The evidence points to just this sort of policy behavior by the medieval Church in the matter of many salvation-related issues in general, and in that of marriage regulations in particular.

Endogamy, Inheritance, and Economic Interests

The incest prohibition was defined and redefined by the Church throughout the Middle Ages, and its manipulation was a central "public-interest" pretext for entry into the marriage market.[4] Church regulations over endogamy (marriage within a kinship group or "inbreeding") varied widely over the early medieval period. Initial regulations against marriage among kin in the second degree prevented the marriage of first cousins. Over time, these regulations were extended to the third and eventually to the seventh degree (sixth cousins), making marriages between second and more distant cousins sinful (incestuous) in the eyes of the Church. By altering and enhancing marital regulations, the Church increased its ability to attach the assurance of salvation to the marriage contract. This served not only to increase Church control over the matrimonial process, but it also provided ample opportunity for rent extraction through dispensations and exemptions. Monopoly benefits accrued to the Church in a two-pronged fashion. Direct benefits flowed to the Church in the form of the fees exacted for exemptions. Indirect benefits also accrued as a result of Church regulation. These involved the suppression of dynastic development that lessened external threats to the power and authority of the Church.

Eligibility Rules

The recurring controversy that centered around incestuous marriages began as early as the fourth century. The first prohibition against marriage to cousins came under Emperor Theodosius I (ca. 385), although dispensations were sometimes awarded to allow such marriages (Goody 1983, 55).[5] Secular law maintained no prohibitions against the marriage of first cousins in the sixth century, as documented in Justinian's *Institutes*, where it is stated that the children of brothers and sisters can marry (Goody 1983, 56). The Church pushed the issue of endogamy to the forefront, however, and extended the regulations against relational marriages to the third degree which prevented the marriage of second cousins (individuals with the same great-grandparent). Although such marriages were illegal in the eyes of the Church, there were economic benefits that often accompanied incestuous marriages, such as the ownership of land for the families that arranged these marriages, which in turn strengthened their economic and social position. The prospect of obtaining such benefits frequently created intense rivalry in the marriage market, the actual goal being ownership of the land involved in the marriage contract. As a result, families sometimes used the Church's prohibition of incestuous marriage to accuse competitors of illegitimate intentions (Gies and Gies 1987, 52) to secure land through marriage contracts. Families that invoked the Church's regulations hoped to maintain or secure land for their own families.

Over time the ban of incestuous marriages became a societal norm, thereby fostering practices of concubinage and polygamy from the sixth to the eighth centuries. This predictably led to problems with divorce, with one of the central allowable causes being an absence of mutual consent to the marriage. Since marriages were frequently arranged by parents, potential spouses were not always freely consenting. Like incestuous marriage, divorce was prohibited by the Church. As a result, for a marriage to be dissolved the question of consent became a focal point that provided an avenue for rent seeking.

Arranged marriages were consistent with the practice of consanguineous marriage. The ability to arrange one's own marriage, however, was a clear departure from the control of the family and kinship group and a move toward maximizing one's own utility through a desired, rather than a forced, marriage. This narrower focus on marriage created a diminished emphasis on kinship groups.[6]

Church councils and synods regularly addressed the issue of so-called incestuous marriage, sometimes forbidding the practice in general while at other times delineating violations to a specific degree of kin and the accompanying punishment.[7] The Eastern Church joined ranks with the

Roman Church at the Synod of Constantinople in 1166 when it prohibited consanguineous marriages to the seventh degree of kinship (Smith 1972, 17). Consanguineous marriages within forbidden degrees were allowed to stand a century earlier (if such a marriage had already been contracted), but the new regulation in 1166 eliminated this loophole and declared that any such marriage would be dissolved. The position of the clergy was further reinforced when the emperor, Manuel, established the same regulation in an imperial edict (Smith 1972, 17).

From a public-interest perspective, one would expect the eligibility rules aimed at preventing incest to be absolute, or nearly so. Even in the absence of concrete genetic knowledge or scientific rigor, longtime historical experience should provide reasonable guidelines as to how far down the blood line relatives could safely proceed in marriage. Church regulations, however, followed a seemingly erratic pattern that is difficult to reconcile with absolute guidelines. In the fourth century the Church prohibited marriage between first cousins, but not between more distant relatives. In the fifth century it raised the guidelines to prohibit marriages between aunts or uncles and nephews or nieces. In the sixth century it extended the prohibitions to include marriages between fifth cousins—at a time when secular law contained no prohibitions against marriage between *first* cousins.[8] In the ninth century it made marriages between sixth cousins illicit. And in the thirteenth century, bowing to external pressure, the Church deregulated slightly by reverting back to prohibitions against marriage between third cousins.

There is no apparent evidence that the progressive restrictions imposed by the medieval Church on Christian marriages conveyed widespread health benefits on society, but there is ample reason to infer that the regulations imposed additional costs on certain individuals and groups within society. One such cost is borne by those couples who get caught in a "regime" change. A couple who married legally under one set of regulations might find themselves in violation of a new (unanticipated) regulation. Before the twelfth century, the Church allowed earlier marriages to stand in the face of progressively stricter standards, effectively minimizing this cost, but the Synod of Constantinople (1166) revoked this practice, declaring earlier marriages invalid. This new doctrinal position, which opened up many additional opportunities for rent seeking on the part of Church officials, as we shall soon see, is difficult to reconcile with a public-interest theory of Church policy.

Illegitimate Heirs: Kinship and Inheritance

Economic posturing in the form of land acquisition and estate building through consanguineous marriages became increasingly common in the

Middle Ages. The Church and the state joined forces and enhanced marital regulations by increasing the degree of kinship that defined incestuous marriage in the eighth century (Gies and Gies 1987, 83–84).[9] One example of indirect rent-seeking activity is that the Church hoped that by further restricting marital options, the incidence of heirs would decrease, thereby *increasing* the likelihood of inheritance for itself.[10] In other words, the Church's regulation of endogamy led to a diminution in the number of heirs, legitimate and illegitimate, thereby enhancing the Church's ability to acquire estates for itself and preventing dynastic growth that could challenge its authority.

In the essentially feudal, decentralized, and localized environment of the early Middle Ages, it is likely that economic growth occurred principally within families, that is, within kinship units. Nonpartible inheritance laws helped keep wealth "in the family," and in-family marriage mergers were but another device ensuring economic strength within the dynastic family. Restrictions on endogamy, therefore, would tend to decrease the number of heirs. Dynastic development depended to a greater degree on *external* alliances in both earlier and later periods, but especially in the latter. As communications and transportation improvements reduced transactions costs of nonrelated family mergers, endogamy regulations most likely furthered economic growth and development.

While secular law did not prohibit endogamy, it did regulate the ability of children from such marriages to inherit an estate. From the moral standpoint of the Church, however, if heirs begotten from such unions were illegitimate, it follows that the Church would deem such marriages as illegitimate or invalid. Even though the Church couched its regulation in terms of public interest (e.g., health concerns and broadened community ties), the evidence points, at least in part, to the private interests of the Church as a motivating factor of its regulations. If individuals continued to engage in endogamous marriages, the Church stood to gain through inheritances, since the existence of legitimate heirs would be lacking. By promoting exogamy, moreover, the Church's position of authority, and hence its income stream from the faithful, were secure. In promoting its regulations then, the Church was employing a "win-win" strategy from which it could secure revenue while maintaining its societal influence.[11]

On more than one occasion, Church synods issued regulations restricting the ability of offspring from consanguineous marriages to inherit an estate. While illegitimate children in most societies could secure an inheritance through a will, the Church was able to nullify this result through its power to confiscate estates according to its marriage regulations. Justinian proclaimed that succession for children of incestuous marriages was prohibited while the Synod of Douci in 874 instructed restraint from marriage to the seventh degree of kin. To bolster its ruling, the synod noted that children of such marriages were prevented from succession to an estate according to Roman law. Furthermore, the Synod of Trosle in 909 reaffirmed that no legitimate heirs could be born of consanguineous marriage (Smith 1972, 14). The Lateran Council of 1123 echoed the same sentiment when it declared that anyone who contracted an incestuous marriage was considered "incapable of succeeding to an inheritance" (Smith 1972, 17).

Papal decrees were also issued to address endogamy and the issue of inheritance. Pope Gregory I was the first to address the issue when he extended the regulation to the seventh degree, basing his judgment on the secular law that forbade succession to relatives in the seventh degree. According to Smith (1972, 28), the Church "erroneously combined the Roman law of intestate succession with the provisions in respect to incest and fallaciously asserted that the Romans had barred marriages up to the seventh degree of blood relationship."[12]

Smith (1972, 8) also notes that according to the Church, the primary reason for preventing marriage among blood relatives was that "the bonds of charity were multiplied and more widely disseminated by marriage of non-relatives." However, the Church's promotion of exogamy posed less of a threat to the papacy than marriages within the family. By encouraging mergers among families, any single family would have more extensive kinship ties, but the family itself would possess less dynastic power than if marriage had occurred within the family.

The endogamy regulations imposed by the Church were contrary to previous custom. Lynch (1992, 290) notes that some societies promoted endogamy, particularly among first cousins, because it secured property within the family. While exogamy might *seem* to pose more of a threat to the Church, the centralization of wealth within the family through endogamy facilitated the development of dynasties, or potentially quasi-monarchies—both of which could pose a serious threat to the authority of the Church. Consequently, exogamy was encouraged because it was the lesser threat. Clearly, extending the regulation to the seventh degree made legal endogamy nearly impossible and provided ample opportunities for rent seeking with respect to marriage dissolution as well as through Church exemptions of consanguineous marriage in exchange for a fee. Table 1 provides information on some of the fees set up by the Church to grant exemptions for a marriage within forbidden degrees. The exemptions granted are constructed from late-fifteenth-century documents (Lunt 1934, 2:524–26) when marriages were forbidden up to the fourth degree of kinship. Fees addressed different degrees of consanguineous marriage, whether the marriage was contracted knowingly in the said degree, contracts that were not consummated, and dispensatory letters.

Table 1   Fees for Church Exemption of Consanguineous Marriage

Degree of Consanguinity or Affinity	Fee (in grossi)
Third- and fourth-degree exemption	27.5
Declaratory letter	7.0
Dispensatory letter	7.0
Seal of dispensation	5.5
For the box	1.0
Ignorantly contracted in illegal degree	18.0
Payment to the writer	9.5
Knowingly contracted in illegal degree	20.5
To the writer	10.5
To the sealer	7.5
To the proctor	?
Declaratory letter allowing third and fourth degree	7.5
Clandestine contract ignorantly contracted	18.5
Contract in fourth degree, not consummated	20.5
To the writer	9.5
To the sealer	7.5
To the proctor	?

Source: Lunt (1934), 2:524–26.

The fee schedules established by the Church did not constitute user fees in the traditional sense; rather, they were fees charged for services at prices above marginal cost. While it is clear that Church-provided services had positive costs associated with their provision, the monopolistic price structure imposed by the Church is inferred by observing its consumers. The majority of consumers of Church exemptions were the wealthy, not the poor. The Church permitted the poor to plead *in forma pauperum* and pay nothing for their case, but since excommunication was a potential penalty for delinquency of payment, most consumers who could afford exemptions paid the court fees (Helmholz 1974, 161; Ingram 1987, 57). A menu of user fees connected "value received" to particular services as individuals self-selected products on the basis of demand elasticity.

    Evidence that nobility were afforded dispensations in return for sizable sums is plentiful. For example, Vatican archives reveal that in March 1480, Maximillian, Duke of Austria and Burgundy, paid 2,250 ducats for a "matrimonial dispensation"—a not-inconsiderable sum at the time (Lunt 1934, 2:525). Inflation in late-sixteenth-century England, moreover, motivated the Church courts to begin fixing prices for exemptions in the early seventeenth century (Ingram 1987, 58, 72). By setting fees at levels comparable to fees in the previous century, the Church not only maintained the demand for its court services, but stood to actually increase demand for its services since its fees were relatively lower than other courts as a result of price fixing. Although the Church might have maintained that its price fixing was done to preserve the affordability of its services, economic theory suggests that the presence of competition in the sale of the assurance of salvation, following the onset of Protestantism, was the underlying cause of maintaining prices at sixteenth-century levels.

In the face of extensive prohibitions on consanguineous marriage it became relatively easy to find or invent a kinship tie in the seventh degree or less. Those seeking a divorce (the regulated) could hire lawyers and copyists to trace their genealogy, looking for a kinship tie (Gies and Gies 1987, 140). As regulator the Church was interested in repelling testamentary challenges brought by surviving family members against bequests of property to the Church (Brundage 1987, 140). By raising regulations against consanguineous marriages, the Church had a means of refuting potential claims to land from relatives of the testator increasing the likelihood that the Church could retain property rights to such land. There is, moreover, clear evidence that exemptions were made in return for fees and that high fees were paid by nobles.[13]

An economic hypothesis would infer that the Church's endogamy regulations typified its rent-seeking behavior. By heightening the regulation on the degree of kinship, the Church effectively limited dynastic development that could have rivaled the power of the Church.[14] Through its regulations the Church could suppress secular development and simultaneously sustain demand for its primary good—the assurance of salvation.

Papal Enforcement: The Case of the Nobility

Kings were particularly persistent in their pursuit of wealth through marriage, regardless of the regulations the Church had instituted by the twelfth century (Gies and Gies 1987, 133–35). Evidence of papal enforcement of marriage regulations regarding kinship ties appears throughout the Middle Ages, including Popes Nicholas I, Innocent III, Gregory VII, and Boniface VIII, spanning from the ninth to the early fourteenth century.[15] For example, Popes Nicholas and Hadrian enforced regulations against wrongful termination of marriage by Lothair II, King of Lotharingia, and his first wife, Teutberga, so that he could take a second wife Waldrada (Smith 1972, 74–76). A famous example of papal enforcement involves the case of King Robert the Pious of France (996–1031), who married Rozala, a claimant to the throne of Italy. Robert dismissed her, saying she was too old but actually he had only married her for political gain. His next wife, Bertha, was the daughter of the King of Burgundy. The marriage did bestow some political gain but they were related within the third degree of kinship (Smith 1972, 77–78). Gerbert, the Archbishop of Rheims (who later became Pope Sylvester II [999–1003]), refused to permit the marriage, but the ceremony was performed anyway. Smith notes (1972, 80) that the Synod of Pavia in 997 decreed that "King Robert, who took to wife his relative, against apostolic prohibition, be called to satisfaction, together with the bishops consenting to this marriage. If they refuse, they are to be deprived of communion." A visit from Abbo, the abbot of Cluny, failed to persuade Robert to obey the pope, so a council was called to Rome in 998 that pronounced a sentence of anathema (a formal excommunication) on Robert if he did not separate from Bertha and do seven years of penance for his sins (Smith 1972, 81). After failing to obey, the pope and his cousin, Emperor Otto, blackmailed Robert to relieve the pope and his monks at Cluny and Fleury from secular supervision (Duby 1978, 46–48). Robert finally conceded because it facilitated a legal divorce that enabled him to marry a third time. His third marriage was successful in producing two male heirs.

In the eleventh century, William, Duke of Normandy (who later became known as William the Conqueror), married his "distant" cousin, Mathilda of Flanders. They were married in about 1050 in the face of papal opposition that arose because of their kinship. Their defiance of the papacy led to their excommunication and the placing of Normandy under an interdict. As the price of lifting their excommunication, Pope Leo IX insisted that they undertake some great work on behalf of the Church. The result was the construction of the Abbaye aux Hommes by William and the Abbaye aux Dames by Mathilda in Caen, the ancient capital of the Normans. The Abbaye aux Hommes, constructed at great cost, remains one of the most complete and important Romanesque churches in France.

The varying degrees of sanctioned endogamy during the early medieval period altered the relative price of marriage to market participants from a microanalytic perspective. Search costs for Church members seeking a mate rose precipitously—especially in the agrarian environment—as the prohibition reached the seventh degree of kinship. Such prohibitions (coupled with divorce prohibition and other constraints) reduced the marriage rate by increasing the relative utility of remaining single. There is also evidence of increased concubinage and prostitution in the ninth century at the height of the endogamy prohibition.[16] Prior to Church regulations, the concubine was considered a part of the household and the children legitimate. However, concubines also became a specific target of Church regulations, wherein the Church began to classify the offspring of a concubine as illegitimate, and as a result, the children lost their claims to any inheritance (Goody 1983, 76). Had the Church permitted the children of concubines to be classified as legitimate, it would have decreased the Church's rent-seeking prospects by decreasing the incidence of exemptions that the Church could have granted for a fee. Furthermore, by defining these children as illegitimate, any estate bequeathed to such an heir was subject to confiscation by the Church (Goody 1983, 77). Concubinage was officially prohibited by the Fifth Lateran Council in 1514, and those found in violation were often fined (Brundage 1987, 514–15).

By the year 1100, the Church had managed to emerge as the leading interpreter of endogamy regulations using ancient secular prohibitions against incest as its entrée into the marriage market. The stage was now set for Church dominance over marriage as a social institution in the later medieval period.

Doctrinal Innovations Regarding the Marriage Contract

Church theologians and canonists were in pursuit of a definition of Church-sanctioned marriage as early as the eleventh century, although the Penitentials or penance manuals of the early Church were suggestive of later Church efforts (McNeill and Gamer 1990, 78, 96). While Church control over endogamy was in place much earlier, controversies over definitions arose among Church officials because of differing interpretations and degrees of emphasis placed on mutual consent as well as whether sex was necessary to render a marriage contract valid.[17] Additionally, the nature of the consent was important in the eyes of the Church. A contract to marry was typically upheld by the Church if the consent was a present rather than a future promise to marry (de presenti as opposed to de futuro). Also, the Church had long maintained that sex for pleasure was a sin and that even within marriage (from at least 525), self-control and discipline regarding the purpose and frequency of sex were appropriate. This interpretation diverged from the secular view that did not perceive sex itself as sinful. As a result, the emphasis on the sinful nature of sex by the Church contributed to its emphasis on mutual consent rather than arranged marriages. This distinction became the point of departure from secular law and diminished the power of parents in arranging marriages to solidify family lines and protect family wealth (Duby 1978, 7–8; Donahue 1983, 144; Houlbrooke 1985, 340; Gies and Gies 1987, 137–40).

Church-sanctioned marriages (apart from the issue of kinship) were redefined throughout the Middle Ages to require increasing levels of involvement in the marriage process by Church officials. Not only did such involvement make the Church a central figure in the marriage market by creating new behavioral constraints on the attainment of salvation, it also enhanced its authority in hearing marriage cases. The Consistory courts were the courts of the Church that heard marriage cases. As Church regulations surrounding the marriage contract changed, the incidence of court cases brought before the Consistory courts increased which allowed the Church to capture more rents in the form of legal fees and fines.

The Fourth Lateran Council (1215) ordered that synods, a meeting of a diocese's clergy, be held annually. These synods were typically the source of the regulations and doctrinal innovations created by the Church to enhance its control during the Middle Ages. Some of the legislation was instituted on the local level by bishops whereas others were papal decrees.[18]

Documentation of Church regulations and the enforcement of canon law in the Middle Ages are most readily available from England. The regulation that mutual consent constituted a marriage was explicitly stated in the mid-1200s to prevent the nonconsensual arrangement of marriages involving minors to "promote the common good" of the families (Sheehan 1978b, 17). It seems, however, that the Church increasingly stressed the need to perform the marriage ceremony publicly and officially within the Church. The Synod of Nantes (1386), for example, addressed the high incidence of clandestine marriages (Brundage 1987, 501). The Church found it difficult to prove that consent existed in such cases since there were often no witnesses to the marriage. Clearly, the influence of outsiders on a marriage was primarily relegated to notification of a kin tie or some other reason why the marriage should not be permitted. This too was a process supervised by the Church through its local agent, the parish priest. At this time a marriage that was not publicly announced or blessed by a priest was considered sinful but was nonetheless binding. With this interpretation marriage became attached to the primary and most important good of the Church—the assurance of eternal salvation.

Church Court Proceedings: Incidence and Expense

Efforts to decrease the role of parents in arranging marriages as a means of economic and social climbing in the twelfth century were part of the public-interest argument that the Church developed in emphasizing a shift to the canon law of marriage (Donahue 1983, 145–46). Additional motivations in accord with apparent concerns for the laity included the notions that people could not regulate marriages themselves, that marriage was indissoluble, and that marriage between kin was incestuous. The Church courts became recognized as the forum for marriage cases, having maintained that such cases were beyond the realm of secular courts (Gottlieb 1980, 49–50; Brundage 1987, 223).[19]

In medieval England, a Consistory court was the bishop's court of canon law. Consistory courts existed in each diocese and were presided over by an official, who represented the bishop, and a judge. A court of audience of the bishop had jurisdiction as well (Morris 1963, 152; Helmholz 1974, 1). These courts were largely concerned with marital problems among the laity, typically including the enforcement of marriage contracts, annulments, and judgments for adultery. The officials of the Consistory courts were lawyers and were often in the service of many bishops, which made it necessary to appoint a deputy to oversee the court (Morris 1963, 153–54). By 1350, a permanent commission was established to oversee the Consistory court. Typically, the court met for two day sessions each month.

An examination of court procedure by Helmholz (1974, 114) reveals that proceedings were typically short for marriage cases, often requiring only one hearing. Expediting the process was in the interest of the Church since once the fees were exacted on the parties to the suit, the Church could capture more rents from hearing more as opposed to fewer cases. By tying up the court for one session per case, on average, the Church could accomplish the goal of hearing more cases while at the same time increasing society's dependence on Church courts. The average time to settle cases which involved more than one hearing was still reasonably quick and ranged from approximately four to seven months, depending on the difficulty of the case.

Cases among the wealthy provided a rent-seeking opportunity for the local bishop since he often adjudicated cases involving the upper class himself. For example, one case involved Margery Paston who had married her father's bailiff and sought to dissolve the marriage. The bishop handled the case personally, and the case was never brought before the Norwich Consistory court (Helmholz 1974, 161). In addition, Smith (1972, 14–15) explains that in a synod held under the direction of Henry II of Germany in 1002,

> the assembled prelates were chided for their apathy in enforcing the law of the Church. The king was reported to have declared that "among many things which are to be corrected in our kingdom and in your parishes is that relatives, very close to each other, are joined in marriage; so that, not fearing God and not revering men, they do not shrink from associating in marriage with a relative even of the third degree which is horrible to say; and they do not fear to violate the line to the seventh degree which the sacred canons order to be observed." The bishops were much embarrassed by the charge. Many of them knew that they had consciously relaxed the laws in the interest of their friends.

A ripe environment for malfeasance was provided the bishops who could price discriminate in this manner.

Enforcement of the Marriage Contract

Enforcement of regulations concerning legal marriages varied within the Church through differing regional alliances with medieval families and the threat of the loss of eternal salvation. Canon law was formally presented as a ruling legislation over marriage by Pope Alexander III in the late twelfth century and was the prevailing law in most countries in western Europe until the Council of Trent in 1563, when a priest's blessing became a requirement to classify a marriage as valid (Donahue 1983, 144–45). Diminution of the occurrence of clandestine marriages was the "public-interest" purpose of the regulation, but the new rule clearly provided rent-seeking opportunities. Once again the Church had redefined a valid marriage and increased the requirements that were attached to the ultimate product of eternal salvation.

Evidence is indicated by the court cases concerning clandestine marriage reported from two English parishes in Table 2.[20] The number of cases between 1615 and 1629 ranged from eight to twenty-two and the sentences ranged from dismissal to excommunication. The couple was not the only recipient of a sentence—ministers and witnesses were also subject to a sentence of penance or excommunication. The small number of cases heard on an annual basis, with the penalty of excommunication being the most common, served to decrease the incidence of clandestine marriages in England. All things being equal, higher penalties served as a deterrent to clandestine marriage, particularly due to the inelastic demand for the assurance of salvation. The mere threat of excommunication was the ultimate weapon of the Church in medieval society, since threats and sentences effectively ostracized an individual from his or her community. Logan (1968, 68) reports about 17,000 excommunications in England between 1250 and 1534 from existing files.[21] Many more probably occurred, most often for cases concerning marriage contracts.

Parishes and Church Rents

Court fees and enforcement policies are consistent with Church rent-seeking activity in counties and parishes throughout England and France. Some indication of the magnitude of Church rents in the medieval period can be found in the county and parish data of medieval England.[22] The total population of England's thirty-nine counties in 1086 was 1,099,766 and had doubled to 2,073,279 by 1377 (Russell 1948, 247). By 1801, the total population for these plus two additional counties had risen to 9,476,700. Population growth in England between the fourteenth and sixteenth centuries was meager, with only 2.5 million people in England by 1500 (Ingram

Table 2   Clandestine Marriage Cases in Salisbury and North Wiltshire

Incidence of Cases

1615	8	1623	22
1616	4	1624	21
1617	3	1625	13
1618	2	1626	13
1619	4	1627	8
1620	2	1628	8
1621	15	1629	13
1622	12		

Treatment of Offenders	Couples	Officiating Ministers	Others Present
Dismissed	22	5	4
To prove regular marriage	11	—	—
Excommunicated/absolved	32	4	29
Excommunicated	58	3	10
Penance	6	—	2
No recorded sentence	19	7	10
Total	148	19	55

Source: Ingram (1987), 216.

1987, 72), but it increased rapidly to nearly 10 million by the onset of the nineteenth century.

Recalling the taxation schedules, court cases, and schedule of legal fees presented earlier, with the total number of parishes in 1801 reaching 10,141 (Wrigley and Schofield 1981, 620), it is clear that the probable magnitude of potential and actual rents captured by the Church through ecclesiastic courts over the medieval period was enormous. Considering that in England there were thirty-nine counties in 1086 and 10,141 parishes by 1801, an average estimate of the revenue accumulated by the Church in England alone amounts to a range between roughly £27,888 and £31,184 per year.[23] Based on these estimates, the total revenue collected from Church courts throughout England and Europe in the Middle Ages would have been quite extensive.

Records of marriage litigation suggest that the Church was relatively successful in its bid to overcome secular law and enhance its own control and influence in society. Had the Church not been able to command such an influence, the number of cases brought before Church courts would have been significantly fewer, particularly since the issue of indissolubility would not have become the cultural norm. The high number of cases brought to prove that a marriage indeed existed would not have been necessary since clandestine marriages—resting on mutual consent to avoid arranged marriages in the face of indissolubility—would have been fewer.

A dissoluble marriage would have had a relatively low opportunity cost for the partners to the marriage since an escape mechanism would have been in place. Concubinage and prostitution would not have been important medieval institutions if a low-cost escape was possible (Otis 1985). With dissoluble marriage the need to prove contracts and consent would not have been so great, and the Church would not have had such extensive access to the marriage market to secure rents.

New constraints undoubtedly affected individual utility for parties to marriage. Assurance of the contract would have yielded positive utility for women, but such assurances (regarding property and obligations in the event of dissolution) could have been provided by civil authority. Disutility from higher search costs for a partner plus the *highest* possible costs to non-Church sanctioned dissolutions or the recourse to prostitution or concubinage (*loss of eternal salvation*) were most certainly nontrivial accompaniments to the Church's takeover of the marriage contract. It seems plausible to argue, therefore, that the Church was, in fact, selling marriage contracts at rates above marginal cost. Monopoly was a factor in the sale of marriage services by the Church as it was in other aspects of medieval social interactions.

Price Discrimination in the Sale of Marriage Services

Evidence consistent with monopoly and rent-seeking activities of the Church in the marriage market is strengthened by policies that constitute price discrimination. Wealthy Church members, as we have already noted, always had access to special dispensations and treatment from high clerics for a fee. Individuals with differing elasticities of demand for Church-related marriage services simply self-selected purchases among the particular services offered.

Regulations and enforcement mechanisms were applied unevenly *among countries* as well. Specifically, new regulations developed by the Church threatened the loss of eternal salvation (excommunication) for clandestine marriages in France much earlier than in England. The takeover of the marriage market, in other words, was less complete in England than in France. Cases involving marriage were treated differently in England and France. For instance, England treated *de presenti* clandestine marriages (a contract with present mutual consent) as civil cases while in France *de futuro* clandestine marriages (a promise to marry in the future) were regarded as criminal cases. Such countrywide differences in the impact of Church regulation is not surprising as the Church was merely responding to constraints and changes in constraints. When considering Church enforcement in England and France, England had a more entrenched secular tradition than did France, making enforcement against malfeasers much lighter than in France. This strong secular tradition and the growing regulatory power of the Church were probably not inconsequential when considering the success of the Reformation in England.

Records indicate a higher incidence of criminal cases in France that were brought by the bishops' courts and a higher number of civil cases in England. Differences between the marriage cases brought before the French and English courts are gleaned from an Ely Act book that documented Church court cases between 1374 and 1382 and from a court register of the bishop of Paris between 1384 and 1387 (Donahue 1983, 149–50). More than 50 percent of the eighty-nine marriage cases heard in Ely were clandestine *de presenti* marriages whereas there were sixty cases brought in Paris to dissolve *de futuro* marriages. The Ely book revealed no cases involving *de futuro* marriage or separation cases (there were 120 separation cases in Paris), while the Paris register showed no cases involving annulments (there were twelve in Ely) and only three cases involving *de presenti* marriages (Donahue 1983, 150).

There is significance in these differences. The largest number of cases in both England and France involved enforcement of a marriage contract. But the primary difference was that in Ely, cases were concerned with whether an actual marriage existed (*de presenti*), while in Paris the issue was enforcing contracts to marry (*de futuro*). In Ely, the cases involved the thrust of Pope Alexander's regulations—*which considered clandestine marriages valid.* In Paris, Alexander's regulations were not brought to bear since the issue was a promise to marry without sexual relations. Other records from the English courts in York and Canterbury as well as from the court at Chartres in France support these differences in legislative patterns (Helmholz 1974, 28n.14; Donahue 1983, 151). The occurrence of cases seeking to uphold *de presenti* marriages did not decrease until the Council of Trent in the sixteenth century.

Economic theory suggests that more than the prevention of clandestine marriage was at stake in the new regulations established by the Church at the Council of Trent. The new regulations created a barrier to entry in the marriage market, particularly in France, where the regulations served to alter the price of marriage. Use of excommunication and the criminal classification of clandestine marriage in France prevented other forms and definitions of marriage from occurring. In addition, the expenditures incurred by the Church to develop and implement the new aspects of canon law in an effort to increase the rent stream from the laity constituted a higher cost for society.[24]

The strict interpretation of canon law in France was a control mechanism jointly enforced by parents and the Church. England lagged behind France in decreasing the incidence of clandestine marriage because automatic excommunication was not used as an enforcement mechanism for some time, thereby leaving the price of a clandestine marriage lower than a Church-approved marriage. Thus, for some time the *full* price of clandestine marriage (relative to a Church-approved marriage) was relatively higher in France than it was in England. Since parental consent and marriages consistent with Church regulations represented a lower cost alternative to clandestine marriage, there was a lower incidence of clandestine marriages in France and consequently an increase in the number of cases involving *de futuro* marriages.

Recall that the price to enter into a clandestine marriage rose because of the threat of losing the assurance of eternal salvation. Since England was not as persistent as France in conveying the loss of salvation when clandestine marriages occurred, more clandestine marriages occurred in England. A stronger secular tradition with a greater emphasis on individual rights and values would contribute to an explanation for the laxity in interpreting the canon law respecting marriage.

Although cases involving *de presenti* marriage in England were generally not considered criminal and typically did not require a payment to remove excommunication, the Church was able to use the courts as an avenue to extract rents in the context of dispute resolution regarding the validity of marriages. Clearly, there was a sufficient number of such cases to keep the courts busy, with litigants paying court costs to the Church.

Stronger influence of family authority existed in France early in the Middle Ages and explains, at least in part, the efforts by the family to align with the Church to promote regulations. The regulations increased the economic benefits to the family through contract mergers in the form of marriage and to the Church through fines, court costs, and the costs associated with a Church-sanctioned marriage. Ultimately, the continued presence and enforcement of canon law in England led to the same results as in France—a decrease in the number of clandestine marriages. Perhaps French aristocrats discovered earlier than their counterparts in England that allegiance with the Church in the case of marriage was mutually beneficial. But the evidence seems clear that a form of price discrimination for marriage services existed between France and England for a significant part of the medieval period.

Conclusion: Marriage, Rent Seeking, and Welfare

The efforts by the medieval Church to usurp secular law and gain control of the marriage market involved substantial costs for both the Church and society. The Church invested resources in a sprawling bureaucracy that enforced and collected rents. Presumably, as wealth was redistributed from the faithful to the institutional Church, these costs were more than offset by the revenues received. But society paid in the form of wasted resources, higher prices, and reduced consumption (especially fewer clandestine, or private, marriages). On Becker's (1981) authority, it can be argued that clandestine marriages maximized the utility of the marriage partners relative to what they would have obtained from arranged marriages, and hence the marital share of household output to individuals in a clandestine marriage was likely to be higher than in a Church-approved marriage. Moreover, as Tullock (1967) reminds us, monopoly rent seeking involves considerable dead weight loss to society.[25]

Medieval Church marriage regulations must, of course, be placed within the broader context of the monopoly over the sale of assurances of eternal salvation. Intertemporally the Church had to maintain demand by suppressing heresy (restricting entry), expanding markets, and convincing society to change its cultural (and economic) norms. The creation of canon law and the Consistory courts provided a fruitful avenue for extracting rents from the laity while maintaining an appearance of providing a public service—upholding marriages or granting annulments on a case-by-case basis.[26]

A number of microeconomic effects undoubtedly accompanied Church involvement in the marriage market. As women became increasingly reliant on the Church to enforce their marriages, their allegiance to the Church increased. The allegiance of men might have decreased, however. The full costs of marriage and the opportunity costs of marriage outside the Church both rose. The ultimate good sold by the church—the assurance of salvation—was successfully attached to the marriage contract. Those who sought to marry outside the Church were excommunicated, fined, and sometimes left with sizable legal fees, payable to the agents of the Church's Consistory courts.

Even at the peak of Church monopoly, religious regulations and constraints were only partially effective in achieving spiritual or moral goals. Prostitution and concubinage in France and elsewhere reveals that, even within the context of Church-defined marriage that included indissolubility, other institutions emerged to provide a safety valve. Church monopoly could only partially overshadow social practice even in the Middle Ages. Actual and economizing practices in courtship and marriage, aided by advancing technology and civil law, ultimately made particular Church constraints less and less effective if not moot for most modern societies.

The static model of monopoly rent seeking that underscores the analysis in this chapter emphasizes the opportunities and motivation for institutional rent seeking, but it does not explain institutional change over time.[27]

NOTES

1. Becker suggests that the customs and traditions that accompany and define marriage evolve through time as a function of economizing activity by the parties to the marriage contract. For example, in societies where divorce and recontracting are prohibited, *ceteris paribus*, longer searches by market participants, higher search costs, fewer marriages, and more prostitution and concubinage can be expected. Although he sketches some of the features of the "anthropological traditional family," Becker did not seek to analyze the effect of Church-mandated rules on the functioning of the market. Presumably, he would agree that behavior regarding courtship and marriage, as well as the utility produced within (and without) that state, are related to the rules, regulations, and institutions of any *given* time. For an alternative treatment that also interprets marriage as a contract, but compares an "old marriage" (e.g., Church-approved union) with a "new marriage" (i.e., after changes in the divorce laws in the 1960s), see Brinig and Crafton (1994). To further complicate matters, recent scholarship has revealed that same-sex unions have been sanctioned and idealized as "marriages" in Western societies for over two thousand years (Boswell 1994).

2. "Peter's Pence" was originally imposed in England, Poland, and the Scandinavian countries. It required local parish churches to make an annual payment theoretically amounting to a penny per household (Lynch 1992, 179).

3. In some cases, monopoly power can be leveraged into other markets, as when a monopolist produces complementary or vertically related products (Ordover et al. 1985; Kaserman and Mayo 1993). Thus, if marriage and salvation are regarded as *complementary goods*, monopoly power might be leveraged from one market to the other in order to maximize profits. A monopoly over both markets would potentially yield larger profits than the sum of single monopolies over each, due to the optimal pricing of the two related goods. However, the vertical coordination problems faced by the medieval Church, and its power to price discriminate (in the second degree) lead us to the simpler characterization.

4. The "incest taboo" (i.e., father–daughter, mother–son, or sister–brother) is both ancient and universal. Fisher (1992) argues that it had emerged among Cro-Magnon peoples for a number of social, economic, and political, as well as biological, reasons. The taboo on such close couplings is shared by other species to the extent that some biologists argue that human incest taboos derive from animal nature. The interesting point is that harmful gene selection and the production of disease take a number of generations of close inbreeding and that *some* inbreeding (of, say, first, second, or third cousins) might be necessary to highlight positive traits. Some inbreeding and outbreeding may be necessary for a vital gene pool (see Fisher 1992, 251, and the evidence she cites on 349n.22).

5. It is not known if the prohibition was directed at first, second, or distant cousins. However, it seems likely from the chronology of regulation against consanguineous marriage that the prohibition was not yet directed toward a distant kinship tie.

6. While the emphasis on mutual consent as opposed to arranged marriages

promoted the interests of the individual marriage partners, some families continued to align their economic interests through arranged marriages. Arranged marriages were permissible if an exemption was obtained from the Church for a fee. For example, an exemption that allowed nobles to marry in the second degree (first cousins) has been estimated to cost 100 grossi (Lunt 1934, 1:129n.549). Grossi were roughly equivalent to twelve English pennies (pence) and were over 90 percent silver in content (Lane and Mueller 1985, 10–11).

7. The Synod of Agde in 506, for example, forbade incestuous marriage in general, whereas the Synod of Epaon in 517 prohibited marriage among first cousins (Smith 1972, 9–10). As early as 531 at the Second Synod of Toledo, excommunication was the proscribed punishment for individuals marrying blood relatives—the penalty to be suffered for the number of years one was "polluted by the stain of the blood of his kin" (Smith 1972, 10). Other synods that proscribed excommunication as a punishment for endogamy include the Synod of Clermont in 535, the Trullan Synod of 692, the Roman Synods of 743 and 826, the Synod of Garonne during Gregory VII's pontificate (1073–1086), the Council of Nimes during Urban II's pontificate (1087–1099), and the Synod of Dioclea in 1199 (Smith 1972, 10–18).

8. According to Goody (1983, 56), Roman law as codified in Justinian's *Institutes* specifically allowed marriage between the children of brothers and sisters.

9. The Church couched its regulations as being in support of the interests of the marriage partners. Since marriage was perceived as a sacred bond by the Church, its validity should rest on mutual consent and not the economic interests of families. The private interest of the Church reveals, however, that the regulations tempered the economic strengths of families and brought more control as well as estates to the Church.

10. See also Brundage (1987, 193), Herlihy (1985, 12), and Goody (1983, 215) for more details on bequests to the Church in this manner. Such opportunistic behavior dovetails with policy manipulations regarding the usury doctrine in later centuries. De Roover (1948a, 157n) reports cases of after-death Church claims on restitution for usury in the late fourteenth century. These *incerta* claims (with unknown victims) were expropriated by ecclesiastic authorities (see Chapter 6 for details).

11. A growing sentiment for priestly celibacy in the tenth and eleventh centuries might also be explained in terms of a growth in the value of the Church's property holdings. A relatively decentralized and poor Church has everything to gain from encouraging almost any enthusiastic adherent to join the priesthood. As power centralized in the Roman papacy and as Church wealth began to grow, the relative cost to the Church of downstream priests who were married tended to rise. Priests with children would have been especially apt to appropriate parish properties and revenues for their families, thus reducing Church wealth through inheritance. Given the great difficulty of monitoring distant agents during medieval times, the doctrine of clerical celibacy minimized the risks of priests appropriating Church property. This would have risen as the Church began to take on the internal organizational characteristics of the M-form firm at the beginning of the second millennium.

12. Secular rent seeking existed along with the rent-seeking behavior exhibited by the Church, as indicated by King Pepin (751–768), who perceived the increasing economic strength of families as a threat to his authority. Following the Synod of Comiegne in 756 (or 758), which ruled that marriage in the third degree of kin should be nullified, Pepin threatened secular punishments against individuals who scorned the acts of the synod (Smith 1972, 12). Pepin joined with the Church in extending marital regulations to prohibit marriages among descendants of a grandfather five times removed, when previous regulations only prohibited marrying a first cousin (marriage in the second degree of kin). First employed in the ninth century, the self-interest of both the Church and the throne led them actively to institute new legislation, hoping to safeguard and maximize their own opportunities for economic benefits.

13. There is strong evidence that aristocratic endogamy continued through exemptions granted when the interests of the Church were at stake (Duby 1978, 30–57). Since parish registers were not maintained, it is difficult to examine the incidence of marriage among kin. However, the ecclesiastic books reveal that approximately 50 percent of the spouses were from the same parish and thus possibly related (Hanawalt 1986, 81). High transaction costs involved in finding a mate in largely rural parish environments promoted marriage within the parish and increased the probability of a distant relation between spouses. Lynch (1992, 290) notes that it was likely in rural areas that many marriages probably could not have withstood close checking with regard to the regulations concerning kinship ties.

14. As the Church gained in power relative to secular authorities, other tensions emerged. The issue of papal investiture, whereby appointments to offices were issued by the Church, was a continuing point of conflict between the Church and monarchs. For example, in 1335, Pope Benedict XII declared that appointments could be made only by the Church to fill offices such as the head of a church, monastery, priory, and other offices, some of which were secular (Lunt 1934, 2:228).

15. While some specific examples of papal enforcement are detailed later, see Smith (1972, 54–156) for a more complete account of enforcement by the popes over this time period.

16. For example, a synod at Avignon prohibited clerics and married men from frequenting brothels, while a synod at Bourges in 1031 issued the regulation that allowed remarriage after a separation due to adultery (Brundage 1987, 201, 525). Several synods prohibited clerics from marrying or having concubines, including the Synod of Pavia (1022), the Synod of Bourges (1031), the Synod of Rome (1059) by Pope Nicholas II, the Synod of Gerona (1068) by Pope Alexander II, and the Synod of Rome (1074) by Pope Gregory VII (Brundage 1987, 218–19).

17. Conflicts in definition and interpretation of particular offenses riddled the early Penitentials of the decentralized Church. The nature of abortion and the penalties attached thereto provide an interesting example. In the seventh-century Penitential of Theodore it is written that "Women who commit abortion before [the foetus] has life, shall do penance for one year or for the three forty-day periods or for forty days, according to the nature of the offense; and if the later, that

is, more than forty days after conception, they shall do penance as murderesses" (McNeill and Gamer 1990, 197). This and other early written "rules" suggest that abortion is not murder until after forty days, a policy that obviously received much attention later by the Church. It goes without saying that a total prohibition of abortion tended to increase church membership.

18. These regulations were selectively enforced, taking hold much later in England (1753) than in France and on the Continent. This kind of "price discrimination" is discussed later in this chapter.

19. Data are from the bishop's court of Salisbury (excluding Berkshire) and the archdeacon's courts of Salisbury and North Wiltshire from 1615 to 1629.

20. It appears that marriage cases most often resulted in excommunication for failure to heed the orders of the judge. For example, one case in 1418 resulted in excommunication when Margery Langford who was married to Richard Clyderowe failed to follow the instructions of the court (Logan 1968, 51n.42).

21. The population in England in 1430 was estimated at 2.75 million people (Wrigley and Schofield 1981, 546). This adds some perspective to the significance of the total number of excommunications between 1250 and 1534. The deterrent effect of the high penalty was probably not insignificant.

22. Due to data limitation, but in an effort to accurately reflect the number of parishes and growth over the medieval period, the counties included are those that were in existence in both 1086 and 1801, whereas the number of parishes in each county are those that were in existence in 1801 (Russell 1948, 247–48; Wrigley and Schofield 1981, 621). The number of parishes in Yorkshire is the sum of the parishes in East, West, and North Riding in 1801. The names of some of the parishes were abbreviated between 1086 and 1801 by dropping "shire."

23. These figures were arrived at using the conversion £1 = 20s = 240d. The lower estimate of £27,888 was based on a case brought to the archbishop's court in York in 1367 which cost 55s. as an average fee (Helmholz 1974, 161). The higher estimate of £31,184 was calculated using the sum of fees paid in the Church court at Salisbury (61.5s.). Each figure was then multiplied by the 10,141 parishes in England to arrive at the estimated range per year.

24. Cases brought before the court alleging *de presenti* marriage after the regulations took hold subjected the plaintiff to automatic excommunication for the purpose of hearing the case (Donahue 1983, 153). This provided a method of generating rent for the Church since a fine was paid in addition to the court costs to bring a suit against an alleged spouse. In France, moreover, it was a criminal act to ignore a contract to marry, and such contracts were generally upheld by the court. Thus, the incidence of clandestine marriages in France was effectively diminished by Church regulations and enforcement at the local level.

25. These costs include all of the costs to maintain the monopoly status, the expenditures of those who compete for the monopoly position, and the resources used by those trying to prevent the monopoly.

26. Even today, those seeking an annulment from the Church face the marriage tribunal of the Church on a case-by-case basis. It is often alleged that obtaining an annulment is contingent on the litigants' willingness to pay.

27. North (1994, 359) has argued, in a manner that we endorse, that the ideal tool of analysis for explaining institutional change over time would be a theory of economic dynamics comparable in precision to general equilibrium theory, which we do not have, nor are we likely to get. In the absence of such a theory, "we can describe the characteristics of past economies, examine the performance of economies at various times, and engage in comparative static analysis." This volume embraces the second-best alternative that North has effectively outlined.

CHAPTER SIX

How the Church Gained
from Usury and Exchange Doctrines

Introduction: The Usury Concept
and the Profit-Seeking Church

Consolidation of Church authority and centralized decision making began to gather force about the eighth and ninth centuries and accelerated in the tenth through twelfth centuries. The status of certain key Church institutions gives credence to this claim. In particular, the medieval papacy launched important efforts to maintain "doctrinal purity." These included assaults on and prohibitions against heresy, witchcraft, and the practice of magic, disputes with papal pretenders, and the waging of holy wars. Furthermore, the Church established particular regulations that constrained practices of members and limited opportunistic behavior of downstream suppliers of its chief product—assurance of eternal salvation. This profit-maximizing behavior included renewed condemnation of simony, restrictions on lay investiture, and limits on the role and jurisdiction of monasteries and churches. In order to collect monetary and other rents, to suppress interlopers, cheaters, and malfeasors, as well as to enforce entry control, the Church established the apostolic *camera*, a corporeal agency (discussed in detail in Chapter 2). Such fundamental institutional changes in the Church had the effect of enhancing rent collections, limiting entry into the market for souls, and creating, enhancing, and maintaining demand inelasticity for its final product.

Perhaps no purely economic doctrine of the Church has had as much attention from scholars as its official position on usury—literally the charging of interest on a loan. A decretum of canon law concerning fornication indicates that to fornicate is always forbidden to anyone, but to trade is sometimes allowed and sometimes not. This same equivocation is mirrored in contemporary treatments of usury that appear to provide a contradictory melange of different viewpoints on the subject.

Some writers have regarded usury as wholly intertwined with theological superstition, without any reference whatsoever to the principles of economics (Lea 1894, 384–85; White 1896, 2:264; Lecky 1897, 2:258). In their view, the eventual withering of the prohibition of usury represented a triumph of reason over authority.

A conventional version of the usury theory rests on the belief that money is sterile. This idea is attributed to Aristotle whose ideas framed much of Scholastic thought, especially that of Aquinas. According to this interpretation, the Scholastics denied the productive use of money. The proper use of money is to spend it, they argued, and one can only spend what one owns. Therefore, the use of money is precisely to transfer its ownership. But if *ownership* is transferred by a loan, a charge for the use of money becomes redundant. Hauser (1927, 54, 60), Thompson (1928, 434), and Troeltsch (1931, 1:320) base their exegeses of medieval texts on this aspect of Scholastic thought.

As a matter of economic doctrine, several writers treat usury as a logical corollary of the theory of just price. O'Brien (1920, 134, 182) and Cleary (1914, 201) advance this view, but Noonan (1957, 398) denounces the connection on the grounds that credit sales involving just price were sharply differentiated by the Schoolmen from credit sales involving usury. Langholm (1984, 15–16, 52–53; 1992) has added his authority to this view, but not unequivocally.

Max Weber (1930) and R. H. Tawney (1926) base their theories of economic history in part on the supposition that the prohibition of usury restricted the development of capital markets and so retarded the progress of production and trade. According to this interpretation, only after the Protestant Reformation did Calvinists abandon the Scholastic attitude toward trade and begin to embrace thrift as a virtue and a business career as a calling sanctified by God. Noonan (1957) and De Roover (1967) flatly reject this view, although they admit that the form and structure of credit markets and banking practices were shaped by the usury prohibition.[1]

From the standpoint of economic history, a public-choice perspective offers a more holistic explanation of medieval Church behavior. To be sure, not all of the above viewpoints express the same concern. Some are matters of exegesis of medieval texts; some explore issues in economic history; and some treat the nature of economic doctrine. Our analysis is singularly focused on understanding economic history from the prospective of a basic economic principle, the self-interest axiom. Within this perspective, we will argue that the Church acted as a monopolist when it lent funds but as a monopsonist or single buyer when it was a borrower of funds. We also explore some aspects of just price in this chapter.

Usury: A Case Study of Monopoly Church Behavior

Paradoxically, the most outwardly economic directive of the medieval Church, the doctrine of usury, has proven most resistant to purely economic explanations. Although the medieval Church's prohibition against usury was a matter of ecclesiastic and civil law, its economic impact was on credit markets and the allocation of resources, and its operation depended on the enforcement policies of a dominant institution that had large, well-defined economic interests.

The Nature of Usury

The idea that interest or "profit" from loans is wrong predates Christianity. The Old Testament (Deuteronomy 13:20) enjoined Jews from taking usury from their "brothers" but not from "aliens." The first official Church prohibition of usury appeared in A.D. 325, when the Council of Nicea banned the practice among clerics. During the reign of Charlemagne, the Hadriana, a collection of canons, extended the prohibition to everyone, defining usury simply as a transaction "where more is asked than is given." Subsequent practice made the ban an absolute prohibition, and for many centuries usury laws enjoyed widespread and official support.

With the revival of learning and trade in the eleventh century, the doctrine of usury came under the scrutiny of Church scholars, and the usual prohibitions were spelled out in detail by Church authorities for the first time. In 1139 the Second Lateran Council denounced usury as a form of theft and required restitution from those who practiced the sinful act. The prohibition was not against gain as such, but against *illicit* gain. Nevertheless, the prohibition came to be even more rigorous than the commandment against murder—it brooked no exceptions, whereas murder was sometimes justified in Christian teachings.

Up to the thirteenth century, the sweeping condemnation of usury by the Church was accompanied by civil prohibitions that varied widely from country to country, both in form and in enforcement. Despite its widespread prohibition, usury was never entirely eradicated in any large part of Europe, nor for any important period of time. Professional pawnbrokers, though sometimes underground, probably always existed in medieval Europe. In fact, where they operated openly, they were licensed by the state, which received license fees.[2] Nevertheless, usury laws had the effect of constraining the use of credit and of altering resource allocation. By the fifteenth century, following a secular decline in the level of interest rates (Homer 1977, 136), usury was treated more as a relative prohibition than an absolute one. For example, in 1452, Pope Nicholas V determined that in Aragon and Sicily a redeemable *census* (a contract similar to a mortgage) was licit provided it did not pay over 10 percent (Noonan 1957, 161).

Usura, from which the word *usury* derives, meant payment for the use of money in a transaction that resulted in gain (i.e., net profit) for the lender; whereas *interesse*, from which the word *interest* originates, meant "loss" and was recognized by ecclesiastic and civil law as a reimbursement for loss or expense. Interest was commonly regarded as compensation for delayed repayment or for loss of profits to the lender who could not employ his capital in some alternative use during the term of the loan. Risk was not generally considered a justification for interest because loans were usually secured by property worth many times the money advanced.

The usury prohibition was not intended to curb the high profits of risk enterprise. The *societas* (partnership) was a recognized form of commercial organization from Roman times. Its profit objective was officially sanctioned, and gains from trade were treated as earnings for effort and risk. The *census* was a kind of annuity and was considered licit. Under the terms of a *census*, the borrower incurred "an obligation to pay an annual return from fruitful property." By its nature, a *census* was not considered usurious.

Moreover, by the thirteenth century, bank deposits had become a form of investment. Merchant bankers paid interest on deposits. As early as the twelfth century, bills of exchange combined foreign exchange with credit, although interest was often concealed in a high exchange rate. In other words, during the Middle Ages, the Church doctrine on usury, existing alongside legitimate forms of interest-taking, helped promote a double standard that became increasingly arbitrary over time, thereby creating opportunities for exploitation by those who made the rules.[3]

Usury as a Tool of Church Monopoly

The price of money, like its analogue, the price of goods, was persistently treated by medieval writers as an ethical issue—they perceived justice rather than efficiency as the appropriate goal of economic policy. Ostensibly, this is consistent with a public-interest theory of corporate behavior. The historical record, however, casts strong shadows on the spiritual argument. It shows, for example, that Church officials frequently manipulated the usury doctrine to create or bolster the monopoly power of the Church.

The purely economic aspects of interest must be examined within a market for loanable funds, while the broader issue of monopoly policy and its specific elements of control require that interest be examined within the economic framework that underlies this study. Within an appropriate framework, the market for loans can be regulated, provided there is an efficient enforcement mechanism. Moreover, the usury prohibition can be absolute or it can be relative. An absolute prohibition would drive the "legitimate" supply of loans to zero, whereas a relative prohibition would restrict interest to some legal maximum.

We do not assert that the medieval Church invented the doctrine of usury, or the economic doctrine of just price, for its own economic gain. Rather, we contend that in spite of its original (and perhaps lasting) concern for justice, the Church recognized, and acted on, the rent-seeking opportunities of the doctrine at a certain juncture in its history. We contend that the medieval Church established de facto dual credit markets. When the Church was a lender, it shadow-priced its loans *inside* the Church at market rates (or above), thus extracting rents. But when it was a borrower, it enforced the doctrine, thereby extracting rents by reducing its cost of credit on certain loans. At other times it used the doctrine to increase contributions and membership. Through selective enforcement, moreover, the Church could increase the supply of loan funds available to itself indirectly by reducing the supply of loans for (laic) consumption purposes.

This hypothesis is consistent with the activities of a rent-seeking monopoly, and it accommodates both monetary and nonmonetary goals, which were often intertwined in the policies pursued by the medieval Church. The chief monetary goal of the Church was to increase its ability to finance its salvation effort; its main nonmonetary goal was to preserve and extend its doctrinal hegemony—that is, to increase demand and lower demand elasticity for final output. Though fragmentary, Vatican records show a pattern of selective enforcement. When it was in the Church's interest to do so, it enforced the usury prohibition to keep its cost of funds low. Moreover, besides the direct use of usury policy to enhance its wealth, the Church made indirect use of it to augment the power of the papal monopoly, including its far-flung bureaucracy.

This hypothesis is not entirely new. Nelson (1947) also found a clear pattern of opportunistic behavior by the Church in its policies on restitution of ill-gotten gains from usury. He also contends that the Church's policies changed over time as it solidified its monopoly status. The most dramatic changes occurred between 1100 and 1550. Usury came to be classified either as *certa*, in cases involving known victims, or *incerta*, in cases involving unknown or unidentifiable victims. Church policy permitted known victims to receive *certae* restitutions, but required *incertae* restitutions to be given to "the poor" or directed to "pious purposes." As one would expect in a rent-seeking society, the practice evolved of issuing "licenses" to certain clerics that entitled them to a percentage of *incertae* restitutions. This, of course, gave the licensees an incentive to maximize the number of *incertae* restitutions they could control.[4] The restitution policy instituted by the Church was analogous to sales-revenue royalties employed in contemporary monopoly arrangements involving franchised firms.[5]

The death of a rich merchant often provided an opportunity for the Church to seize wealth in the name of restitution. A papal decree of the thirteenth century gave the Church power to seize the wealth of intestate laymen and (Church) clerks (Paris 1872–1883, 4:552, 604–5). It was revoked only on the vigorous objection of the lay authorities. Undeterred, the pope laid claim in the same year to the profits of deceased usurers in England, naming the Brothers Minor (an order of clerics) as his proctors. The Brothers were directed specifically to "inquire concerning living [and dead] usurers and the things wrongfully acquired by this wicked usury . . . and . . . compel opponents by ecclesiastical censure" (Paris 1872–83, 4:564–65).

Church officials routinely looked the other way for favored transgressors (e.g., the Medici) but continued to condemn "manifest, public usurers," such as the Jewish moneylenders, when it was in their interests to do so. Nelson (1947, 120–21) observed that the Church's selective enforcement dichotomized the medieval merchant-usurer into "two disparate figures who stood at opposite poles: the degraded manifest usurer-pawnbroker, as often as not a Jew; and the city father, arbiter of elegance, patron of the arts, devout philanthropist, the merchant prince." He concluded that the Church's restitution policies spawned opportunities for economic growth (i.e., the rise of temporal and market power) in pre-Reformation Europe. But Nelson only saw the tip of the iceberg.

The Church as Borrower. The papal treasury was both a demander and a supplier of loans. Although records are sparse and loan terms were often camouflaged in papal rhetoric (e.g., references to "gifts" instead of interest), it appears that the *camera* borrowed frequently on favorable terms. While the Medici Bank was paying between 5 percent and 10 percent on deposits in the fifteenth century (Homer 1977, 107), the *camera* was paying loan rates between 2.3 and 6.6 percent, according to information contained in the Introitus and Exitus Registers (Schulte 1904, 5–7; Arias 1905, 548).[6] One entry in the Obligations Register of the *camera* for the year 1436 refers to two "pure and gratuitous and friendly loans" of 1,900 gold florins each (Clergeac 1911, 254).

Papal demand for loans was ostensibly heavy, especially during the Crusades and other territorial conquests (see Chapter 7). Beginning in 1245, the papacy accumulated large debts in its attempt to gain control of the

Kingdom of Sicily, although the terms of such loans are not known. Lunt (1939, 227) reports, however, that the loans bore interest and that the Italian bankers to whom the debts were owed were pressing Pope Urban IV for payment in 1262. Despite the absence of complete and detailed records on the Church's borrowing, it appears that loan activity continued unabated throughout the medieval period. A cameral document of 1492 lists forty-seven papal creditors to whom the *camera* owed a total of 128,424 ducats, which was approximately half of its estimated income that year (Clergeac 1911, 268–71).[7]

The Church as Lender. On the supply side, the medieval Church's role as lender is more obscure and more difficult to trace. Some ecclesiastic historians maintain that the papacy was not a lender and that its revenues came entirely from taxes, traditional dues, and tithes. However, Vatican documents suggest that the apostolic *camera* routinely loaned money "in-house" to its own clerics for a wide variety of purposes. The most common circumstance was one in which illiquid clerics were forced to borrow in order to make required payments to the *camera*. Most of the papacy's lending activity was done at arm's length, through papal bankers who were not clerics but who nevertheless operated as agents of the papacy. Often the *camera* factored loans incurred by clerics who were required to pay a lump-sum tax (*servitia*) to the papacy on being raised to the episcopate. These loans were contracted with the license of the pope, and amounts were usually guaranteed by the property of the borrower's church, as well as the pope's. In such matters the pope designated special clerks to execute the rigorous ecclesiastic penalties and processes that would be directed against the borrower if he should fail to meet the terms of the contract with the bankers. According to Lunt (1939, 472), "The borrower paid to the bankers for the accommodation sums which were equivalent to modern interest in all but name." Other documents suggest that those prelates paying *servitia* were often forced to borrow from the *camera*, or its bankers, at usurious rates (Snape 1926, 103–4; Lunt 1934, 2:236–39, 257–59).[8]

Tyerman (1988, 206) argues that from 1100 to 1250, monasteries "occupied a central position in private crusade finance, to their undoubted material advantage. They rapidly emerged as major institutions of capitalist enterprise, acting as bankers and financiers, as well as territorial empire builders." On the other hand, Snape (1926, 119) reports that medieval monasteries typically incurred heavy debts, especially throughout the thirteenth century. It was not unusual for the pope to use his influence on monks and clergy to facilitate payment of amounts owed to the papacy. Pope Alexander IV, for example, attempted to force English prelates to lend a large sum of money to Henry III for immediate application to the debt

Henry owed the papacy. The English monastic writers whose houses were affected attribute the plan to the Bishop of Hereford, who falsely represented himself as the agent of the monasteries and pledged them to repay certain loans to Italian bankers that the religious communities neither authorized nor received. Under this pretense, the bishop borrowed money from the merchant bankers, remitted it to the *camera*, and left the monasteries holding the bag. Interest and expenses paid by the unwilling borrowers ran between 16 and 21 percent and the monks were threatened with excommunication if they did not pay (Lunt 1939, 267–72, 286).

Throughout the Middle Ages, the Church's tax and loan policies were intricately bound together in a way that encouraged vigorous participation in loan markets. As the Church's expansionist policies put greater pressure on its cash flow, it routinely borrowed advances against the collection of revenues, then raised taxes to cover the cost of loans. New and higher taxes raised the debt burden on prelates and encouraged more loans at the lower levels of Church administration to pay the debts incurred at the higher level.

Vatican documents reveal a hard-nosed treatment of delinquent borrowers. In the first year of his pontificate, Pope Urban IV (1261–1264) wrote to bishops in England, Austria, Spain, Germany, and Scotland threatening excommunication if their loans were not repaid in a timely fashion (Lunt 1934, 2:240–41). On many occasions, the pope also intervened to assist papal bankers in collecting debts, both from the clergy and the laity (Lunt 1934, 1:329–31, 333–37). The unpopularity of Italian merchant bankers in England was attributed to their charging interest on loans. In 1235 the Bishop of London excommunicated the Italian merchants in that city and ordered them to leave, but the merchants overcame that obstacle with the help of the pope. On at least one occasion, some Italian merchants in London who were arrested for usury claimed that they were papal agents (Lunt 1939, 600).

Overall, it appears that the Church operated on both sides of the loan market. It borrowed freely from its own (merchant) bankers and quietly made usurious loans to its prelates (or forced them into such loans), while outwardly declaring public usurers anathema.

Usury and Other Church Objectives

The doctrine of usury was used in creative ways by the medieval Church, as demonstrated by papal behavior during the Crusades, which created an enormous demand for capital and manpower.[9] The Church responded with extra taxes on its priests and parishioners, including the imposition of income taxes on the clergy. However, manpower needs were more difficult to fulfill. In its drive to secure more fighting personnel, the Church used its usury doctrine as a carrot and stick to increase enlistments. It selectively absolved guilt and dispensed restitution for usurers who volunteered to fight the infidels.

The exhortation of Pope Innocent III (1198–1216) to his clergy in 1199 illustrates the vigor of papal attempts to encourage certain behavior by establishing the proper incentives. On this occasion, usury figured prominently. After encouraging the enlistment of combatants to the Crusades, the pope declared:

> If, indeed, any of those departing thither are held bound by oath to paying usury, do you, brother archbishops and bishops, force their creditors throughout your dioceses with the same coercive measure, with the obstacle of appeal taken away, that, absolving them from the oath forthwith, they desist from the exaction of further usury. But if any creditor should force them to the payment of usury, do you force him by a similar measure of coercion to the restitution of it, with appeal removed. Jews, indeed, we order to be compelled by the secular power to remit usuries to them; and, until they shall have remitted them, we order all communion to be denied them by Christ's faithful by sentence of excommunication, both in merchandises and in other things. (Lunt 1934, 2:86)[10]

According to Tyerman (1988, 196) the Church's edicts of 1146 and 1187 to 1188, exempting Crusaders from paying usury on past loans and exempting payment of usury on any new loans contracted while a Crusader, encouraged Crusaders to seek long leasing arrangements rather than short-term loans. In the final analysis, the papal exemptions served to destroy a Crusader's credit by exposing lenders to additional risk. Tyerman (1988, 197) concludes that "these decrees . . . represent either the height of naivety or, in view of the church's role as the main source of ready cash, the depth of disingenuousness, an attempt to consolidate a near monopoly."

Persistence of the Usury Doctrine

Although conventional economic wisdom denigrates the doctrine of usury as outside the standard logic of economic theory, it offers little in the way of explanation for the doctrine's endurance over centuries. Was the doctrine of usury simply a bad idea that became increasingly anachronistic as economic markets slowly advanced, or were there identifiable economic reasons why the doctrine persisted during the Middle Ages?

Existing explanations of usury, as noted in the introduction to this chapter, stress doctrine more than policy. They imply that from an economic standpoint, usury was a bad idea that somehow lingered too long. Such explanations may be classified into three categories. The first approach seeks to understand medieval Church practice by emphasizing the role of theological dogma. A second approach attempts to elucidate the doctrine of usury by exegetical analysis of medieval texts. A third approach concentrates narrowly on the nature of economic doctrine, seeking lasting contributions to economic analysis.

The explanation of the medieval doctrine of usury offered here differs from existing ones in three major respects: (1) it emphasizes the policy or *practice* of usury rather than the doctrine; (2) it treats usury as merely one of many policy variables at the Church's disposal in its efforts to achieve certain objectives; (3) it presupposes actions by Church officials based on the theory of bureaucratic-monopolistic behavior. This approach leads to the conclusion that the doctrine of usury persisted because it was in the medieval Church's interest to regulate loan markets. Specifically,

1. In cases where the papacy was a borrower, it had an incentive to develop and enforce policies that enhanced its wealth at low cost.
2. In cases where the papacy was a lender, it had an incentive to adopt practices designed to preserve and enhance its monopoly status.
3. In cases where the papacy was neither lender nor borrower, it had an incentive to adopt and maintain policies that enabled it to further its wealth or influence, including the collection of rents and the control of entry.

We do not imply that the usury doctrine was not used for other, more indirect, rent-seeking purposes. Indeed, it was used to punish the Church's enemies directly. One decretum, interpreting a text from St. Ambrose, indicates that it is permissible to demand usury from "enemies." Enemies, it seems, were the likes of Saracens, heretics, and infidels. Not only did the Church benefit directly from its development and selective enforcement of the usury doctrine, the doctrine was used in direct assaults on entrants and potential entrants by the centralized Roman Catholic establishment.

Usury and Just Price

A considerable body of scholarship has declared that the canonical doctrine of usury was only part of a larger issue—that is, "just price." This purported relationship between the two doctrines is a popular notion, albeit incorrect in our view. The concept of just price dates from the twelfth century and owes its origin to the revival of Roman law that took place about that time.

Roman law offered two doctrines pertinent to the sale and price of economic goods. The principles of *laesio enormis* was a remedy available under Roman law that enabled a litigant to sue for recovery in cases where the price received in an exchange was less than half of the just price. This principle was supplemented with a second, *Licet contrahentibus invicem se naturaliter circumvenire;* that is, parties to a contract are free to get the better of one another. Free bargaining, then, helped to determine the just price, in other words, the market price. In practice, *laesio enormis* came into play only in cases where fraud, intentional misrepresentation, or some other shady manipulation was employed in an exchange.

This was the basis for the canonical doctrine of *justum pretium*, or just price. To the canonists, the just price was merely the current price as determined by the free market, *or* as determined by the state. It is important to note that *justum pretium* explicitly acknowledged efforts by government to regulate price.

Prices were in principle free to fluctuate, within the bounds of just price doctrine; *justum pretium* was neither a requirement that prices remain fixed, nor a version of the labor theory of value. The notion of the just price or market price was not applied to loans; hence, usury was not a problem of just price in canon law (Noonan 1957, 89).

However, the canonists did in fact hold that a price could be *unjust* under some circumstances. The doctrine on unjust price was termed *pretium affectionis*, which translates as "price discrimination." An unjust price occurred when one party to an exchange took advantage of some weakness or dire necessity to which the other party was subject, or alternatively when the price was "artificially fixed." This meant that the exchange was affected by monopoly or collusion. The canonists, like their Roman predecessors, treated monopoly as a kind of intentional fraud. According to canon law, monopoly profits were *turpe lucrum*, which meant that such profits were subject to restitution—exploited consumers could claim the gains a monopolist made at their "expense."

The Church did not prohibit *all* price fixing or all monopolies. The canonists restricted their prohibition to cases involving private monopolies, and thus did not define government-provided or Church-sponsored monopoly rights as unjust.[11] They generally approved of government policies that restricted competition, and those that regulated exchange. The official Church doctrine expressly allowed the government to regulate prices for purposes of the "public good."

Friedman (1980) argues that the doctrine of just price was a rational policy under the relevant economic circumstances that describe the medieval context. He argues that whereas the neoclassical economics textbook account of the efficiency of free markets normally presumes a highly competitive market composed of large numbers of buyers and sellers with easy access to reliable information, in medieval times markets for most goods and services tended to be characterized by extremely small numbers of buyers and sellers. Under these conditions, bargaining problems were very widespread. Sometimes trades involved a transaction between a monopoly producer and a monopsony consumer, more commonly, one or both sides of the market involved very small numbers of bargaining agents, considerable collusion, and highly impacted information flows. Price, in short, was highly indeterminate in practice. As Friedman (1980, 235–36) explains:

> a market price is only well defined when there are many buyers and sellers. Such a situation was far from universal in the medieval economy. Both the writers in the Scholastic tradition and Aristotle, their primary source, were largely concerned with exchanges involving small numbers of buyers and sellers. As the situation approaches closer and closer to the pure case of bilateral monopoly—one buyer and one seller—the price at which a good can be bought or sold becomes increasingly indeterminate. The purpose of the doctrine of just price was to determine the price in such noncompetitive situation.

Friedman concludes that the doctrine of just price was at heart a kind of *arbitration procedure*, that is, a set of guidelines intended to help resolve the conflicts that were endemic in circumstances where competitive markets and determinate prices were absent. The just price doctrine implied that a price should be sufficient to permit the full recovery of reasonable costs by the seller, a rough approximation of the long-run equilibrium price we would expect to see in a competitive market. According to Friedman (1980, 237),

> In the normal non-competitive case the merchant's costs would be the same as those of a merchant in the competitive market; hence the market value of the good would be within the bargaining range and would provide a reasonable arbitrated price. In the exceptional case in which a good was worth more than its market price to the seller, the just price would be adjusted upward accordingly.

Friedman is correct in noting the proliferation of barriers to price competition from a number of sources during the Middle Ages. Many of these barriers were erected and maintained by government. For example, municipal governments raised considerable revenue from the sale of monopoly franchises, which were an important component of the medieval "monopoly problem." Similarly, the guilds that were so widespread during the time and dominated so many craft markets were essentially creations of government in almost all cases—created and supported by legal sanction of various sorts.

The guild system was an example of government-sponsored cartelization. A local group of producers practicing a particular craft would obtain sanction from municipal authorities to forbid the entry of new competitors into the local market, without first securing, the permission of the guild. These organizations tended to be composed of groups of small independent masters (a sole proprietor) and represented local cartels. They frequently entered into open agreements with one another to fix prices and restrict output, with government approval and support.

Scholastic writers diplomatically tended to avoid direct confrontation with guilds, since these organizations represented a major source of monopoly power in the Middle Ages, and Church authors recognized this fact. A few Scholastic philosophers spoke out against the monopolistic practices of the guilds, and sometimes even criticized the award of special privileges to guilds by municipal governments. Their vigilance, though relatively weak, probably deterred some especially blatant abuses of medieval consumers by guilds with monopoly power, but that economic benefit was indirect. The fact is that the Church did not actively campaign against the system of guild–cartels.

During the Middle Ages, governments intervened extensively in the operation of private markets, and the bulk of this regulation was implemented by the municipal authorities of cities, towns, and boroughs, although the central (royal) government was also involved in France and England (De Roover 1958, 428). This regulatory activity included substantial efforts designed to fix prices, an issue not broached by Friedman.

Medieval price regulation tended to be extensive, but was usually limited to a range of goods considered "necessities," that is, wheat, bread, meat, wine, beer, and so on. Legal prices of the period were normally ceiling prices, but price controls at times tended to extend to a more inclusive set of objects, and some writers insisted that government price controls should be extended to all commodities.[12] Superficially, the Church would seem to have implicitly supported this governmental price fixing, given the fact that the "scholastic authors were full of illusions about the omniscience, honesty, and efficiency of public authorities" (De Roover, 1958, 429).

These price regulations were disorganized and tended to work at cross-purposes with each other For example, even though by the later Middle Ages the prices most frequently fixed were ceilings imposed on markets for foodstuffs, candles, wood, and building materials—supposedly on behalf of consumers—wages earned by those same consumers were widely and regularly the object of *maximum* legal rates (Cipolla 1963, 405). As one scholar notes, "there were laws, of town origin, aiming to enforce competition in the things the townsmen bought, while the guild regulations [supported by municipal grants of monopoly privilege] limited and controlled the competition in the things they sold" (Clark 1939, 23). De Roover (1958, 430) characterizes medieval government price regulation as "a tale of woe." Price fixing often led to the emergence of underground market activity and widespread concealment of existing stocks of goods. In many cases, price controls were enacted largely due to the demands of violent mobs, who threatened the lives of public officials if the latter failed to "do something."

The Church's canon law, not to mention its moral authority, tended to influence government policy at the margin. Price fixing was a political action driven by rent seeking. The actual legal price (or other rationing policy) ultimately took the form it did as an expression of the interests of the highest "bidding" group. Becker (1985) argues that in a modern democratic setting, the economic policies that eventually dominate and become actual tend to be those that have the relatively least negative impact on overall efficiency because deadweight cost produced by efficiency-reducing regulations represents potential gain for interest groups. Thus, price controls, enacted in a modern context by a democratic government, should tend to resemble the structure of prices that would have expressed themselves across a free competitive market at least as a long-term proposition.

But the context of medieval public policymaking was fundamentally different given the extremely high transaction costs associated with political markets in the medieval period. Government regulations in general—whether of price or other market variables—tended to be more erratic, and more commonly at odds with economic efficiency. If, say, the municipal authorities decreed a massive reduction in the legal price of wheat after being physically intimidated by a violent mob of economically unsophisticated medieval consumers, the result of this far-from-equilibrium effective price might be substantial reduction in economic efficiency (including redistributive effects). To return to the example, suppliers of wheat might respond by withholding their output, and large numbers of misguided consumers might die as a result. As a point of fact, much medieval municipal price fixing occurred during famines and other temporary shortage situations, which were very common given the undeveloped nature of the general economy. The just price doctrine, insofar as it focused implicitly on the idea of the competitive price as the model, may have stiffened the spine of municipal authorities in their price-fixing activities. From this perspective, the official doctrine of the Church, in other words, may have helped restrain municipal economic policymakers from economically inefficient behavior.

Set against this possibility are the effects of the Church's prohibition of certain types of "speculation." This prohibition did not include all buying and selling for profit—for example, the purchase of goods at a low price and sale at a higher price in the same place. Rather, the Church's prohibitions related to what we would now term forward markets and spot exchange —the purchase of goods now at one price and the later sale of them at a higher price. The economic value of such speculation is now understood as the transfer of goods through time from periods of plenty to those of scarcity. The canons of Gratian found it "dishonest to buy grain at harvest time in order to sell it for a higher price in time of famine" (McLaughlin 1939, 96). This speculation, according to the canonists, is a flagrant case of *turpe lucrum*—dishonest gain in the form of buying at a low figure to (later) make a profit. Thus, while the just price qua market price interpretation of Church exchange regulations might have had a marginal impact on the behavior of local government authorities, other aspects of the just price doctrine clearly had an opposite effect on economic efficiency.

"Dishonest speculation" was only one clash with Church doctrine. In addition, cupidity (the inordinate love of money) and self-interest were generally condemned by the Church (and still are) (Chapter 9), although moderate income from trade and freedom of bargaining with restrictions were legitimized. Enforcement of the "Christianized" Roman law of *laesio enormis* and transactions generally were selective on occasion in *favor* of Church interests (McLaughlin 1939, 127), with the prohibitions of *turpe lucrum* (acts from love of gain) more often officially directed at the clergy than at lay traders. Accommodation of moral opinion to the growing level of transactions appears, in other words, to follow the same pattern as doctrinal manipulation of the usury prohibition.

Conclusion: Usury and Economic Opportunism

Throughout this book we argue that the institutional framework of the medieval Church provided many opportunities for rent seeking and created numerous problems of enforcement for ecclesiastic authorities. The medieval Church's treatment of usury, in practice as opposed to authoritarian doctrine, provides a case in point. The famous medieval doctrine of just price almost certainly provides another example of opportunistic behavior. Of course, the full extent to which ecclesiastic "managers" took advantage of existing rent-seeking opportunities, and promoted additional opportunities to obtain economic rents, remains problematical, due, among other things, to limitations regarding the quantity and quality of data. Economic theory can give us a window into economic history but it cannot write the historical record for us.

Like other forms of legislation and regulation, the medieval doctrine of usury can be understood in terms of the interest-group theory of government. In this interest-group setting, Church policy emerges to promote the monopoly-bureaucratic interests of the ecclesiastic organization and its temporal satellites. This does not mean that the medieval Church originally formulated its usury doctrine for this purpose, because it is a matter of record that the doctrine preceded the organizational Church. It does suggest, however, that the Church framed and altered the doctrine to suit its institutional interests during the Middle Ages.

It is our view that some historians of economic thought have tended to overintellectualize the doctrine of usury, which is the one aspect of the Church's complex regulatory framework that has typically drawn the most attention. Others, like Nelson (1947), who saw opportunism in the Church's policy on restitution, have stopped short of a complete and adequate interpretation. A number of economic historians, following Weber and Tawney, have argued that the medieval Church's usury prohibitions impeded the development of capitalism. Contrariwise, our analysis suggests that the Church's success at rent seeking through usury and other monopoly-maintenance policies may have inadvertently and unintentionally *encouraged* temporal market developments.[13]

In a masterful study of medieval economic doctrine, Langholm (1992) describes the doctrinal interplay between psychological-religious attitudes and emerging economic man. He notes that the economic doctrine of the medieval theologians were "a set of compromises, codes of economic conduct which must be operational while abandoning as little as possible of the Christian vision of society" (Langholm 1992, 565). He further notes that the Smithian concept of self-interest (*avaritia*) was antithetical to the fundamental vision of a Christian economy where self-love was one of the seven deadly sins. Yet the substance of the Church's positions on usury (and on other medieval doctrines such as just price) appears to reveal overt self-interested behavior on the part of Church officials. Although the effects of the usury doctrine on economic growth remain an open question, we believe that additional research along the lines suggested here has the potential to supply logically consistent answers to such fundamental historic-economic puzzles.

NOTES

1. Joseph Schumpeter (1954, 104–5) credits the Schoolmen, not Aristotle, with the origin of a theory of interest. He assigns discovery to the Scholastic writers of the following causal propositions: (a) interest is essentially a monetary phenomenon; (b) interest is an element in the price of money (although medieval writers did not fully appreciate the nature of interest as an intertemporal premium, they helped clear the way for the fundamental logical problem involved); and (c) the fundamental factor accounting for a positive rate of interest is the prevalence of business profit.

2. Before the Renaissance, the legal limits on personal loans from pawnshops ranged from a low of 10 percent in Italy to 300 percent in Provence. In the four-

teenth century, the Lombards often charged 50 percent, although the most common legal pawnshop limit in effect was 43 1/3 percent. Monarchs, such as Emperor Frederick II (1211–1250), often paid interest of 30–40 percent to creditors, especially when collateral was not liquid. Commercial loans commonly fetched interest rates between 10–25 percent depending on the adequacy of commercial credits (see Homer 1977, 89–103).

3. De Roover (1967, 266) notes that pawnbrokers and small moneylenders were the main victims of the Church's campaigns against usury, "but the big bankers with international connections were left undisturbed. Far from being censured, they were called 'the peculiarly beloved sons of the Church' and prided themselves on being the Pope's exchangers."

4. Tawney (1926, 43) cites the case of a Paris bishop who urged a usurer to dedicate his ill-gotten wealth to the building of Notre Dame Cathedral rather than make restitution. And De Roover (1948a, 157n) relates a bizarre example of the Church's restitution policy in the late fourteenth century involving the will of a notorious Florentine usurer, Bartolomeo dei Cocchi-Compagni. According to De Roover:

> The will called for complete and unconditional restitution to all persons who could prove that they had been wronged by the testator. Despite this provision, all the bequests in favor of the Church were paid in full prior to any restitution. What remained of the estate did not suffice to satisfy all the claimants. Moreover, the archbishop of Florence was awarded by the executors a grant of 100 florins . . . [and] Bartolomeo dei Cocchi-Compagni was buried in state under the steps of the high altar of Santa Maria Novella.

5. See Rubin (1978) for the stylistic argument regarding the modern franchising firm.

6. Part of this difference may, of course, be explained by lender perceptions of differential risk. Lenders may have perceived loans to the apostolic *camera* as low-risk bonds because they were often secured by proceeds from *servitia*, a service tax paid by prelates who received an office from Rome.

7. Based on figures published by Lunt (1934, 1:13–14), annual papal revenues averaged slightly more than 200,000 florins during the first half of the fourteenth century, rising to somewhere around 250,000 florins per year during the second half of the fifteenth century.

8. In the case of Lord Burkard, the Bishop of Constance (Germany), the total expenses of his confirmation at the hands of Pope Pius II (1458–1464) was 3,316 gold florins—about $17,000 in today's money (Lunt 1934, 2:286–87). Other bishops paid similar amounts to be confirmed.

9. Support for the Crusades may have been eagerly provided by Italian merchants, who provisioned most of the pope's armies.

10. Since Jews obviously could not be excommunicated, the policy of "anathema," or "shunning," was often applied, whereby the faithful were forbidden to trade or otherwise communicate with those "shunned." In this case as in others, the Church used spiritual sanctions to achieve economic ends indirectly. The practice

of using the usury doctrine to achieve other ends indirectly apparently continued even into the post-medieval era. Pope Julius II (1503–1513) granted jurisdiction over usury cases to the Spanish Inquisition, although usury itself did not constitute heresy. The people who had been traditionally detested as usurers and who had inspired the creation of the Inquisition were the Jews, many of whom by this time were "converted" and assimilated into Spanish culture and government. The Church's action was therefore controversial, and in 1554, it revoked the power of the Inquisition to prosecute cases involving usury (Kamen 1985, 200). Evidence suggests that the Inquisition itself was a means of collecting rents, since confiscation of property was the standard punishment prescribed by canon law for heresy (Lunt 1934, 2:369). Kamen (1985, 146–54) found that although the initial confiscations carried out by the Inquisition were very large, inquisitorial budgets were persistently in deficit, mainly because the bureaucracy became bloated as its revenues increased. Contemporary observers quickly concluded that the search for heretics was really a search for property.

11. See the discussion of the Church-owned Tolfa alum mines in Chapter 2.

12. For example, a Frenchman by the name of Jean Gerson (1362–1428) advocated this point of view, on the grounds that no one should presume to be wiser than the lawmaker! See De Roover (1958, 425).

13. Ullman (1972, 292) makes a connection between papal fiscal policies and the rise of European nationalism, but does not go so far as to make the same connection to the emergence of capitalism. Lane (1966, 67–68) and De Roover (1967, 271) disagree on whether the doctrine of usury fostered or retarded economic growth.

CHAPTER SEVEN

How the Church Profited
from the Crusades

Introduction: Religion and Violence

The religious wars between East and West (and sometimes between eastern and western Europe) that pitted the medieval Christian Church against the Moslem "infidels" have come to be known simply as the Crusades. The most intense conflicts between the Latin Church and the Moslem forces that controlled Jerusalem and other Holy Places occurred between the eleventh and thirteenth centuries (1095–1274). These conflicts had an impact on the economic development of Europe and also on the intertemporal prospects of the Latin Church as a monopoly provider of salvation.

In this chapter we seek to provide an economic rationale for what superficially seems incongruous activity for a religious institution dedicated to the nonviolent teachings of Christ. How does one explain such nominally un-Christian activity as violent warfare against another religious sect? We maintain that the institutional behavior of the Latin Church that manifested itself in the Crusades was motivated in large part by the desire to protect its monopoly position and to expand its market areas. The former may be analyzed as a supply-side response and the latter as a demand-side response.

Because the Latin Church "sold" a pure credence good—a system of belief promising eternal salvation that was not subject to "external" verification—challenges to its credibility could, *ceteris paribus*, impose economic loss. Moslem encroachment and occupation of Jerusalem and the holy shrines of the Near East, by denying access to pilgrims from the Latin Church, made it difficult for the Latin Church to maintain the quality and credibility of its product. Consequently, the Moslems imposed higher production costs

on the Latin Church, and the Crusades were an incongruous but predictable response to the market challenge raised by the spread of Islam.

Our tendency to stress economic elements at the expense of spiritual or
other noneconomic elements in the analysis of institutional Church behavior does not prove that other factors did not affect Church policy. Rather,
we stress the economic factors because they are vital to the interest-group
theory of institutional behavior, and because this latter theory is greatly
underrepresented, certainly as part of an overarching strategy, in historical arguments about the medieval Church. A popular view, though one not
held by all medievalists, was that the Crusaders were not motivated by
profit. In fact, however, the papacy held out the prospects for economic
gain as a motivation for Crusaders from the very first crusade (Lunt 1934,
1:244).

In some cases naive economic analysis has been employed to buttress
this view. For example, the fact that many Crusaders had to finance their
participation in the Crusades by selling their family lands (patrimony) for
cash has been cited as evidence that profit seeking was not a significant
motivation among participants. It is true that liquidating land in western
Europe on the eve of the First Crusade was financially hazardous because of
depressed agricultural production and low land prices. It is also true that such
sales required the agreement of *all* family members. But these combined
circumstances do not necessarily support the "obvious" conclusion drawn
by Riley-Smith (1981, 13–14): "It makes sense to suppose that they (the
Crusaders), and especially their families, were moved by idealism."

Such simple statements overlook the possibility that the rush to raise
cash might have been motivated by a competition to claim economic rents
in the Holy Land before they could be dissipated, not unlike the kind of
activity in North America touched off by the California or Alaska gold
rushes. In place of the conventional wisdom we advance a public-choice
perspective, in which the purported philosophical and ideological arguments of certain proponents of specific public policies can be shown to be
compatible with the capture of rents by those proponents. We believe that
this perspective is appropriate to most historical investigation, including
the Crusades. While our interpretation does not deny the presence of
extenuating noneconomic circumstances, it flatly rejects the notion that
Crusaders (both direct participants and ecclesiastic instigators) behaved
irrationally in the economic sense, or that religious zeal was everywhere
and always the driving force behind crusade activity.

All of the Crusades, including those to the Holy Lands and to the Baltic
and Russia, may be seen as an essential part of a general wealth-maximizing
strategy and as a form of "public policy" devised by the Latin Church to
accomplish its general goals. The medieval Church was, in the main, *the*

public sector (a kind of multinational government) in medieval western Europe. It levied taxes, maintained a court system, and provided most of medieval society's "welfare transfers." It was also the largest single property owner in western Europe. As a dominant economic player in medieval society, the Church was faced with the inevitable problems of maintaining the value of its capital stock, expanding its market area, and maximizing the value of its assets. Under these circumstances it would have been foolhardy not to devise public policy to protect its interests. In all likelihood the Crusades were a vital part of that strategy—a kind of "foreign policy" in a different world in which governments as we know them today were prehistorical.

As a general wealth-maximizing plan, the Crusades must be viewed as a long-run strategy. Although they occasioned some wealth destruction in the short run, the plan was aimed at long-run economic efficiency and at increasing the value of Church investments. The structural changes launched by the Crusades probably affected economic growth rates in western Europe, and undoubtedly led to some expansion of Christian civilization in eastern Europe as well. But it is likely that these were unintended rather than intended consequences of the medieval Church's public policy.

Warfare as a Means of Achieving Market Dominance

In the business world a dominant firm can be expected to resist serious challenges to its market position. The nature and success of such resistance depend on the relative power of the market participants and the institutional constraints imposed by society. By the eleventh century, the Church had achieved a dominant position in the "market for religion," but this had not always been the case. Almost from its inception the institutional Roman Catholic Church had to face adversity and hostility, but as its membership grew, it gradually consolidated power and influence. Always central to the maintenance of its position, however, was the claim of credibility, and as the purveyor of a pure credence good, the Church persistently sought to increase and protect its "credibility capital."

Warfare was an integral part of medieval society. Even before it attained the height of its power and influence, the Church relied on the military might of others. In 853, for example, Pope Leo IV appealed to the Franks for military assistance in the defense of Rome against the Saracens; and in 878, Pope John VIII enlisted soldiers in the cause of the Church (i.e., protection of papal property) by promising them "heavenly reward" (Brundage 1982, 18). Where convenient, the Church also enlisted the aid of secular governments to protect the credibility of its spiritual claims, particularly the enforcement of laws against heresy in the later Middle Ages (Chapter

4). Each of these episodes can be regarded as an investment in the preservation of the Church's spiritual capital, which is what constituted the foundation of the Church as a firm.

The First Crusade, then, was neither an isolated nor an unprecedented event. What was unprecedented was its audacity and scope. Given the nature and background of Christianity, the First Crusade was based on an astonishing and radical premise: that it was legitimate for the Christian Church to pursue its ends through military means. Whether one accepts this premise or not, it is our contention that the train of military expeditions undertaken by the medieval Church from the eleventh century onward generated substantial economic costs *and* benefits, both of a direct and indirect nature.

The First Crusade as a Case Study

Although our analysis applies to the medieval Crusades in general, we focus primarily, though not exclusively, on the First Crusade in this chapter for several reasons: (1) it is the most extensively studied of the eight Crusades; (2) it is the one that historians have pronounced most obviously "religious" in motivation; and (3) the crusading army was almost entirely raised, supported, and directed by the Church itself (in later years, various nation-states became more directly or indirectly involved in the crusading conflicts).

Supply-Side Response. As we saw in Chapter 2, vertical integration was central to the economic interests of the Latin Church because credence on the part of its customers was vital to the present and future stream of revenues that flowed to the Church. We can interpret the Church's initiation of and participation in the Crusades as another attempt at vertical integration, that is, a supply-side response to external market threats.

The precise historical trigger point of any major military conflict is always difficult to ascertain, but certain events transpired during the eleventh century that may have influenced the timing of the decision by Pope Urban II to call for a military solution to a mounting problem. These events, which carried a number of specific economic implications, combined to sway public sentiment in western Europe toward a major military campaign. The object of the campaign was to oust the Turks from the Holy Land. After capturing Palestine and Anatolia from Byzantium in the late eleventh century, the Seljuk Turks began, around 1085, to harass Christian pilgrims to the Holy Land and tax them to an unprecedented degree.[1] European traders also encountered high levels of interference in their day-to-day operations in newly held Turkish territories. In particular, Italian merchants from Venice, Genoa, and Pisa faced prohibitive tolls and tariffs, plus general hostility to their trading activities. To be sure, these hostilities were long-standing. Italian city-states fought the Saracens for four centuries prior to the ascendancy of the Seljuk Turks, suffering "endless raids and plunderings" (Krueger 1969, 40). Thus, the Seljuks merely continued and exacerbated an old annoyance, causing hostilities to accelerate into a major grievance on the part of the Italian merchants, who looked to the Vatican, their partner in many financial arrangements, for relief. Of course, the Church also had a strong incentive to protect its primary capital asset: its proclaimed role as the sole representative of God on earth. The customer appeal of all of the services offered by the Church to its members pivoted on the credibility of this overarching claim.[2]

Any challenge to the credibility of the Church's unique relationship with God, if successful, could impose a huge capital loss, and the events leading up to the First Crusade seemed to muster just such a threat. If the Church could not protect the pilgrimage rights so vital to its central claim as God's sole representative on earth, then neither could it preserve its vast political influence or its dominant share of the market for religion.

Demand-Side Expansion. In the late eleventh century, the market position of the Latin Church was threatened from the East on two fronts, one from without and one from within. The external threat was Moslem expansionism into the territories of the Near East. The internal threat was a growing separatism in the Eastern Orthodox Church. The First Crusade gave the Latin Church an opportunity to gain supremacy in the Near East that would allow it to enter a lucrative new market for religious services. Both Islamic and Byzantine governments had forcibly blunted the Latin Church's missionary efforts in the Near East, effectively blocking the establishment of local churches and the conversion of local inhabitants. New markets meant new members, and new members meant new revenues. In addition, the Vatican favored the establishment of a "buffer zone," composed of conquered territories that would protect the Church's western European market from competitive entry by Islam.

Pope Urban II gave voice to his concern about the mounting threat to the Eastern and Western churches posed by the rapid spread of Islam after the death of Mohammed. In calling the First Crusade from Clermont on November 27, 1095, Urban II stressed the importance of maintaining doctrinal (and political) hegemony over the Moslems: "All Christendom is disgraced by the triumphs and supremacy of the Muslims in the East. The Holy Land . . . is profaned and enslaved by infidel rulers. Those who lose their lives in such an enterprise [crusading] will gain paradise and remission of their sins" (Tanner et al. 1926, 265). Interestingly, the steady spread of the Moors through Syria, North Africa, and Spain during the seventh and eighth centuries, though viewed with some alarm by the Latin Church, did *not* prompt a holy war; yet the fall of Antioch to the Turks in 1085 and the Moslem revival in Spain and Africa shortly thereafter did. What might account for the different response at a later date?

We believe that the answer rests on two grounds. First, the Church was a more mature firm with far greater resources in the eleventh century than it was in the eighth century.[3] Second, the threat posed by Islam in the eleventh century was viewed by the Vatican as more intense, multifaceted, and dangerous, in part, because the internal cohesion of the Church had been damaged. A more intense and complicated threat evoked a more intense and complicated response. Thus, the Latin Church launched both demand-side and supply-side initiatives.

The demand-side justification for the Crusades was characterized by the Church's vigorous efforts to establish doctrinal hegemony over competing religions. Complicating the struggle for doctrinal hegemony was the fact that the medieval Christian Church consisted of two major branches— the Greek, or Eastern Church, and the Latin, or Western Church. Internal doctrinal discord between these two branches had been building for many years prior to the conquest of the Holy Land. A formal split between the Latin and Greek churches occurred in 1054. There followed a great schism that witnessed the almost comic mutual excommunication of the Patriarch of Constantinople by Pope Leo IX and of the pope by the patriarch (Newhall 1963, 20).

This schism established the Eastern Church as a competitor rather than a partner of the Western Church, and in this disunity the Eastern Church lost ground to Moslem competitors. Urban II tried to reunite the Greek and Latin churches through negotiation, but failed. He was soon presented an opportunity to accomplish reunification by other means, however. Near the close of the eleventh century, Alexius, the Byzantine emperor, who had attempted to resist the invading Turks, was facing a new enemy, the Normans, who were allied with the Latin Church. In March 1095, Alexius sent messengers to Pope Urban's council at Piacenze seeking mercenaries in return for negotiations on Church unity (Mayer 1972, 7–8). The messengers appear to have exaggerated the danger to Byzantium, but the Latin Church nevertheless saw an opportunity to seize control of a world market. By one account, "in papal circles men came to hold the opinion that only drastic measures could save Byzantium—and at the same time the Christian Church in the East—measures which might then lead to a reunion of the churches under the primacy of Rome" (Tanner et al. 1926, 88).

The Vatican thereby anticipated the benefits of a successful "holy" war against the Turks. Victory would enable the Latin Church to recapture and enlarge market areas in which its services could be sold to new converts. It was critical that the Latin Church have a monopoly on the *definition* as well as the means of obtaining its product in order to prevent market encroachment by non-Christians or by its former organizational partner, the Greek Church. The eventual recapture of Antioch and the (albeit temporary) rescue of Palestine in the name of Christ were major events in economic history. Not only did it consolidate the monopoly power of the Latin Church, it also demonstrated that the Western Church was capable of sanctioning rebellious activity by its Eastern counterpart.

It is, of course, difficult to aggregate all of the Crusades together or to generalize from one to another. Moreover, we cannot analyze the motivations of each crusade in the space allotted here. Although a complete analysis of the issue requires more depth and breadth, we believe a historical inquiry that exposes the rent-seeking opportunities of decision makers is capable of adding much insight and understanding. With regard to the First Crusade, it is clear that the veneer of religious motivation was more easily placed on it than on later Crusades. Between 1095 and 1274, Crusades were launched against the Moors in Spain, the pagans in northeastern Europe (i.e., the Baltic Crusades), heretics in southern France and Germany, schismatics in Greece, and, of course, the Moslems in the Holy Land, Egypt, and North Africa. "Till at last," according to Runciman (1954, 472), "the crusade came to mean any war against the enemies of papal policy." Indeed, in later Crusades, the Byzantine empire itself was dismembered, and its capital, Constantinople, sacked by soldiers of the Latin Church.

The "Business" of Crusading: Revenues and Costs

A businesslike approach to decisionmaking means that the decision makers carefully weigh the full (present and expected) costs and benefits of contemplated actions. There is sufficient reason to think that the Church, in its economic calculation of whether to launch a specific crusade, behaved in a businesslike way. In trying to reconstruct the historical environment, it is difficult to identify and assess all of the relevant costs faced by the Church on the eve of the Crusades. Obvious short-run costs included the expenditure of outfitting and maintaining armies. Long-run costs, including relevant opportunity costs, such as the risks of alienating huge segments of rival populations from Christianity, may well have been more significant. These latter costs varied with the direction of the crusade. In other words, because of the ultimate failure to maintain control of Palestine, the Near East Crusades were more costly than those in eastern Europe where conversions to Christianity continue to yield returns up to the present day. Although a firm conclusion about the ultimate profitability of the Crusades is near impossible, we contend that the short-term and long-term revenue prospects have so far remained relatively unexplored, and, in all probability, vastly understated.

Direct Rent Collections

Cloaked in the rhetoric of religious fervor, the Crusades promised substantial direct benefits to the Latin Church and offered significant prospects of indirect benefits. Although not fully accountable, large revenues accrued to the Church directly from conquest and control of the Holy Land. These direct revenues came chiefly from tourism, the sale of relics, new taxes, and, to a lesser extent, from new "products."

Revenues from Tourism and Relics. From the fourth through the eleventh centuries, pilgrimages to the Holy Land became increasingly popular among the members of the Latin Church. It was widely believed (a belief encouraged by the clergy) that a pilgrimage to Jerusalem and other holy places conferred spiritual advantages on the pilgrim, ranging from the cure of bodily ills to the absolution of sins and the increased likelihood of entering heaven. In addition to religious conviction, many pilgrims were basically tourists enthralled by the adventure and excitement of the visit.

Thus, pilgrimages were an abundant source of revenue to the Church as pilgrims made donations to abbeys and churches en route as well as at their destination. Religious tourists usually reserved the largest donations for places connected with major events in the life of Christ. Consequently, monasteries and churches tended to locate so as to "enshrine" the holy places and thereby control access to the holy sites. For example, the Church of the Holy Sepulchre in Jerusalem was a major attraction because of its location at the tomb of Christ. Regardless of whether these "donations" are understood as gifts bestowed from religious conviction or the price of a ticket to see a major attraction (e.g., the Disneyland phenomenon of our own time), the revenues were potentially vast.

In terms of "demand" religious relics were also highly prized by the Church as a revenue source, but unlike the Holy Places, relics had the added advantage of being pure credence goods that were portable and easily smuggled.[4] Thus, they were bought and sold in an active market. Willing buyers were those churches not located in the Holy Land that nevertheless wished to increase their "tourist revenues." The possession of relics such as the bones of the apostles and saints, pieces of the True Cross, the Holy Grail, and so on were in great demand by local churches because they acted as major drawing cards for pilgrim-tourists, who were expected to make donations at the site of worship. The Vatican clearly understood the financial benefits that derived from monopolization of the supply of holy relics, which provided yet another rationalization for the Crusades.[5]

The demand for holy relics, always intense in the Middle Ages, received additional impetus during the great period of cathedral building in western Europe. The creation of architecturally bold and awe-inspiring Gothic cathedrals was itself an astonishing example of how the Church was able to refine its product. Poor and uneducated peasants marveled at the glories of heaven suggested by towering vaulted ceilings and beautiful stained-glass windows and trembled at the fearsome threat of hell reflected in the cold stare of decorative stone gargoyles. Church music was yet another input helping to assure Church credentials as a monopoly supplier of God's wisdom and favors. Not surprisingly, medieval cathedrals became key factors in the economic development of entire towns (much as sports complexes are today in large cities), and a high-quality relic collection was as much a draw as a well-crafted cathedral. In fact, the two were highly complementary. Because the Holy Land and its environs had been the scene of many spiritual events in the Church's early history, these places "became a mine for the pious and a boon for the enterprising" (Prawer 1972, 183). Unfettered access to the "relic mines" therefore provided a key economic rationale for the Crusades.[6]

To be sure, an active trade in relics preceded the Middle Ages, but the frenzy seems to have been renewed and intensified with the coming of the Crusades. This new frenzy spawned many problems of internal control for the Church, some of which it was powerless to remedy. Forgeries proliferated from the very start, and competition among local churches frequently got out of hand. Thurston (1913, 737) reported problems as early as the fifth century, when monks "seized upon certain martyrs' bodies by force of arms, defying the authority of the bishops." St. Augustine denounced impostors in the early Church who wandered about in monks' habits making profit from the sale of spurious relics. Moreover, the quest for authenticity often led to bizarre behavior. According to Thurston (1913, 737), Egbert, the Bishop of Trier, tested the authenticity of what was purported to be the body of a venerated saint by tossing "a joint of the finger of St. Celsus wrapped in a cloth into a thurible full of burning coals . . . during Mass, after the offertory had been sung, . . . which remained unhurt and untouched by the fire the whole time of the Canon."

Authentic or not, inventories of the great relic collections, such as those of Rome, Aachen, Cologne, Naples, Salzburg, Antwerp, Constantinople, or Sainte-Chapelle (Paris), were "advertised" in order to increase demand. This kind of hype merely served to increase the number of forgeries that continued unabated.[7] At the Council of Lyon in 1287, the pope was given final authority in disputes involving the authenticity of relics, but there was little that the Church could do in suppressing forgers. As a practical matter, effective policing was impossible as long as the Church attempted to monopolize the supply of relics and artificially inflate their prices. Moreover, it is not clear that the Church had a financial interest in discouraging counterfeits, as long as the relic, real or imagined, served the purpose of attracting tourists and providing revenues.

Taxation and Interest Revenues. Another economic aspect of the Crusades is that they provided a powerful fiscal rationalization for new taxes. According to Gilchrist (1969, 38):

> The papacy . . . sanctioned special taxes to pay for the expenses of the war, e.g., tax of one-twentieth for three years on all ecclesiastical revenues (Lateran IV) or one tenth for six years (Lyons II). This was the first income tax imposed on the clergy, and it set a precedent in both ecclesiastical and secular administrations. Also fines for blasphemy, contributions by penitents, bequests in wills, special levies by secular rulers were imposed.

Many historians accept the premise that these revenues more or less matched the actual expenditures of the Crusades. However, this premise cannot be firmly established because detailed financial data for these revenue flows is virtually nonexistent. Thus, the possibility exists that the Church received a net revenue surplus (i.e., excess of crusade revenues minus crusade expenditures). Finucane (1983, 48) notes that by "the end of the thirteenth century, the call to crusade seemed to many, both clerical and lay, to be no more than a thinly-disguised way to raise money for both kings and popes for a variety of purposes unconnected with the Near East." According to Lunt (1939, 607–8), the Church raised forty-three new levies between 1188 and 1326, an interval that covered most of the crusading period.

Possibly the most neglected and least understood rent-seeking device used by the Church during the Crusades was its creative use of the usury doctrine to increase revenues (Chapter 6). As a lender, the Church itself made enormous profits on loans to Crusaders who required cash to finance their soldiering. As Tyerman (1988, 28, 204) notes," [crusaders] needed cash, and the commonest source of cash in the twelfth century was religious houses." A soldier in the Middle Ages was attracted to warfare as a source of plunder, but like most entrepreneurs, he needed financial capital to launch and sustain the enterprise. In the case of the Crusades, none other than the Church itself offered banking services to its enterprising soldiers.[8]

Once again, if we consider the Church as an M-form firm, it is relatively easy to rationalize its lending activities. The Church faced heavy fixed costs connected with the maintenance of its far-flung bureaucracy, but it also received an immense cash flow from taxes on its members, from contributions of the faithful, and from the earnings of its monastic estates. A large part of this cash flow was diverted to the provision of expensive public goods, such as churches and cathedrals, but it is also likely that its cash flow grew over time. Although we are too far removed from circumstances to know for sure, it is possible that from time to time the Church was awash in cash. If so, the Church would have come under increasing pressure to find profitable outlets for its excess liquidity at a time when capital markets were not well established. Therefore, the Church would have had a strong incentive to promote or manipulate institutional arrangements that would allow it to loan its excess liquidity at attractive rates of interest. The long-standing church doctrine of usury was a potential impediment to such activity, but we have already seen (Chapter 6) that the Church was innovative and selective in its application of this doctrine.

A prominent and telling example of how the Church behaved as a sophisticated monopolist seeking to accomplish multiple objectives is presented by the conjunction of its efforts to recruit Crusaders on the one hand, and its ability to innovate at the doctrinal level on the other. A papal bull relating to the Second Crusade declared that Crusaders were to be exempted from paying usury—that is, they were held sinless for borrowing at interest in order to finance their crusading activities. Of course, lenders were under no legal obligation to lend at zero interest, and any such law or decree seeking to force them to do so would have been completely unenforceable. Thus, the intent of the "exemption" was to dry up secular sources of loan capital, giving the Crusaders "little recourse but to borrow from the church itself" (Tyerman 1988, 196–97).

Although canon law technically prohibited usury by *all* lenders, including the Church itself, evasion of the law by clerics and monks was relatively easy. The most common device employed was the disguise of a loan as an intertemporal "exchange." Another common ploy was the exchange of "mutual gifts," for example, a tract of land offered to a church or monastery, with the clerical institution later reciprocating by transfers of cash or supplies. On more detailed examination, these disguised loans were frequently made at extremely high effective interest rates.[9]

Buy-Backs of Crusading Vows and Crusading Indulgences. Another direct source of revenue from the Crusades was the "buy-back" of crusading vows by those who subsequently regretted their pledges. The usual penalty for reneging on a crusading vow was excommunication, but the Church offered an alternative whereby the "contract" could be bought out at a fee. This option was not available on a regular basis until 1220, but earlier selective exceptions were made. The practice became rife as the Crusades became less popular. As one historian put it, "while prelates spent their money on fine horses and pet monkeys, their agents raised money by the wholesale redemption of Crusading vows" (Runciman 1954, 339).[10]

Officially, the cash payment demanded of a *crucesignatus* seeking to revoke his contract was equivalent to the expected cost of his journey to the Holy Land, following a principle established by Pope Innocent III at the Fourth Lateran Council. But Tyerman (1988, 193–94) claims that actual payments were often lower (which may have been calculated to encourage more redemptions). Revocation payments were supposedly earmarked for expenditures on Crusades, but since cash is fungible, we cannot be sure that they were not spent on other things (e.g., traveling expenses for Church officials).

As an inducement for individuals to enlist in its crusading armies, the Church devised several doctrinal innovations. One such inducement was the crusading indulgence. Technically, an indulgence provides remission of the penalties imposed on sinners, not forgiveness of the sin itself (which was reserved only to God). However, local agents of the papacy (with the tacit approval of Rome) often fostered the belief that indulgences wiped away sin itself. If we consider penance as a kind of "sin tax," which it obviously was, then we may regard the crusading indulgence as a kind of "tax credit." Originally granted only to soldiers who fought in the Crusades, eventually the awarding of indulgences was so commercialized that the Church openly sold these tax credits for cash payments, thus providing another source of revenue tangentially linked to the Crusades.

At first, revenues from indulgences were collected by local prelates who delivered and allocated the proceeds locally to finance the crusading effort. But gradually papal administrators took control of the flow of funds. Lunt reports that as early as 1200 there were suspicions that the insertion of papal envoys into the collection process meant that some money would never go beyond Rome. He writes that after 1261,

> the regular collectors of papal revenues usually treated the money derived from crusading indulgences as they did any other which came into their hands by reason of their office and assigned it to the papal camera. . . . Money derived from the crusading indulgences thus flowed into the papal coffers from the thirteenth century to the time of the protestant reformation. The volume of receipts appears to have increased notably in the fifteenth century. (Lunt 1934, 1:121)

Indirect Benefits from the Crusades

In addition to the direct benefits that accompanied crusading activity, the Church stood to gain from certain indirect benefits as well. By combining the "crusading spirit" with its usury doctrine, for example, the Church was able to repress Jewish interests and thereby restrain a doctrinal competitor. In 1199, Pope Innocent III directed secular authorities to coerce Jews to remit usuries to crusader-creditors, threatening excommunication to any Christian who trafficked with those Jewish merchant-bankers who failed to heed the directive (Lunt 1934, 2:86). While ostensibly made to encourage crusader enlistments, it is clear that such a decree also erected entry barriers into loan markets to secular lenders, thereby affording more profit opportunities to the ecclesiastic lenders.

Peace, Order, and Authority. Pope Urban II inherited the so-called investiture controversy when he ascended to the papacy in 1088. This controversy, which had extensive economic implications, was a dispute over who had final authority over "local" ecclesiastic appointments and over policies relating to Church property (as indicated in earlier chapters). Throughout the eleventh century, secular rulers increasingly laid claim to rights of appointment and control regarding local Church matters. Given the structure of medieval society, Urban II found himself in a ticklish situation. He wished to free the Church from secular power even as the Church often depended on the authority of secular powers to carry out its spiritual directives.

According to Runciman (1954, 471), "One of Pope Urban's expressed aims in preaching the crusades was to find some useful work for the turbulent and bellicose barons who otherwise spent their energy on civil wars at home." Thus, the Crusades were conceived in part as a means of promoting peace and order in western Europe by redirecting the military fervor and resources of feudal factions toward more distant targets. The Church stood to gain from the successful redirection of conflict away from the home front. Dead parishioners do not pay tithes. Moreover, local Church property was vulnerable to expropriation during domestic conflicts. Home conflict also deterred economic growth and the development of trade in western Europe, whereas the Church stood to gain from economic growth and trade development in two principal ways: appreciation of its assets, particularly its vast landholdings, and a higher percentage "take" from tithes and bequests. Runciman's judgment is affirmed by Duncalf (1969, 242), who maintains that Urban II "intended that the crusade should benefit the people of the west by substituting foreign war for private warfare at home."

It should be noted, however, that another big advantage to the papacy was possible if the Crusades were successful. The unification of the feudal orders of western Europe under the rubric of a *spiritual* goal would serve to reaffirm the *political* primacy of spiritual over temporal authority. Such consolidation of power would strengthen the monopoly of the Church over "official" codes of behavior and curtail opportunistic rent seeking by down-stream ecclesiastic firms that sought to conspire with local nobles.

Commerce and Trade. The interest-group theory advanced here also contributes to an improved understanding of the ambiguous stand that the Church took toward trade and trading rights with the infidel countries. Prior to the Crusades, the Church officially denounced trade with Moslems and directed the rectors of cities and districts in western Europe to enjoin Christians against it (Peters 1971, 45). This prohibition persisted even though it was flagrantly violated by Italian merchants, especially the Venetians, who were allied with Byzantium before the First Crusade.[11] The ban remained in effect throughout the crusading era, but despite its force, trade with Egypt soon resumed after the fall of Acre (Lane 1973, 130).

The ban itself, though ineffective, may be explained by two transparent circumstances. Obviously, a party to war does not want to encourage provisioning its enemy. Moreover, anticipating complete victory, the Church may have had designs on marketing East–West trade rights once the lands of the Near East had been secured for Christianity. But the interests of the Italian merchants were too firmly established, and moreover the Latin Church knew that its own fortunes were intertwined with the success of the Italians. The *nouveau riche* merchants enhanced the wealth of the Church not only by increasing the tithe-tax base, but also through large direct contributions to the Vatican's coffers (Atiya 1962, 196).

Italian merchants were so resolved to open new trade routes and to preserve free trade in Moslem ports that they openly discouraged proposed Crusades that would interfere with commerce (Finucane 1983, 162). But, ironically, it was the First Crusade that provided the initial stimulus to expansion of trade with the East. As Atiya (1962, 170) observed, "the resumption of the Eastern trade came as a natural consequence to the [First] Crusade, since merchants from Europe accompanied the various expeditions or followed in their steps and opened up fresh markets in every newly conquered seaport." The Venetians were in the forefront of this development, seeking to monopolize trade and increase profits. According to Newhall (1963, 51):

> Their interest in crusading was free from inhibiting religious sentiment. . . . In general, the naval republics . . . gained, in addition to their share of money, special quarters in captured coastal cities—usually one third of the area—which would be directly under the jurisdiction of the Italian city-state. More significant still were the rights of importing and selling goods in the crusader states without paying taxes. With these advantages, Italian commercial colonies grew up in the Latin Kingdom not subject to the royal government. They monopolized trade and absorbed the revenue of the ports.

Individual Rationality and the Crusades

An important question remains. Was crusading economically rational for
individual Crusaders? Religious fervor may have motivated some Crusaders,
but many (perhaps most) were stirred by the rational pursuit of economic
gain. First, the Church offered payments in a wholly tangible, temporal
sense. Crusaders also received a variety of special privileges, courtesy of
the Church. The most important of these were immunity from secular prosecution and general amnesty from secular taxation for the duration of their
crusading service, but there were other privileges as well.

Salvation

The Church did not exclusively offer temporal rewards, however. The
Church was the monopoly provider of a unique and inelastically demanded
service in the eleventh century: salvation from eternal torment. Christians
were required to perform the sacrament of penance in order to achieve
absolution from their sins. Penance—usually a period of sacrifice and sometimes public humiliation imposed by a priest—was literally a "sin tax."
Crusaders though were absolved from penance with the crusading indulgence, which was one of the canons adopted by the Council of Clermont.
The pope's apparent intention was to grant an indulgence only to those
Crusaders who actively participated in the attempt to "liberate" Jerusalem
and to those whose motives were purely based on religious devotion. The
indulgence was not intended as an offer of the "remission of sins"—which,
according to official Church doctrine, the pope had no power to grant—
but merely for the remission of the *penance* the Church imposed for sins. In
theory, the forgiveness of sins was entirely up to God (Duncalf 1969,
245–46).

Pillage, Plunder, and the Role of Warrior Monks

In addition to both temporal and spiritual "tax holidays" the Church offered
important material economic gains to Crusaders in terms of actual payments.
The rights to pillage and plunder at will without fear of secular or religious
sanction figured prominently in a number of Crusades. Officially, such rights
were legitimate so long as the victims of looting were infidels, such as the
followers of Mohammed and others, but in a number of thirteenth-century
Crusades, these activities were directed at fellow Christians as well (the Fourth
Crusade ended in the sacking of Constantinople).

The Church had long relied on mercenaries to achieve crusading and other
ends, but the ever-increasing need for trained warriors and the inability

to control the excesses of paid armies led to a peculiar theological development in the first half of the twelfth century. The campaigns against the Moslems in Palestine had been assisted by holy orders such as the Hospitallers and the Knights Templars. These were orders of men and women (monks, priests, nuns, and lay persons) dedicated to the spiritual and military aims of the Church in the Holy Land. By 1200, the Knights Templars, Hospitallers, and Spanish Orders were famous and effective, enriched by donations from kings and answerable only to the pope.

Monastic knighthood clearly had pagan origins. In pagan lore the warrior-killer is a hero, but he is a hero that reeks of death. Just as the pagan hero had to be expiated of guilt through dedication to a god (or through other means), the Church had to find a method of sanctifying bellicose behavior and murder. In an example of what has been referred to as the "syncretic genius of Catholicism" (Seward 1972, 4), St. Bernard of Clairvaux justified the warrior monk Crusaders on the basis that the activity conquered two Satans. Vows of humility, chastity, and poverty conquered the Satan within, encouraging discipline and taboo. The Crusades waged by the holy monks conquered the other Satan—the Moslems who were following Satan's foreign policy in attacking Christians (Christiansen 1980, 72–73 passim). As with so many other doctrines of the medieval Church, practical theology was based on economic necessity, as trained killers were transformed into holy warriors.

Crusaders who banded together in the holy orders (e.g., the Knights Templars, the Hospitallers, and the Teutonic Knights) were particularly motivated by taking rewards in conquered territories. Expansion of the Church's dominion and membership through *sanctified armed aggression* was no more obvious than in the Crusades against Eastern Europeans—the Baltic Crusades. Here the German (Teutonic) Knights, whose motto was "he who fights us fights Jesus Christ," were central players in massive land grabs against Eastern Europeans and Russians *already converted to Christianity* but of the orthodox variety. (*The Chronicle of Novgorod,* 1016–1471 [Michell and Forbes 1970] provides a interesting account of the Russian city's dealings with the Teutonic Order.) Originating in Palestine and joined by the "Swordbrothers," a brutal band of private mercenaries (Urban 1975, 91–92), the Teutonic Knights made political and spiritual inroads into eastern Europe that persist to this day. Stark violence accompanied the Knights from the first Northern Crusade in 1147 to the conquest of western Prussia by 1240.

Within the context of brutal power struggles, the lands of Livonia (modern day Estonia and Latvia), Prussia, and large parts of Christian Russia were conquered for Latin Christianity. While the ostensible goal of the Knights was the conversion of pagan tribes such as the Balts, Livs, and Letts, these land-hungry Teutons labeled all who fought against them (the "brethren") as heretics and apostates. Seward's (1972, 1011) account of the Knights' suppression of a Prussian rebellion in 1263 is illustrative: "The Order began a systematic policy of bloody extermination, slaughtering the population wholesale, destroying villages and burning crops. Tribes disappeared without trace, Prussian leaders being hunted down like animals. Brethren copied Prussian tactics, sending raiding parties guided by loyal tribesmen deep into the forests. No quarter was given."

In time the Russians joined "pagans" against the Order, and in 1308, the Archbishop of Riga (in Livonia) begged Pope Clement V to suppress the Knights' persecution of Christians. A similar land grab of the city of Danzig by the Knights elicited a plea for mercy from Polish kings. A typically ambivalent response from the papacy was the result. Territorial ambitions of the Knights ended in the establishment of Ordensland (the settlement of Prussia) in the fourteenth century. The Knights ran the *Ordensstaat* as a monopoly, with exclusive rights to trade franchised from the pope. Jews were eliminated from the state. By the beginning of the fifteenth century, the Order had created the first modern state consisting of fifty-five towns, forty-eight fortresses, unified laws and administration, coordinated foreign policy, trade, and industry. While conversion of heretics and pagans might have been the stated goal of the Baltic Crusades, the result was a lasting expansion of territories under the spiritual-economic control of the Latin Church. Theological inventiveness gave legitimacy to executions and property grabs—a doctrinal twist that was clearly wealth maximizing from the Church's perspective. In the end the murderous incursions of the holy fighting orders did much to further the demand-side market-expansion policies of the medieval Latin Church monopoly in the Baltic region.

Conclusion: Crusades and the Wealth-Maximization Hypothesis

In this chapter we have argued that the Church received substantial revenue and rent flows from the Crusades, and that it also took advantage of opportunities and circumstances in the crusading era to secure other valuable advantages as well. Although the Church did not permanently hold on to all of the conquered territories (Acre returned to Moslem control in 1291), two centuries of expansion in the Holy Land allowed the Latin Church to solidify its monopoly status and enhance its potential for economic wealth. In the Baltic region particularly, the Church was able to extend its sphere of influence because of the severe blow dealt to the Greek Church and to Byzantium. By virtue of conquest, the Latin Church acquired the rights to supply "essential" dogma and salvation services. In this sense the Crusades had the intended impact of repelling many of the market incursions made against Christianity by rival religions.

The macroeconomic effects entrained by the Crusades may have been even more important in the larger scheme of things. Market expansion by the Church also allowed a strong coattail effect, as many individual Crusaders also made fortunes in the conquered territories. Riley-Smith (1981, 27–28) recounts the example of Godfrey of Bouillon, who acquired the castle and estates of Tilbesar, which so visibly enhanced his wealth that it "may have contributed to his election as ruler of Jerusalem." Nor was the newly acquired wealth confined to the subjugated regions. Italian merchants and their city-states also gained enormously. According to Hitti (1985, 38), "Trade—at least in the case of the Genoese, Venetians, and Pisans, the shrewdest money-makers of the age—was a primary motivation of the venture [crusading]." These returns to the Italian city-states took several forms: relaxation of trade barriers imposed by the Moslems, expansion of commerce in the Near East, and direct profits from the provisioning of the crusading armies.

As suggested earlier, Venice came to dominate the market for provisions and the larger trade with Palestine. Venetian merchants eventually acquired a large and extensive array of special trading privileges and tax exemptions in the Holy Land (Robbert 1985, 389). One incident alone gives considerable insight into the extent and value of Venetian holdings in the Holy Land. Hitti (1985, 38) records that the Venetians lost in one day, from a single warehouse in Beirut, 10,000 dinars worth of pepper, "a figure which gives an idea of the enormous riches accumulated in the agencies of factories of the Levant." And Gilchrist (1969, 37–38) adds that "the crusades led to profits all round, not, as many think, derived largely from war booty, but from the grant of commercial privileges that followed the setting up of Christian kingdoms in the East. The towns of Venice and Amalfi, and later Genoa and Pisa, grew rich on these profits."

The increase in personal wealth that accrued to the traders who participated in the Crusades contributed directly to the development of a new and wealthy social class in Europe, the merchant class. These merchants, "having made large fortunes in foreign trade, one after another promptly reinvested a good portion of their profits in town houses, farms, and often in manors and noble estates" back home (Bautier 1971, 107), providing impetus to the domestic economy. Moreover, Eastern European merchants shared in the gains and thereafter became supportive members of the Latin Church (Seward 1972, 105).

Economic activity, of course, has a way of gaining and maintaining momentum. It seems likely that the Latin Church's pursuit of spiritual and material gains over two centuries of crusading activity would create unintended spillover effects in Europe's secular economy. The entrepreneurial spirit fostered and extended by the Crusades undoubtedly created political and economic forces that could not be easily curtailed when the Crusades were over. The rise of the merchant class hastened the breakdown of the old feudal economy. The wealth and power of the emerging merchant class had to be reckoned with, as it pushed more and more for urban emancipation. According to Bautier (1971, 106), after the Crusades "there were constant clashes with the emperor, who upheld the old order and was committed to the defence of imperial rights. There were also collisions with the pope; all too often the popes were concerned with protecting their own temporal interests, and those of the bishops, which were adversely affected by urban emancipation."

The Crusades ultimately affected the fortunes of the Church in other adverse ways, with consequent long-term effects. Although the Latin Church made important market inroads in the Baltic (where rent flows continue to be generated to the present day), it was not able to maintain its supremacy in the Near East. Indeed, the enmity it created among Moslem populations still persists today. By failing to control the holy places, the Church may have permanently damaged its credibility and reduced the long-run value of the credence good it sells.

NOTES

1. Even before 1085, Christian pilgrims to the Holy Land exposed themselves to hardship, ill-treatment, and various taxes, but the severity of these measures imposed by the Seljuk Turks suggests that certain of their rulers were more interested in discouraging pilgrimage rather than raising revenue.

2. As we have argued earlier, the quality and reliability of the Church's output could not be determined after "purchase," in the conventional sense. Even the purported ability of the Church to intervene in the temporal world on behalf of believers was based on the premise that the Church was God's representative on earth. In economic terms, prayer was a kind of "technology" for manipulating the physical environment. Church doctrine included the belief that divine intervention in the temporal world was always potentially available through the prayers of the faithful, aided by members of the clergy. Thomas (1971, 25–50) notes that the essential difference between the prayers of a churchman and the incantations of a magician was that the latter were assumed to work independently, whereas the former were contingent—a prayer would only work if God so willed. The Church, in fact, taught that "prayers might bring practical results, but they could not be guaranteed to do so" (Thomas 1971, 40). Despite this inherent uncertainty, prayer was encouraged and directed by the clergy and popularly regarded as a powerful tool in everyday medieval life.

3. Consider, for example, how the evolution of the doctrine of indulgences, which became increasingly commercialized over time, provided the Church a major

cost advantage in raising armies by the time of the Crusades. It was common for the Church to offer participants in the Crusades a "crusading indulgence" that promised remission from the penance attached to personal sins. This benefit bestowed on the Crusader was a form of in-kind payment that lowered the cash "wage" that the Church would otherwise have had to pay.

4. The remains of the holy martyrs and saints, especially after several centuries (dust and bones), were easily transported and "divisible." Forgeries, moreover, were easy to pass off given the high costs of communication and transportation between towns and villages, especially prior to the eleventh century. The incidence of duplicative forgeries, in nearby locales particularly, must have declined as all kinds of transaction costs began to decline in the later Middle Ages.

5. A superb account of the social and symbolic implications of *furta sacra* (sacred thefts) of relics between the ninth and eleventh centuries is given by Geary (1990). In the context of accounts of the translation of relics, that is, the stories of their movement from place to place, Geary studies both commercial and ecclesiastic thefts and their significance for religion and medieval society. Relic thefts by monks and other religious authorities, especially given the belief that the relic *was* the saint and therefore *agreed to be stolen* (!), were even sanctioned by the Church. The papacy clearly looked the other way when an active and illicit trade benefiting merchants and customers began to take place in Roman relics from the catacombs and elsewhere around the city. This was, according to Geary (1990, 53), an advertising bonanza for the papacy and for Rome as the center of Christianity.

6. According to Tyerman (1988, 205), "Relics from the East, such as the Holy rood of Bromholm, could transform the material fortunes of a local church or religious house. From an early date interest in the crusading ideal prompted patronage not only of the military orders but also of other religious orders associated with the Holy Land, such as the Augustinian canons of the Temple of the Lord in the twelfth century, or the Carmelite friars in the thirteenth." An attractive relic collection and the tourists it would attract could even make up for other economic deficiencies of a town in economic recession (see Geary 1990, 130).

7. According to MacKay (1852, 356), "a grove of a hundred oaks" could not have furnished all of the wood chips purported to be of the "True Cross," and the supposed "Tears of Mary" would, if collected together, "have filled a cistern."

8. The Church may have seen this as a necessary cost of mobilizing "holy" armies, but we can also interpret the loan activity of the Church during the Crusades as a less risky and less costly, albeit indirect, way to share in the spoils of war.

9. Tyerman (1988, 197) cites one blatant, but presumably not atypical, arrangement of mutual exchange that was highly lucrative for the "lender," that is, the Church:

> While Philip Basset gave the abbey of St. Benet Holme his marsh and a flock of three hundred sheep the monks promised to give Philip fifteen marks immediately and to pay an annual rent of five marks, of which seven years were to be remitted from the departure of the crusade. . . . On the lowest cal-

culation of the remitted rent . . . abbey was making a profit over its investment of one hundred thirty-three percent spread over seven years—not a bad return for an age and an institution which frowned upon usury and for a deal with a man supposedly immune from it.

10. Reports on the Crusades written by clergy and sent to the pope, although discrete in their criticisms of papal policy, were frank enough in stressing the shortcomings of the Church. The *Collectio de Scandalis Ecclesiae*, for example, focused on the corruption of the clergy and the abuse of indulgences (see Throop 1940, 69–104).

11. Newhall (1963, 33) writes that "when in 1082 the Byzantine Empire was under threat from invasion by the Normans, it allied itself with the Venetians. The price for the Venetian alliance was control of a quarter in Constantinople with commercial rights vastly superior to those of any other Italian city."

CHAPTER EIGHT

Product Innovation in a Doctrinal Firm

Introduction: Purgatory as Doctrinal Innovation

One of the proven strategies for maintaining market dominance is successful and timely product innovation—the systematic alteration of a product to meet changing conditions of market demand and supply. Inasmuch as a major product of the salvation "industry" is religious doctrine, the medieval Church might have been expected to engage in doctrinal innovation in response to threats of market encroachment. In this chapter we attempt to show how the medieval Church used the doctrine of purgatory in a way consistent with such a response.

The word *purgatory* suggests not so much a *place* as an other-worldly experience between heaven and hell. According to Christian teachings, purgatory is a sojourn where the spirits of those who die in a state of grace pay in torment the debt due for their unexpurgated venial sins and for their mortal sins that have been forgiven but not atoned. The doctrine of purgatory, as opposed to the belief in purgatory (which is much older), emerged in the Middle Ages and became part of the Catholic Church's penitential system. Unlike secular jurisprudence, however, the Church's penitential system extended beyond the temporal world into the afterlife. This system, which evolved over a thousand years, consisted in the thirteenth century of the doctrine of purgatory, the doctrine of the "treasury of merits" (which included the practice of "selling" indulgences), and the practice of praying for the faithful departed (Pelikan 1984, 4:249). The medieval Church's penitential system, and its perceived abuses, eventually served as the lightening rod for the Protestant Reformation, especially the attack on Church doctrine spearheaded by Martin Luther.

Purgatory is unusual among Church doctrines insofar as it has little if any scriptural basis. According to Le Goff (1984), the doctrine was invented by the Church in the twelfth century. It was rejected by the Protestant Reformation in the sixteenth century, but defended and retained by the Catholic Church. Within Catholicism it remains uniquely Western, never having been accepted by the Eastern Church. Medieval Church historians admit purgatory as a doctrinal *innovation*, but economic historians have heretofore offered little or no economic analysis of the subject.

Our analysis applies principles from the economics of innovation to analyze the invention of purgatory. Following Dosi (1988), we emphasize the main characteristics of the innovative process, the factors that encourage or impede the development of new ideas, the processes that determine the selection of particular innovations, and the ultimate effects of new innovations on industry structure. Our analysis is necessarily constrained to the explicit and implicit economic incentives facing the institutional medieval Church at a time when its "market position" was challenged by new and varied institutional rivals. Our central thesis is that the Catholic Church faced economic incentives that encouraged the invention of purgatory. The new doctrine provided a means whereby the Church could increase its revenues and simultaneously increase communicant satisfaction. This analysis is consistent with and amplifies the conclusions reached about purgatory by LeGoff (1984, 168–69, 217), that (1) the authors of the doctrine used it as a weapon in the battle against heresy; (2) purgatory forms a *system*, along with the distinction between mortal and venial sins, auricular confession, and indulgences; and (3) purgatory was an important political force in the hands of the Church, enabling it to extend its power over the faithful into the world beyond death.

Opportunity, Perception, and Entrepreneurship

From the fall of Rome to the rise of Constantinople, the Catholic Church slowly moved toward dominance in the market for religion. The broad ideological divisions were between paganism and Christianity on the one hand and Judaism and Christianity on the other. Other competing sects within each of these broad divisions remained small, splintered, and mostly ineffectual, posing no serious challenge to the large groups.

From the seventh to the eleventh centuries, neither the social structure of western Europe, the basically monastic character of religious culture, or the range of intellectual inquiry that later spawned the growth of philosophical heresy fostered widespread dissent. From the eleventh century to the fifteenth, however, dissenting movements appeared with greater frequency, attracted more followers, acquired deeper philosophical and theo-

logical dimensions, and increasingly occupied the time and mind of the
ecclesiastic and civil authorities (Peters 1980, 3). Lambert (1977, 24, 39)
identified nineteen heresies in the West during the eleventh century alone,
a substantial increase over the previous century, yet less than the number
that emerged in the following century.

The medieval Church attempted to deal with heterodoxy chiefly by
persuasion or by force (Chapter 4). Persuasive methods to convert heretics
and preserve the faith included penitence, reform, exhortation, instruction, and
propaganda. Forceful methods involved legal coercion against heretics
and their supporters. The best-known manifestations of force employed by
the medieval Church in the defense of faith include the Albigensian Crusade of 1208 to 1229 and the Inquisition.

A third avenue of protecting the Church's quasi-monopoly position,
generally underemphasized in historical studies, is doctrinal innovation,
of which purgatory is the most striking example. Facing a "critical problem" of the sort described by Rosenberg (1978), that is, a decline in devotion and the loss of members (and revenue) to rival sects, the medieval
Church used the doctrine of purgatory as a means to maintain or enlarge
its "market share."[1]

The Market for Purgatory: Inducements and Appropriability

The invention of purgatory may be viewed as a consequence of the interplay between various sorts of market inducements on the one hand and
opportunity and appropriability combinations on the other (Dosi 1988,
1141). *Appropriability* in this context refers to those technical and institutional properties that permit innovations (which become rent-yielding
assets) and protect them, to varying degrees, against imitation by rivals.

Consider the idea of purgatory in a market context. Purgatory represents
the expiation of sins, a "forgiveness" of earthly transgressions that readies
the soul for entry into heaven.[2] The closest analogue to purgatory in the
business world is bankruptcy legislation, which, like purgatory, "forgives"
past errors and offers the businessperson a second chance to "redeem" oneself commercially. As such, bankruptcy laws lower the cost to potential
entrepreneurs of participating in economic enterprise. In similar fashion,
purgatory had the effect of giving sinners a "second chance" to prepare
themselves for heaven. Thus, purgatory offered hope, and hope can be big
business![3]

The basic outline of the purgatory doctrine may be set forth briefly as
follows. The Church held that sins had to be paid for either in this world
or the next. Payment was proportioned to guilt. Grievous offenses (i.e.,
mortal sins) condemned one to hell if the offender died unrepentant. Pur-

gatory was of no consequence in such cases. However, sinners who repented and received absolution from a priest retained the opportunity to enter heaven, provided they did penance. Before purgatory came to be official doctrine, sins could be atoned on earth only by good works, that is, payment rendered directly within one's earthly lifetime. The invention of purgatory essentially introduced a means of "deferred payment," which not only allowed atonement to be postponed beyond this life, but also allowed third parties to make payments on behalf of the deceased. The subsequent sale of indulgences meant that the Church accepted monetary payments in lieu of good works. The Church recognized, and tapped, a ready demand by the faithful for support of their relatives and friends in matters beyond the grave.

With a strong demand base, the doctrine of purgatory gained rapid and steady acceptance over the next two millennia, and as it did the Church was alert to entrepreneurial opportunities. For example, initially the doctrine identified purgatory as a time of punishment during the *entire* interval between death and resurrection. But the issue of time became malleable in the hands of the ecclesiastic policy makers. An element of calculation was introduced whereby the exact time of deliverance from purgatory depended on the quantity and quality of sins to be atoned and the intensity of suffrages offered by the living for the dead. This accountancy, in turn, gave new force to the system of indulgences—the practice of selling release time from purgatory—which, according to Lea (1896, 3:28), "led naturally to the mercantile treatment of sin and pardon . . . in which the sinner is taught that God keeps an account with him, which is to be paid, it matters little how."[4] Indulgences also widened consumption alternatives for the faithful by providing the choice of paying for sins with money rather than with deeds.

Demand Considerations

Consider the comparative–statics context of a simple market model. Before purgatory the "price" of sin for a Catholic desirous of heaven was the amount of good works imposed by the Church to atone for bad deeds. Freed from its moral baggage, the concept of sin fits the definition of an economic "good"—namely, an action that produces (illicit) pleasure. Before purgatory more sin could be "purchased" if one was willing to pay the price established by the Church, and the price was a specified amount of good works. Until the practice of selling indulgences was joined to the doctrine of purgatory, good works, not money, were the "currency" of redemption.

Likewise, if virtue is regarded merely as the ransom for sin, it takes on the aspects of an economic "bad," no matter how "good" it may be conceived in moral terms. This apparent perversion of customary usage must be imposed because it goes to the heart of the analysis. It underscores the fact that virtue and sin are both complex forms of human behavior that involve varying degrees of "goods-character" and "bads-character."[5] One degree of complexity is imparted by the element of risk that enters into the price of sin, insofar as no one knows the exact time of his or her death. This uncertainty exposes sinners to the prospect of dying in an unrepentant state, thereby being condemned to hell without benefit of remedial "cleansing" in purgatory. Another degree of complexity consists of the theological differentiation between "mortal" and "venial" sins.[6] Theoretically, a mortal sin is an "all-or-nothing" act, so that attempts to model behavioral choices involving mortal sins must resort to zero-one variables at the commission of the act. Choices involving venial sins, however, may be modeled as smooth and continuous functions, assuming the properties of the standard demand curve.

There is every reason to believe that at least venial sin is a desirable good for most consumers (except in a few extreme cases, e.g., sainthood). Other things equal, a member of the Church will commit more sin as the "price" of sin declines; in other words, the demand curve for sin is downward-sloping.[7] Some consumers, moreover, are always at the margin, in the sense that if they perceive the price of sin to be too high, they will search for alternative moral codes that attach a lower price to sin. One aspect of Christian life in the Middle Ages is that the availability of alternative moral codes was tightly constrained and more proscribed than it is today: heretics, Jews, and Muslims, for example, were treated as "outsiders" and officially denied entrance to heaven.

Purgatory had two consequences that tended to lower the price of sin. On the one hand, it allowed payment to be deferred to some future, mostly unknown, time and circumstance. If the Austrian economist Böhm-Bawerk was right, that consumers suffer from persistent myopia about the future, this opportunity to defer payment meant a perceived reduction in the current price of sin.[8] On the other hand, the Church's use of indulgences, the value of which depended almost entirely on purgatory, had the effect of lowering transaction costs to those sinners with high (time) opportunity costs. The time cost involved in doing good works could be the same for two people with the same guilt, but the full cost would be higher for the one whose time was more valuable.

An obvious paradox posed by this kind of analysis is difficult to resolve on purely moral grounds. Why would the Church introduce a doctrinal innovation that encouraged sin? Again, there is an economic answer: the Church wanted to increase its membership and prevent existing members from defecting to alternative religions that offered assurances of salvation at a lower price. In other words, at least in part, purgatory is a market response to doctrinal competition. In the vernacular of economics, there is strong evidence that purgatory constitutes a "market-pull" rather than a "technology-push" innovation.[9]

It has been observed that innovations, when they arise, come in clusters. This "cluster effect" was especially obtrusive in the doctrinal activity of the medieval Church during the thirteenth century. No less than three interrelated innovations emerged within a short time span—purgatory, indulgences, and auricular confession.

The question of whether purgatory singularly and causatively induced the requirement of auricular confession, or vice versa, is difficult to resolve. Murray (1981, 279) notes that before the thirteenth century, outside of monasteries and except as an immediate preparation for death, the practice of confession was far from universal. Auricular confession was not required as an annual duty until the Fourth Lateran Council in 1215, an event coterminous with the centralization of power over indulgences in the hands of the papacy under Innocent III. The theology of penance also changed at this time, shifting from a subjective to an objective criterion. Whereas before mere contrition was sufficient, after the Fourth Lateran Council the specific grant of absolution by a priest was required. This objectification was the Church's way of providing a more solid guarantee of salvation. Purely subjective standards of contrition, after all, might not provide sufficient information to illiterates regarding whether or not they would be saved. Insofar as the medieval world was basically authoritarian, members of the Church were most likely solicitous of someone in authority validating their contritions.

Le Goff (1984) places the birth of purgatory in the twelfth century. So the idea already had currency while the innovative changes in confession and indulgences were emerging. Originally, indulgences were merely the substitution of pious works for part or all of the penance prescribed in the confessional. An entirely new concept of indulgences arose in the thirteenth century when theologians developed the idea of a "treasure of merits," that is, the belief that the passion of Christ and the superabundant merits of the saints gave the Church an inexhaustible treasure that it could apply at will to satisfy sins by offering God a quid pro quo. Thus, good works became commodities capable of being transferred between traders. A further feature was that good works became "public goods" because the Church held that communication of good works to others does not diminish their utility to the performer. The doctrine of the treasure of merits also contributed to the concentration of authority over indulgences in the hands of the Vatican. Obviously the right to disburse "funds" from the treasure had to be closely guarded.

The entrance of the papacy into the market for indulgences may be taken as indirect evidence that the practice was lucrative. Insofar as the doctrine of purgatory emerged as a weapon against heresy, it is not surprising that the Crusades provided the initial backdrop for the commercialization of indulgences. In the first year of his pontificate, Pope Clement III (1084–1100) urged his bishops to collect money for the Crusades and authorized them to grant remission of sins to contributors in proportion to "the quality of the person and the quantity of the subvention" (Lunt 1934, 2:486–87). By the end of the twelfth century, the custom of selling indulgences in connection with the Crusades was well established, the market having developed to the point that those who took vows to fight could redeem their vows by money payments, which elicited the same indulgence as the pledge to fight. Thus, Lunt (1934, 1:118) observed that "the grants of indulgences to crusaders helped to develop and stimulate the financially profitable traffic in the redemption of crusaders' vows" (Chapter 7).

It is difficult to draw definitive conclusions about the growth of revenues from the sale of indulgences because most of the receipts do not appear to have routinely passed through the papal treasury until the fourteenth century. Lunt (1934, 1:121) maintains that the volume of receipts from crusading indulgences increased notably in the fifteenth century, which was the approximate time that Pope Eugene IV (1431–1447) began the practice of profit-sharing between the papacy and the local churches. The share of indulgence revenue taken by the pope was commonly one-third or one-half, although there were instances of as much as two-thirds being diverted to papal coffers (Lunt 1934, 1:114).

As noted in the preceding chapter, the Crusades were coercive actions against heretics and the like. Indulgences were also connected with noncoercive activities; in fact, those indulgences that produced the most revenue for the medieval Church were issued in connection with jubilees, which were special Christian celebrations spaced one hundred years apart. During the jubilee of 1300, Pope Boniface VIII (1294–1303) began the practice of issuing a plenary indulgence (i.e., complete remission of sins) to those pilgrims who visited Rome a specified number of times during the jubilee year. Although there was no direct fee for this indulgence, visiting pilgrims left large voluntary offerings at Vatican churches (Lea 1896, 3:205). The Vatican was astute enough to recognize a financial windfall. Merchants and politicians were also quick to recognize the beneficial effects of the jubilee, and in an early example of the "convention city" lobby, a Roman delegation successfully petitioned Pope Clement VI (1342–1352), the fourth Avignon Pope, to shorten the interval between jubilees. The pope obliged by cutting the interval between jubilees in half, and according to Kelly (1986, 219) the jubilee of 1350 produced large economic benefits for Rome.[10]

Thereafter, the voluntary offerings left by pilgrims visiting Rome provided a rich, occasional source of direct income to the papacy and indirect income to the city of Rome.

Under these circumstances, public-choice theory predicts that city fathers outside of Rome would have lobbied the pope to extend the benefits of the jubilee to their cities as well. Historical records do not permit the actual documentation of lobbying efforts, but it is a matter of record that Pope Boniface IX (1389–1404) extended the privileges of jubilees to cities (and countries) beyond Rome by making indulgences obtainable for the cost of the journey plus the amount the pilgrim might have offered at the Roman shrines (Lunt 1962, 468).[11] Since Boniface IX was residing in Rome and presumably facing strong political pressures from Roman aristocrats and merchants, the relative political demands should have favored keeping the money at home. If pilgrims had difficulty getting to Rome, however, dispersion of benefits provided additional sources of revenue that would otherwise be lost. Thus it was that the new rules allowed seekers of grace who were "truly penitent and confessed" to be granted an indulgence in return for a certain number of visitations to specified neighborhood churches in their own locale.[12]

Over time, the interval between jubilees was gradually shortened to twenty-five years or less; the amount that the recipient of the indulgence had to pay was reduced from the whole cost of a journey to Rome to about one-fourth as much; and profits were divided between local churches and the papacy.[13] Pope Clement VII attempted to build additional demand for jubilee indulgences by suspending all plenary indulgences administered locally the year before the jubilee of 1525 (Lunt 1962, 465,498).[14]

Supply Considerations

Churches commonly "sell" a variety of "products" to their members, including solace in this life, an array of "social services," and, most important for the current analysis, assurances of eternal salvation for those who adhere to specified codes of moral behavior. From a customer viewpoint, purgatory was valuable because it provided a "second chance" to be saved, especially if one died without benefit of clergy. Consequently, it could be expected that purgatory would have a positive impact on Church membership, religious participation, and Church revenues.[15] Given the level of anticipated demand for purgatory, therefore, was it reasonable to expect an economic benefit net of costs?

Many writers have drawn a connection between a firm's size and its ability to successfully marshall resources needed to develop and introduce innovations. In this connection, the medieval Church had a distinct advantage because by the twelfth century it dwarfed other religions in terms of wealth and power. Since the inventors in this case were church theologians (i.e., the Scholastics), it is also important to note that the Church had invested heavily over the centuries in building a *knowledge base* capable of supporting doctrinal innovations.[16] In other words, it could draw on information inputs, specific knowledge, and human capabilities, at a relatively low cost.

In addition to its production and distribution cost advantages, the Catholic Church operated within a legal and institutional framework that allowed it to protect its doctrine as a rent-yielding asset. The medieval Church held wide sway over the minds and fortunes of Christians, a fact reflected in the close connection between civil and ecclesiastic governments (Southern 1970, 24). Yet Christianity was, and is, more of a transnational force than a transcultural one. Within the confines of Western Christendom, appropriability conditions favored the medieval Church. Outside of those confines it was more difficult for the Church to appropriate economic rents.

Innovational Externalities

Technological innovations typically involve "public" and "private" aspects, and the appropriability of economic returns from innovation clearly depend on the latter. We have already noted how the synergy between purgatory and the doctrine of treasure produced positive externalities for the faithful. It is possible that this doctrinal synergy generated a structured set of innovational externalities which the Roman Church attempted to internalize as a collective asset, one that became institution-specific, and, as such, shaped the incentives and constraints to further innovations that could be expected to arise from a given set of economic signals. In other words, a major innovational step like purgatory, when linked with confession and indulgences, may have set the innovational trajectory of the Catholic Church from that point onward, establishing a kind of "doctrinal irreversibility" that could be expected to constrain future innovational patterns in the face of economic or doctrinal rivalry.

Thus, when confronted with the challenge of the Protestant Reformation, the Catholic Church found its ideological maneuverability severely constrained. For example, Pelikan (1984, 4:274) notes how the Reformation forced the Catholic Church from a "pluralist" to a "particularist" position on key doctrinal issues, including the nature and locus of authority, the doctrine of justification, and the doctrine of original sin.

Ultimately, the issue of whether purgatory is a technological improvement or a demand improvement is problematical. On the one hand, it might be regarded as a technological improvement from the standpoint of a large, well-organized priesthood acting as intercessionary agents in the salvation industry. On the other hand, the absence of purgatory from most Christian religions, as well as from Islam, which also has a well-defined, but more materialistic, heaven and hell, suggests that purgatory was a demand improvement within the context of a fairly well-developed penitential system. Regardless of its categorical status, however, purgatory can be treated as a unique *innovation* because heterogeneous religions, like heterogeneous goods, are most susceptible to specific improvements.

Effects of Innovation on "Industry" Structure

Studies in the economics of innovation usually take care to distinguish between the factors that *induce, stimulate,* or *constrain* innovative change from the *outcomes* of the changes themselves (e.g., Dosi 1988, 1145). In like manner we may examine the effects of purgatory on "industry" structure, taking it as axiomatic that industrial performance and industrial structure are *endogenous* to the process of innovation, imitation, and competition.

As a supplier of ideology and other intangible products, the medieval Church enjoyed certain monopoly advantages, including market dominance, "brand loyalty," the ability to segment markets by different demands, and institutional barriers that prevented arbitrage and retrading. In sum, the conditions were ripe for engaging in price discrimination, an opportunity given new vent by the introduction of purgatory. Given the somewhat ambiguous distinction between mortal and venial sins (intention, not action, was the controlling factor), what the faithful required was a method of discerning between the two sins and a means of obtaining individual guidance on appropriate penances.

The confessional at once provided this service and gave priests a unique device for discerning levels of individual demand among penitents In any specific locality or parish, especially in the agrarian setting of medieval Europe, most parishioners were known to the priests (Le Roy Ladurie 1978). Murray (1981, 303–4) notes that confessors commonly had long-term associations with their penitents that gave them intimate experiences of other people's lives. This knowledge included the income profile of each penitent and other pertinent characteristics regarding wealth and tastes. Consequently, penances in the form of direct, charitable donations or the sale of indulgences could be meted out by the priest-confessor in close accord with the individual's demand for salvation. In these circumstances, markets were more or less naturally divided because arbitrage and retrading were impossible. Moreover, the secrecy of the confessional precluded tariff schedules from being published.

Official Church documents (e.g., papal bulls dealing with indulgences) sanctioned differential pricing, broadly conceived. Vatican financial records, in fact, provide surprising detail. There is one recorded instance of a three-tier pricing system, whereby the highest price was paid by the rich, the next highest by those of modest means, and the lowest by everyone else (Lunt 1962, 494). In Scotland during the jubilee of 1475, a five-tier pricing schedule was imposed (Lunt 1962, 586). By far the most elaborate recorded differential pricing scheme was drawn up by Jasper Ponce, the papal agent to England during the pontificate of Alexander VI (1492–1503). Ponce's schedule of "gifts" for a plenary indulgence included three categories of givers (i.e., laymen owning substantial *real* property; laymen owning substantial *movable* property; and *clergy* owning substantial real property). Each category contained four to seven separate tariffs based on discrete ranges of annual personal income (Lunt 1962, 60–4).[17]

It follows that the doctrine of purgatory provided the Church an opportunity to enhance its revenues and its power by offering differential prices for assurances of salvation to different demanders. The fact that different demands existed among occupational groups is clearly established by Le Goff (1984, 328), who notes that the doctrine of purgatory had special appeal to the members of certain professions who were generally held in contempt by society, for example, usurers, barber-surgeons, and so forth.

During the Protestant Reformation, Luther made purgatory a central aspect of his brief against the Church. Most especially, Luther denounced the Church's revenue-maximizing efforts involving the sale of indulgences, eventually choosing to abandon altogether the belief in a third world between heaven and hell. Other nascent sects who raised similar challenges to the Church's doctrinal authority followed suit on this issue. Thus, Protestantism came to distinguish itself from Catholicism by eliminating the "middle man." In Protestant religions the sinner is required to deal directly with God; he must be guided by individual conscience, as long as life lasts, in expressing repentance and offering self-improvement that may win justice from his Creator. Protestantism in general comprises a set of beliefs that is less authoritarian than Catholicism.

The analysis presented here provides some useful insights into why Luther, Calvin, Zwingli, and other reformers returned to the all-or-nothing circumstances of heaven and hell. Over time, the Church employed increasingly intricate price-discriminatory schemes in its sale of indulgences, thereby moving closer and closer to first-degree price discrimination, and capturing most, if not all, consumers' surplus. Faced with an increase in the full price of salvation, certain (Roman Catholic) demanders were likely pushed to the margin of purchase. Luther's innovations provided an all-or-nothing offer of the afterlife with a still lower entry price (i.e., salvation was determined by faith alone). The proof of this proposition is that Luther successfully used the financial abuses of the Church regarding indulgences as a handle to gain entry into the market.

In the end, Luther and other religious entrepreneurs gained customers by offering consumption choices that moved some individuals to higher indifference curves by changing the budget constraint. This seems consistent with Pautler's (1977) results that Church membership responds to changes in relative price. Ultimately, the Catholic Church's shortsighted attempts to milk consumers' surplus from the faithful were self-defeating, and eventually purgatory, indulgences, and confession lost force in religious markets subject to considerable competition, for example, in the United States. Centuries of super competitive returns from price discrimination prior to the Reformation were clearly beneficial to Church interests.

Another factor in the success of the Reformation may have been the production technology of religion. Luther may have been justified in claiming that the complex Catholic religion was no longer believable. After all, if promises were all that mattered in religion, Reverend Ike would dominate the U.S. religious market. Other technical and cultural factors obviously shaped the Reformation, too. Thus, the invention of printing, the spread of literacy, the growth of self-consciousness that accompanied the Renaissance, and various other elements of economic and cultural evolution impinge on a general theory of doctrinal change.

On the one hand, an economic interpretation of the invention of purgatory supplements historical explanations of purgatory and the Protestant Reformation. Conversely, applying the tools of contemporary economics to historical processes suggests that, at least in part, the dogma and doctrine of the medieval Church were endogenous to the operation of medieval society. Church doctrines, such as purgatory and usury, were possibly as much a part of the interplay between market forces as they were the result of exogenous Church pronouncements that claimed to define the spiritual and moral interests of the faithful. By the same token, the Protestant Reformation cannot be completely explained by its environmental setting. It should be viewed in part as the outcome of endogenous, economically inspired manipulation of Church doctrine in the centuries before the full-scale emergence of competitive religious markets.

Conclusion

This chapter focuses on innovation as a key element in the episodic behavior of the medieval Church. The basic premise of the economics of religion, combined with the stylized facts of medieval Church history, and accepted principles of the economics of innovation, enable us to establish an economic rationale for the invention of purgatory. This rationale is not merely consistent with the judgment of Church historians, it also points toward a general theory of why institutions and doctrines emerge in the first place and how they change over time. And, indeed, the doctrine of purgatory provides an acid test of the economic versus "other" theories of Church behavior. Here we have a case where the Church lowered the "price" of sin in an effort to increase its revenues. Such behavior clearly contradicts other theories of Church motivation and supports the economic theory.

NOTES

1. Pelikan (1984, 4:249) asserts that once the Reformation got underway, the defenders of purgatory actually "conceded that the system was liable to corruption and *had been invented to compensate for the decline in Christian devotion*" (emphasis added).

2. By treating the subject in the abstract, we may ignore, for the present, the particular *form* of suffering by which redemption is ultimately purchased.

3. Other devices, such as one borrowed from the field of law and economics, might be employed to help understand the Church's invention of purgatory. Purgatory may be depicted as a device to enhance "marginal deterrence." If the option is either-or—speeding either to heaven or hell for the dead soul—gradations of punishment are too few to bring about "optimal" deterrence of sin on earth. As an example, if one is going to hell for some serious infraction such as adultery, why not become a thief as well for earthly profit? Purgatory permitted the Church to more closely match punishment to offense, enabling it to create better incentives (based on marginal deterrence) against the commission of sin.

4. This kind of "spiritual accounting system," while making it easier for the Church to raise revenues, imposed certain recordkeeping costs on the faithful. The problem was how to keep score. Unsure of the size of one's spiritual debt resulting from sinful behavior, the individual nevertheless received concrete information regarding his or her "redemption units," which were defined in the familiar terms of earthly time, for example, days. Depending on the impact of uncertainty and a person's preference for risk, individuals may have overinsured or underinsured against damnation.

5. Bentham (1879, 30) recognized long ago that some forms of human action produce mixtures of pleasure and pain (e.g., childbirth). What was important in his felicific calculus was the (aggregate) *net* pleasure or *net* pain. The same considerations must be invoked, at the micro level, in defining good works and sin as either an economic "good" or an economic "bad" for a single individual.

6. The distinction between mortal and venial sins was alluded to in the fifth century by St. Augustine, in the seventh century by St. Eligius, and in the eighth century by St. Bede. But none of this was Church doctrine in any official sense. Le Goff (1984, 107, 217) insists that the doctrine emerged in the twelfth century

as a response to heretical challenges, and that purgatory comprises a doctrinal *system*, along with oral confession, the mortal-venial distinction, and indulgences.

7. The medieval theologian, Segneri, recognized the economic aspects of sin by comparing penance with "a tax laid by Christ on transgression, similar to the customs duty levied on importations" (Lea 1896, 2:424). Lea (1896, 2:415) added that the practice of selling indulgences fostered "the idea that salvation was a sort of merchandise to be bought and sold, and that sin was a luxury to be safely indulged in by those who could afford to pay for pardon." It may be argued that while the invention of purgatory lowered the price of sin in general, it *increased* the price of venial sin.

8. Eugen von Böhm-Bawerk (1851–1914) studied the individual's behavior with respect to the preference of present over future goods. The uncertainties of life and the expectation that we will be better off in the future are two reasons why one might undervalue the future and overvalue the present.

9. For a discussion of the differences between these two, see Kamien and Schwartz (1982, 33–36).

10. It is interesting to note that Rome returned to the control of the Avignon Pope in exchange for receiving the 1350 jubilee. The Roman merchants and politicians were undoubtedly sensitive to the local economic effects of visitors' spending in their city.

11. A spatial economic theory helps explain the spread of jubilees. The "offering" was what would have been made to go to Rome—aggregate demand for indulgences is increased by spatially spreading out, and Rome is made better off by side payments.

12. Kelly (1986, 231) writes of Boniface IX: "Under him the papal conferring of benefices . . . became a matter of barefaced marketing, with . . . offices sold for cash down to the highest bidder . . . the commercial possibilities of indulgences were exploited to the full."

13. This profit sharing itself was probably an effort by the papacy to keep agency problems under control. As Lea (1896, 3:13) recognized, once the utility of indulgences to the papacy had been demonstrated, "it was part of wisdom to prevent competition, which might destroy their value, if every bishop and every abbot in Christendom was authorized to issue them for the benefit of his cathedral or his monastery."

14. Lunt (1934, 1:124–25) notes that jubilee indulgences were particularly prized by the faithful because it was commonly believed that they "provided pardon of the guilt as well as the penance, a belief which was sometimes fostered by the agents who administered the indulgences locally. The consequence was a ready sale and a large revenue for the papacy."

15. Commenting on the extension of indulgences to the dead, Lea (1896, 3:319) underscored the institutional incentive for the Church to become a product innovator: "the struggling Church would have had slender chance of securing converts if it had disclaimed all power to succor the dead and had admitted that it abandoned them to the justice of God, while proclaiming under divine sanction a code of morality far more rigid than that accepted by the easy-going gentile world, and

insisting on the infinite disparity between the present and future life." The modern day Mormon Church has a rigorous code of earthly conduct and promises salvation for the souls of ancestors of living Church members as well as for living members themselves.

16. Given its institutional makeup, the medieval Church was in fact a kind of early think-tank, perhaps the first formal R&D organization. Through its network of teachers and philosophers, it was actively involved in building a doctrinal *knowledge base*, which, ironically, drew freely from pagan Greek philosophers as a fertile source of ideas.

17. It is important to note that, from a purely technical point of view, first-degree price discrimination in the selling of indulgences would promote economic efficiency in the market for forgiveness.

Summary and Conclusions

The Medieval Church and the Emergence of Capitalism

Introduction: Economics and Religion or Economics versus Religion?

The medieval Catholic Church was an institution with an avowed public interest that nevertheless consistently behaved in a manner that promoted its particular interests. As the foregoing chapters have shown, these particular interests were most often rooted in economic considerations, such as the preservation of market power, the accumulation of wealth, and the pursuit of profits. Consequently, the medieval Church readily lends itself to economic analysis as well as to theological, philosophical, historical and sociological analysis. Many Church historians have understood the economic dimensions of medieval Church behavior, but few have had the economic training and expertise to analyze Church history within the paradigm of modern economic theory. This book attempts to raise the level of earlier analysis that emphasized the economic aspects of religion.

This does not imply that our approach is *against* religion, but rather that a complementary understanding of economics *and* religion are needed to assess the full import and historical sway of the medieval Church. Because the medieval Church was a complex and pervasive organization that mixed worldly and spiritual concerns, no single explanation of its institutional behavior, that is, one based solely on economic reasoning, is likely to resolve all historical issues concerning its effect on medieval society and its influence on modern culture. Nevertheless, as the foregoing chapters have attempted to demonstrate, a monopoly–rent-seeking characterization fits the historical record remarkably well. It also has the advantage of reconciling seemingly disparate practices and pronouncements of the medieval

Church so that they may be seen in a more unified and internally consistent framework. Our approach has been to utilize economic theory to *understand* the worldly behavior of a religious organization, not to question the justification or existence of religion itself.

In the not-too-distant past, public-interest explanations of sociopolitical institutions dominated the analytical landscape, and institutions were largely ignored by conventional economic theory. Today, these "conventions" are breaking down, as important inroads are being made by the particular-interest, or public-choice, paradigm, and institutions are being increasingly treated by economists as endogenous rather than exogenous. Indeed, it has become fashionable to attempt to explain the evolution of institutions and their change over time within the framework of economic theory. This book is in the spirit of these recent developments.

Our analysis is based on the belief that economic motives matter and that incentives are powerful spurs to action. It supports the contention that doctrines are endogenous to their institutional frameworks. What historians call "custom" or "tradition" may often be viewed by economists as the product of predictable motives and actions. In other words, the development of doctrine is affected to some degree by the economic incentives of its proponents, and analysts should be able to trace over time the impact of these incentives on the development of doctrine. The Scholastics, no more than the mercantilists of the next era, were not totally disinterested writers; after all, they were "employees" of the church.

The Medieval Church as a Microeconomic Entity

Administratively, the medieval Church decentralized its day-to-day operations by assigning constrained authority to self-contained operating divisions: monasteries, dioceses, and parishes. The general office maintained an elite staff, the Curia, which advised the pope in his role as chief executive officer. The papal bureaucracy also monitored the behavior of the clergy who functioned as low-level managers of the operating divisions. Corporate strategy was concentrated in the general office of the Vatican, which allocated resources among competing divisions in accordance with overall organizational objectives.

As a loosely integrated monopolist, the medieval Church faced problems of vertical integration. High information and other transaction costs generated problems of rent collection between the upstream monopoly and the downstream agents of the Church. The Vatican used several familiar devices to counter these problems. It attempted to standardize its product with clear definitions of the rules and regulations that its customers were required to follow. It established an elaborate system of penalties designed to enforce its regulations. And it set up mechanisms to repatriate downstream revenues, including profit sharing, lump-sum fees, and various forms of taxation. The repatriation was made primarily, though not exclusively, through the papal *camera*.

Despite inevitable vertical-integration problems, the administrative structure outlined above served the Roman Catholic Church well for many centuries. The medieval Church grew into a powerful monopoly, expanding and consolidating its market power throughout the Middle Ages. Taking advantage of its monopoly status, the organizational Church systematically exploited opportunities to collect monopoly rents. Rent streams emerged from the rules and regulations imposed by the administrative Church in order to thwart opportunistic behavior on the part of downstream suppliers of religious products and services. Partly by design and partly by the nature of the religious "enterprise," most of these rents were difficult to trace, in some measure because the services the Church provided to its consumers were not sold at publicly listed prices, and in some measure because the exchanges were often disguised. Nevertheless, the "otherworldly" nature of the goods and services supplied by the medieval Church does not change the basic economic facts.

Like other prominent monopolies in precapitalism, and especially befitting one with global reach, the medieval Church also functioned as a quasi-government. It routinely provided certain public goods that weak and fragmented governments were unable to supply in the Middle Ages. Among these public goods were jurisprudence, a certain measure of individual security, economic assistance for the poor and disadvantaged, and scholarship—which constituted a kind of information technology. Even as it filled the role of public-goods provider, however, the Church was alert to opportunities to increase its flow of rents, as the foregoing chapters have shown.

Over time, the power and influence of the medieval Church eventually gave way to the forces of market competition. Today the Catholic Church continues to exist, but merely as one religion in a sea of competing faiths. This naturally raises the question of how the medieval Church lost its position of market dominance. The usual answer is that the Protestant Reformation introduced competing sects that gradually eroded the monopoly status of the Roman Church. But this begs the more fundamental question: Why did the Reformation succeed when other separatist movements did not? After all, the Catholic Church had faced competition before, as its many battles with heretics, infidels, and schismatics attest.

The Medieval Church and the Macroeconomy

The dominance of the medieval Church in the marketplace for religious services came to an end as the Protestant Reformation gained a toehold in the sixteenth century. Eventually many Protestant denominations arose throughout Europe, displacing the Roman Church as the One True Church. More than a few scholars have portrayed this development in a positive light, asserting that the displacement of the corrupt and bloated monopoly by organized, efficient, and successful competitors greatly encouraged the development of capitalism in the West. According to this stylized version of the Reformation as a force for economic growth, the monopoly Catholic Church was the villain of the piece, inasmuch as it pursued policies that retarded economic progress.[1]

The Weberian Thesis: Fact or Fiction?

The popular idea that the medieval monopoly Church hampered the growth and development of the European economy and that the Protestant Reformation encouraged and accelerated prosperity was allegedly originated by Max Weber in his classic work, *The Protestant Ethic and the Spirit of Capitalism*, and subsequently echoed by Richard Tawney in *Religion and the Rise of Capitalism*.[2] According to Weber, an ethical stigma attached to business activity during the Middle Ages, and this stigma was the direct result of Catholic teachings. The ethos of medieval Christianity can be summed up in the old judgment passed on the merchant, to wit: *homo mercator vix aut numquam Deo placere*—he may conduct himself without sin but cannot be pleasing to God (Weber 1930, 262). According to Weber (1930, 73), "the feeling was never quite overcome, that activity directed to acquisition for its own sake was at bottom a *pudendum* which was to be tolerated only because of the unalterable necessities of life in this world." Catholic doctrine, in short, failed actively to encourage the capitalist mentality and therefore failed to promote economic development.

Weber singled out Calvinism as a religion that fostered the capitalist spirit, albeit in a rather subtle and roundabout way. Calvinism is based on predestinarianism—the belief that only a select few are predestined for salvation, whereas the bulk of humanity will be doomed to eternal perdition. According to Calvin, God makes this assignment, and it becomes a fixed datum. No human actions or choices can have any influence over the matter. The devout can never know their election or nonelection to eternal bliss, but they could know their "calling." The calling was the responsibility of the individual to discern his role by working in the mundane world to achieve God's will. Unable to determine their destiny,

Calvinists, according to Weber, yearn for a sign that they are on the right track. They found reassurance in the puritanical glorification of hard work. According to Weber (1930, 163, 166), "the Puritan idea of the calling and the premium it placed on ascetic conduct was bound directly to influence the development of a capitalist way of life" because the doctrine bestowed "a psychological sanction" on the profit motive, whereby "the providential interpretation of profit-making justified the activities of the business man." Weber underscored the irony in this unintended consequence of Calvinism, for Calvinist theology is not designed to promote free enterprise; to the contrary, it is less tolerant of "mammon" than the medieval Church. The explicit hostility of Calvinism to capitalism notwithstanding, Weber (1930, 259) argues that "the spirit of ascetic religion nevertheless . . . gave birth to economic rationalism."

Weber's thesis, at least as popularly interpreted, has been enormously influential, despite the fact that it employs tortuous reasoning and commits a basic error. Weber's logic rests on the premise that Calvinism defines "works" to include earthly toil, whereas informed theological authority maintains that the Calvinist "true doctrine of good works" involves spiritual obedience to the Law. It has nothing to do with economic success (MacKinnon 1993, 220). Nowhere does Weber confront the contradiction between his interpretation of Calvinism and the dictates of Calvinist theology, which exhort the faithful on the one hand to "choose that employment or calling . . . in which you may be most serviceable to God. Choose not that in which you may be most honorable in the world; but that which you may do most good and best escape sinning"; and on the other hand decrees: "Above all, God and Mammon cannot be reconciled" (MacKinnon 1993, 222).

There is a growing consensus among historians that the Middle Ages—a time dominated by the supposedly anti-capitalist monopoly Church—witnessed both the emergence and the rapid spread of recognizably capitalist economic institutions. For example, Robertson (1933, 34, 4–41) asserts that capitalism was spawned in the Middle Ages, citing the high level of development of the cloth, woolen, and silk industries in Florence and in Belgium. Tawney (1926, 26) himself, otherwise arguing in the Weberian mold, notes that small-scale capitalism was omnipresent during the Middle Ages, and that large-scale capitalism existed simultaneously in Belgium and Italy. He also maintains that the "capitalist spirit" was alive and well in fourteenth-century Venice, Florence, South Germany, and Flanders, and in fifteenth-century Antwerp; yet all these areas were dominated by the Catholic Church (Tawney 1926, 316). Trevor-Roper (1972, 2–23) argues that large-scale industrial capitalism existed long before the sixteenth century, having developed by 1500 in Antwerp, Liege, Lisbon, Augustberg,

Milan, Luca, Venice, and Genoa. Luthy (1970, 95, 98) goes even further, asserting that the Catholic bastions of Italy and Portugal laid the material preconditions for a modern capitalist economy, and that "Catholic Europe in the fifteenth and early sixteenth centuries reached a level of structural and organizational development which was not to be achieved again for a further two centuries."

Another factual challenge to the popular version of Weber's thesis is the empirical reality that many Calvinist countries were less than glowing capitalist success stories. In Hungary, for example, where Calvinism took rapid root, capitalism did not follow (Hyma 1951, 501); in fact, trade appears to have declined as Calvinism spread (Hyma 1937, 139). During the century of Calvinist dominance in France (1550–1650), capitalism was in decline (Hyma 1951, 503). Scotland presents another apparent counterexample. By the seventeenth century, Scotland had become more thoroughly Calvinistic than either England or Holland, yet industry lagged in proportion to the spread of the doctrine (Hyma 1937, 139; 1951, 503), and the Scottish clergy were vehemently hostile to enterprise (Trevor-Roper, 1972, 18). In Holland, the Calvinist portions of the country were unable to match the enterprise of Amsterdam, which retained the Spanish allegiance (and its Catholic influence) longer than all other Dutch cities. And in America, as Appleby (1984, 9) has observed, Puritan men tended to avoid becoming modern entrepreneurs, choosing instead to settle in as stolid rural patriarchs.

Sombart's Alternative Thesis

At least one historian challenged the popular view of Weber's thesis by turning it on its head. Sombart (1915) argued that it was Catholicism, not Protestantism, that encouraged the development of capitalism. In support of his thesis, he cited many elements in medieval Catholicism that were favorable to the growth of capitalism. For example, the Church rationalized the pace of life by placing strict control over the passions (Sombart 1915, 237–139). Moreover, the Church established an elaborate papal financial system and developed doctrines favorable to the emergence of capitalism. Aquinas, for example, differentiated between borrowing for unproductive purposes and borrowing for productive purposes (i.e., to create capital), advocating the latter over the former. Other prominent Scholastics, such as Antoninus of Florence and Bernard of Siena, advanced this distinction as well. Finally, Sombart noted the successful practice of capitalism in Catholic cities like Antwerp.

In the final analysis, it is not for us to "prove" either of these theses, but it is our observation that Weber's thesis has dominated historical views defining the role of the medieval Church in the development of capitalism.

It is sometimes overlooked that medieval civilization produced impressive cultural and economic achievements that would not have been possible without the active support and encouragement of the monks and clergy of the Catholic Church, who comprised the intelligentsia of that era. The Church played a critical role in economic development by providing vital human and financial capital. According to O'Sullivan (1962, 13), the medieval Church "proclaimed the wise doctrine of a stable coinage and took part in large commercial enterprises." It created reserves of capital; instituted the first system of deposits, credit, and banking; and encouraged efficient changes in the pattern of land ownership. The ecclesiastic estates of chapter, bishopric, and monastery were often the most important determinants of regional economy, and in parts of northern Europe a combination of traders' churches often became the nucleus of new towns (Hilton, 1947, 5).

Economic progress required political and social peace that the Church helped to provide through its general emphasis on peace and good will, and in particular by doctrines such as the *Truce of God*, which surfaced in Aquitaine in the eleventh century. Even the disasters and infamies that accompanied the Crusades can be said to have encouraged individuals to look outward and eastward for a release of their warlike energies. Church doctrine gave a sense of purpose and direction to human labor, without which the acquisitive impulses would have remained stifled and undeveloped (Davies 1967, 66). Finally, the Church supported the rising merchant class in a variety of ways. For example, the monasteries acted as credit establishments, providing lending services to merchants at a critical time before the emergence of banking. Moreover, according to Le Goff (1989, 82), throughout the medieval period "the Church protected the merchant and helped him to conquer the prejudice which made the inactive seignorial class despise him."

Microanalytics versus Macroanalytics

Up until now, neither the accepted version of the Weber thesis or the Sombart thesis have been informed by a detailed analysis of the microeconomics of the medieval Church. The present study, which explicitly adopts a microanalytic approach, can therefore be of service in assessing the merits of one of the larger debates in economic history. Our research into the microeconomics of the medieval Church uncovers certain facts that challenge the logic of an institution at odds with economic development.

First, official Church doctrine in the Middle Ages was not antagonistic to industry and trade. The actual record has been obscured by the seemingly contradictory rhetoric about the evils of greed and the virtues of poverty. To be sure, Church doctrine strongly emphasized the *temptation* that wealth presents: wealth invites sin by tempting one to avarice. But the possession of wealth per se was not a sin, and poverty was not the recommended lifestyle, except for those who expressly pursued a spiritual calling. Even within the Church hierarchy, poverty and rejection of worldly goods was considered acceptable for certain mendicant orders, but was not advocated for the clergy at large. Practically from its inception, the Christian Church defended private property and trading activity. Leading Fathers of the early Church, including St. Augustine, expressed the prevalent view.[3] According to Viner (1978, 86), moreover, "On practically all other matters relating to commercial activity, church doctrine was stated in such abstract or general terms as would not in practice give rise to problems for respectable businessmen." In truth, any other position would have been contrary to the medieval Church's own circumstances regarding wealth. Thus, although the medieval Church never glorified wealth, it did not condemn the pursuit of riches. It essentially placed questions of wealth and property outside of theology, allowing for different lifestyles within and without the organizational Church (Gonzalez 1990, 231).

Second, the medieval Church not only survived but prospered. One of the core propositions of contemporary economics is the survivorship principle. Institutions survive in the long run only if they are economically efficient. An institution that creates a persistent drag on economic development will not last long. In the case of the medieval monopoly Church, the time frame was a very long run—approximately a thousand years. Competitive entry did eventually cut off this institution's long domination, but for centuries the Catholic Church repeatedly and successfully fought off attempts by potential competitors to poach its markets.

Third, the medieval Church was a residual claimant. The fact that it literally owned a large part of the European economy meant that it prospered if the overall economy prospered. In this regard the monopoly status of the Church should have encouraged it to promote economic progress. As we know, economic growth benefits all firms, not just the ones that invest resources in growth. Consequently, any one firm may have a weak incentive to invest in growth. But the medieval Church, by virtue of its monopoly status, had a large stake in economic growth and simultaneously did not face a serious free-rider problem. Recognition of this fact helps us to dispose of one possible confusion. We cannot conclude that because the medieval Church was a monopolist it therefore was more likely to pursue an anti-capitalist policy agenda. On the contrary, its monopoly status seemingly would confer rewards for the opposite type of behavior.

While the above findings cast doubt on the unequivocal pronouncement of the medieval Church's negative role in economic development, the following issues raise perennial questions about its progrowth behavior: the doctrine of usury (and its companion idea of "just price"), the medieval Church's protracted battle against heresy, and the Church's supposed suppression of science and technology. We discuss each of these issues next.

Morality versus Efficiency: Usury and "Just Price." Critics of the economic impact of the medieval Church can make a strong case that one doctrine in particular, usury, produced a significant drag on European economic development. Viner (1978, 86) argues that it was the only Church doctrine with important economic relevance, and that it resulted in serious tension "between the Church and the world of commerce and finance." As we have shown in Chapter 6, the medieval Church manipulated the usury doctrine in order to redistribute income to itself. The general prohibition against usury undoubtedly had a negative impact on the development of capital markets, but it is easy to exaggerate that impact. Some exceptions always existed, and over time the exceptions became more and more common. Early in the Scholastic tradition, the consensus position was that a lender can demand just indemnity from a borrower if the lender can show that making the loan will place oneself at risk of loss. It was customary to distinguish between two components of loss, the actual loss (i.e., *damnum emergens*), and the forgone gain (*lucrum cessans*), or opportunity cost of making the loan.

In the latter case, Scholastic writers engaged in logical semantics. When a lender claimed *lucrum cessans*, the doctrine maintained that he was not actually being indemnified for profit foregone on his money (Aristotelian theory defined money as sterile and thus incapable of producing anything), but rather for the lost opportunity of exercising his own industry. Consequently, proof of intent actually to use one's own money as an alternative to lending it out was required before title to interest could be honored (Langholm 1984, 126–27). This legerdemain robbed the usury doctrine of much of its potential negative force; a market for loanable funds did in fact continue to function, albeit subject to marginally higher transaction costs due to the need to satisfy the legalistic requirement imposed by the doctrine just as it does in the United States today.

By contrast, the "just price" doctrine was a red herring. For all the attention devoted to this issue by modern scholars, in reality the doctrine apparently did not amount to much. Church theologians merely proclaimed that the open or market price was the just price (Gilchrist 1969, 116). The medieval Church neither acted to enforce price controls, or to establish precise standards as to how the just price could vary from the market price. As author of the most exhaustive study of the issue of just price, Langholm (1984, 119) concludes:

Several criteria of fair pricing were recommended, but they were rough rules of thumb only, allowing for "great latitude," as John Duns Scotus (d. 1308) put it. Nor were they meant to apply to all exchanges. The scholastics on the whole favored government price regulations. . . . But the majority of exchangers must needs be left to their own devices, and the most that could be hoped for was that they would take some heed of just norms of their own volition. Anyhow, as long as terms of contract were truly voluntary on the part of both parties to an exchange, there would be no reason for any moral authority to intervene.

Viner notes that for the later Scholastics, the dominant criterion of the just price was the "common estimate," which was the price that would be attained under normal conditions in a competitive market. Consistent with this doctrine, the Scholastics "uniformly condemned all private monopolies and were unenthusiastic about official ones . . . [advocacy] of price regulation thus gave way to advocacy of regulation of the functioning of market institutions in the interest of fair competition" (Viner 1978, 85). In this way, the doctrine of just price lost most of its practical significance. By the end of the Middle Ages, canonistic teaching on the theory of the just price had little import (Viner 1978, 118).[4]

The Campaign Against Heresy. As demonstrated in Chapter 4, the medieval Church maintained its effective monopoly of the market for religious services by vigorous attacks on potential competitors. Since this campaign against heresy has traditionally been condemned by the advocates of a liberal economic order as antagonistic to economic development, it requires closer scrutiny. A complete evaluation of Church policy on this point would have to take into account the complex religious and theological issues as well as the strictly economic. But even on the strictly economic front, the results were somewhat ambiguous. The primary economic goal of the medieval Church in its battle against heresy was clearly the protection of its monopoly rents. To the extent that heretical sects attracted followers from the ranks of the Roman Church, they siphoned off tithes, bequests, and other donations.[5] Superficially, at least, it would appear that resources expended by the medieval Church to eliminate competitors was value lost to society.

Despite the negative impact on society of doctrinal warfare by the medieval Church, there is an aspect of the campaign against heresy that has a positive side, at least insofar as economic development is concerned. Many heretical movements condemned earthly society, preached the sanctity of poverty, taught that labor was sinful, and in so many ways fostered an anti-capitalist mentality among their adherents. Heretics themselves tended to come from the ranks of the poor and from other groups alienated from the existing social order (Mundy 1954, 77). Some heretical sects were nihilistic in their attitude toward worldly affairs. According to Le Goff (1989, 314–15),

> many heretical movements, by condemning earthly society and especially the Church, concealed a very powerful revolutionary ferment. . . . The nihilism which attacked work in particular, for work was more harshly condemned by many heretics than by anyone else—the Cathari *perfecti* were not supposed to work—paralysed the social effectiveness of rebellions conducted under a religious banner. Heresies were the most acute form of ideological alienation.

The fact is that heresy, particularly in the late medieval period, was widely regarded as a crime against the well-being of society—governments often classified it as a form of treason (Jaeger 1961, 21). While this secular disposition toward heresy may simply have been a product of the Church's clout in political matters, it must also be recognized that the medieval Church was widely believed to represent the bulwark of civilized society, and that any threat to it was likewise a threat to civilized society.[6] Viner (1978, 39) adds that many heretical sects, including the Ebionites, the Manichaens, the Carpocratians, the Montanists, the Apostolics, the Pelagians, the Donatists, and others, "gave a decidedly communist slant to the interpretation of the Gospel."

Monopoly, Magic, Science, and Technology. Policies of the Church, either directly or indirectly, altered the economic growth and development of medieval Europe. The ambivalence of the Church's effects on development in dealing with heresy is, as we have seen, an important case in point. We have argued that, with certain important reservations, the Church generally fostered economic efficiency in Europe. But an important counterexample exists in conventional wisdom: the case of Galileo. Galileo was tried and convicted by the Inquisition of heresy for propounding proscribed views on cosmology in 1633, in effect, for claiming that the earth revolved around the sun. (His conviction was only officially retracted by Pope John Paul II.) Some past observers have generalized this case, suggesting that this behavior was typical of the Church's opposition to science and, hence, to economic progress. Was this generally the case and how does our interpretation of medieval Church behavior affect this argument?

The discouragement of superstition (i.e., "magic")—belief in the efficacy of nonmeasurable nonobservable supernatural forces to effect changes in real life—is even more basic than the active encouragement of science. In a similar vein one authority defines magic as the "exercise of a preternatural control over nature by human beings, with the assistance of forces more powerful than they" (Flint 1991, 3).

The early Middle Ages was a time when belief in "pagan magic" was at its height. The popular religion of antiquity that continued unabated through the fifth or sixth centuries in the rural areas of Europe was animistic in character. Powers were vested in the natural world where "every stream, every tree, every mountain contained a guardian spirit who had to be carefully propitiated" (White 1978, 46). If mythological (otherworldly) "causes" formed the basis of arguments concerning the natural world, little progress in science would be expected. As such, pagan magic generated a negative externality for the welfare of society.

The Church fought, from the early Middle Ages, to substitute its own supernatural technology for pagan magic. It systematically condemned, and treated as heretical, belief in the gamut of magical agencies: astrology, divination, the control of the weather by demons, and so on. The Church encouraged belief in the "Power of the Cross" as a supernatural technology, thereby offering consumers its own system of magic. Preternatural control over events was attempted, in this system, by numerous means such as prayer, appeal to saints, and ritualistic observances surrounding sacred artifacts. Pagan magicians were persecuted as heretics; in their place, Catholic priests were offered as agents of the Power of the Cross.

Efforts of the Catholic Church to displace its competitors in the "magic market" would appear to imply a neutral impact on the welfare of society if, as scholars have argued, magic was a real impediment to the emergence of modern science and economic growth. The Church, in this view, merely replaced one form of magic with another form, just as deleterious to economic growth. This view could attain some credence were it not for two factors: the market structure of the medieval Church and the character of the "magic" it sold.

First, consider the monopoly market structure of the Church. In the absence of regulatory intervention, an ordinary monopoly reduces the quantity of output below that which would have been provided in a competitive market. For an ordinary private good, the welfare of society is reduced in consequence. But the market for magic was different. Reliance on supernatural technology by consumers generated negative externalities for society as a whole. The greater the availability of, and reliance on supernatural remedies, the larger the detrimental impact on reality-based science and technology and, by extension, on economic development. If belief in magic reduced the rate of growth in science and technology, it was in the best long-run interests of medieval European society as a whole that the supply of magic services—*whoever supplied them*—be reduced.

The Church accomplished this goal, not because it acted as some kind of beneficent central planner, but as a by-product of its attempt to maximize the returns from its monopoly.

The Church would have provided a service to society by reducing the output of magic even if it had only replaced early medieval and heretical magic with as injurious a form. But there is good evidence that it actually discouraged forms of magic least helpful in terms of science, technology, and economic development. Church magic tended to offer fewer claims for efficacy in affecting practical, mundane matters of everyday life than pagan magic. Instead, it tended to quite tightly focus on the otherworldly problem of salvation and the afterlife. Priests were not agents to whom a person might appeal for help with next year's crop, but were "travel agents of the soul." Thus, by displacing the pagan magic that pretended to offer an effective means for the achievement of practical ends, the Church's attempted monopolization of the magic market helped clear a path for the growth and popular acceptance of science. Superstitious beliefs in a mystical technology that was wasteful and ineffective were discouraged, allowing the easier dissemination of knowledge about technology that worked.

The virtue of "temperance" gained ascendance among the cardinal virtues in the medieval Church. In it, real world labor and (ultimately) labor-saving devices found their grounding in nature. A noted authority on religion and technology described the essential differences between pagan superstition and Christian "magic":

> The Christian saint who displaced the genius loci as the most accessible spiritual entity in the new religion was very different. Although he might have favorite shrines, his ear was omnipresent. Moreover, he was completely a man, and could be approached in terms of human interests. The cult of saints ousted spirits from the material objects of nature and liberated mankind psychologically to exploit physical nature freely. . . . One may regard the popular religion of the Middle Ages as gross superstition and still recognize that, as compared with its equivalent in antiquity, it was vastly more sophisticated, and that its new abstraction of spirit from matter fostered a new flexibility in the human utilization of matter. (White 1978, 146)

Early in the Middle Ages, Church magic was advertised as a technology capable of achieving practical improvements in the everyday lives of believers. Later, official doctrine held that the Church possessed only very limited ability to achieve practical consequences through magical intervention.

The Church also actively encouraged the development of formal science in a number of ways. According to Schumpeter (1954, 81), "the scholastic science of the Middle Ages contained all the germs of the laical science of the Renaissance." Important figures like Albertus Magnus, Roger Bacon, and Jordanus the Nemore played key roles in the history of science and were all monks or members of the clergy. Even the heliocentric theory of astronomy—the ostensible target of the Inquisition in the case of Galileo—originated within the Church.[7]

A quasi-facilitating view of science even emerged within official and evolving dogma in their replacement of pagan supernatural technology. While man's first duty was to God, his second was to know and rule himself. The latter adjuration applied only to the world as revealed by God in the Gospels (and as interpreted by the Church). As such there was "no new science"—only that "revealed" by God through man. Nevertheless, this stance translated into an encouragement or a benign neglect of the advancement of empirical "engineering" technology, particularly agricultural technology. (Engineering advances were separated from science in perpetuation of the Platonic dichotomy between contemplation or speculation and action-based engineering). Generally, the major labor-saving discoveries of the period were empirical and not the result of basic science. Furthermore, in an apparent nod to earlier "rougher" magic of the pagan period, the Church encouraged the development of metalworking and the mechanical clock invented and used by medical astrologers. According to White (1978, 337), "the Church immediately saw in such spectacular devices an unsurpassed means of visual education to preach the coherence and rationality of God's universe."

But other cases are to be set against this facilitating attitude. In 1633, Galileo Galilei was condemned by the Holy Inquisition for his insistence that Copernicus's theory of a heliocentric universe was in fact correct, and that, consequently, the scriptural claim (that the Earth was the center of the universe) was wrong. Galileo got into trouble because he held the Copernican system to be true and not simply a "conjecture." As such, he frontally challenged the veracity of the Church in its claim to be the infallible interpreter of infallible Scripture. The actual impact of the censure of Galileo on the progress of science is highly problematical, but the intent of the Church was clear.[8]

By persecuting Galileo and other high-profile challengers to its doctrinal hegemony, the Church was acting to protect the stream of rents it obtained from being the monopoly provider of supernatural technology. The Church obtained contributions, in part, due to its claimed ability to provide useful understanding of the natural world. The issue of heliocentrism was probably not of great importance to the Church in any direct, practical sense. But the Church's credibility as the monopoly interpreter of the interaction between supernatural agencies and the natural world was at stake.[9] If the Church's official interpretation of Scripture was wrong, then the entire edi-

fice of its supernatural technology was weakened, perhaps gravely. The (possibly more important) advances in practical engineering technology, directed primarily toward agriculture, did not actually present such challenges.[10]

The ambivalence of the Church toward "science" was much the same as it was to usury, heresy, or marriage. The Church, in the long run and in the face of the Protestant Reformation, stood to gain large returns from the emerging development of capitalism in Europe. A more efficient manner of protecting its reputational capital was to implement careful reinterpretation of the physical implications of Scripture, so as to avoid unnecessary doctrinal conflicts with emerging science. This is the course the Church, in fact, gradually adopted, a tactic that helped support its long-term interests.

Conclusion: Micro Efficiency versus Macro Welfare

Most historical studies of the medieval Church that come within the purview of economists have focused on the Church as a force in the macroeconomy of western Europe. The prominent theories regarding the role of the medieval Church in retarding or promoting economic development are those of Weber-Tawney and Sombart-Schumpeter. This work departs from previous studies by adopting a microeconomic approach.

What a microeconomic study of the medieval Church reveals is that the Church was locked on the horns of a dilemma. On the one hand, as a residual claimant with a direct stake in a large part of the European economy, the Church stood to gain from economic development that would augment its already considerable wealth. On the other, many of the elements of economic development accelerated the political and economic decline of agriculture, the rise of individualism and its spirit of competitiveness; and so on. As complex multinational firm, the Church responded to worldly events: sometimes consolidating or expanding its market power; sometimes expanding the production of public goods; sometimes "defeating" the forces of economic growth; sometimes altering the environment that encourages growth and sometimes merely guarding the status quo; but all the while seeking opportunities to increase rents within the constraints of its overall corporate (and spiritual) mission. We have examined a number of examples of how the Church molded doctrine and institutions in its own interest, and there are undoubtedly many more.

Our study emphasizes that an institutional approach to the Church must be carefully divorced from its doctrinal or ideational orientation. Although not a matter of "faith and morals," that is, although not officially covered under papal infallibility, recent papal encyclicals have *not* been supportive of the "capitalist spirit," if that means justification for the Smithian view self-interest. In these matters the Church is following doctrine develop

in the Middle Ages. Three recent encyclicals issued by Pope John Paul II, along with recent "Pastoral Letters" of American bishops, appear to throw cold water on capitalism as it is commonly understood.[11] In 1981, the encyclical *Laborem Exercens* supported union developments to achieve "social justice"; in the 1988 encyclical, *Sollicitude Rei Socialis*, the Pope levied broadsides against both liberal capitalism and Marxist communism; in *Centesimus Annus* (1991), John Paul cited weaknesses in democracy, defending communal action as an appropriate avenue for achievement of human rights. Official Catholic social and economic policy emphasizes serious restraints on private ownership of property and unlimited acquisition of material goods. It has defended state subsidies to family farmers with a strong agrarian bias. The ideal society that still shapes Catholic doctrine is that of the feudal state, with its simple technology, its small communal living, and its dedication to things spiritual. From an ideational perspective at least, it is difficult to disagree with Langholm (1992, 564–65) who argues that, despite pragmatic adjustments, fundamental Church doctrine is antithetical to Smith's concept of self-interest as the guiding motive of capitalism.

A microeconomic study of the medieval Church suggests that either of the two competing hypotheses—Weber's on the one hand and Sombart's on the other—are too facile. Both theories oversimplify the macroeconomic role of the medieval Church because they are not rooted in thoroughgoing microeconomic analysis. The medieval monopoly Church generated net rents for its owners, and the creation of these net rents generated some deadweight loss to society. But the size of this social waste remains problematical. Its magnitude is not likely to be discovered by macroeconomic inquiries of the traditional type. Microanalytic inquiry is more apt to uncover the motivation, complexity, and sometimes ambiguous results of the medieval Church's actions and the consequent impact on its members, as well as on society at large.

The ultimate value of a monopoly–microanalytic study of the medieval Church is that it provides a coherent and modern framework from which to analyze the economic functioning of a large, ongoing, historically pivotal, institution. We have asserted that such inquiries are capable of yielding important generalizations regarding the Church and its economic impact on society through the ages.

Additional, even more microanalytic, studies (e.g., at the parish or diocesan level) may provide valuable insights into individual, household, and family behavior, as well as to particular institutions such as inheritance, customs, and changing legal structures over the period. We concede that purely economic studies of the medieval Church are incapable of explaining, let alone resolving, the character of spiritual or religious belief and related historical events. Holistic explanations, especially those that include eco-

nomic motives, have great appeal in explaining particular episodes.[12] The point is that spiritual and other hypotheses may be developed that are observationally equivalent to economic hypotheses. Nevertheless, the economic approach is an important alternative means of organizing research around "religious" institutions.[13] We conclude this study, therefore, with a call for the use of modern economic theory to further study particular institutions at particular places and times, in order to penetrate the historical mysteries of the medieval Church.

NOTES

1. See, for example, Henri Pirenne (1937, 48–49), who asserts that "the attitude of the Church . . . towards commerce [was] not merely passive but actively hostile"; and that the merchant is rarely ever able to please God."

2. Whether Weber actually sponsored this popular and often-cited "thesis" is most unclear, although we adopt the popular version here for purposes of strong contrast. It is important to acknowledge that what we have called the "popular" interpretation of the Weber, the Sombart and, to a large extent, the Tawney theses may seriously misrepresent the intellectual task they set for themselves. Weber's stated goal was to attempt to ascertain the strength of religious forces in the qualitative formation and the empirical expressions of the capitalist spirit. Clearly, Weber was too much the scholar not to admit that capitalistic institutions were operative in the city-states of Italy, Babylonia, China, and the Iberian peninsula in the pre-Protestant period. More important, perhaps, Weber and Sombart were primarily interested in an ideational view of Catholicism and Protestantism—the Geist or ethos of the era as we noted in Chapter 1—rather than the impact of this or that institution on existing practices or economic institutions as we are here. Weber did *not* claim that the medieval Church was opposed to capitalism. He merely argued that Catholic teachings did not promote the "capitalist spirit," whereas Protestantism, or at least one kind of Protestantism (Calvinism) did. Whether the Roman Church's teachings currently support the "capitalist spirit" is also unclear.

3. According to Frend (1971, 331–32), Augustine shared fully in the socially conservative, landowner approach to the donatist controversy.

4. This does not deny that government price controls were widespread, or that they were often framed using the language of "just price." Gilchrist (1969, 116–18) provides a list of detailed examples of price fixing by secular (local) governments during this period.

5. As Runciman (1982, 116, 125) put it, regarding the dualist heresy: "The heretics preached apostolic poverty and attacked the growing luxury and political activities of the Church."

6. Interestingly, Aquinas likened heresy to counterfeiting: "Heresy is a sin which merits not only excommunication but also death, for it is worse to corrupt the Faith which is the life of the soul than to issue counterfeit coins which minister to the secular life. Since counterfeiters are justly killed by princes as enemies to the common good, so heretics also deserve the same punishment" (quoted in Southern 1970, 17).

7. Nicolaus Cusanus, who was the first thinker in medieval times to develop the basic idea, was even a cardinal. The great Copernicus himself was a doctor of canon law, lived all his life in Church circles, and Pope Clement VII actively encouraged his research.

8. The irony of the whole episode is that it surely served to accelerate the popular knowledge, and eventual acceptance of, Copernicus's idea. The Holy Inquisition provided heliocentrism with an advertising windfall. The Galileo case seems to have done little to hamper the growing acceptance of the Copernican idea, and the Holy Office devoted no further resources to similar persecutions. The importance of the condemnation on the technology of Galileo's time or on that of the following 200 years is equally problematical (White 1978, 132).

9. It is worth emphasizing how difficult it was, as a practical matter, to challenge the Church's credibility with a new scientific theory. Time and again the Church made clear that it had no objection to the popular discussion of scientific conjectures. This applied even to those that appeared inconsistent with accepted Church interpretation of Scripture, so long as the infallibility of Scripture was not directly challenged.

10. This point is the basis for the assessment of White (1978, 22): "The chief glory of the later Middle Ages was not its cathedrals or its epics or its scholasticism: it was the building for the first time in history of a complex civilization which rested not on the backs of sweating slaves or coolies but primarily on non-human power."

11. Encyclicals do not carry the might of papal infallibility, but they are considered to be solemn pronouncements of high theological significance. The "faithful," members of the Church, nominally remain free to follow their own conscience, although debate and dissent have received severe censure under the present administration of the Roman Church.

12. One obvious matter that requires resolution is the form and timing of the Protestant Reformation. Was the Reformation a case of "competitive" entry into the market for salvation, or were the multiform state monopolies over religion that it spawned antithetical to the competitive supply of religious services? These and other questions await further research.

13. The reader may refer to the earlier discussion in the preface for suggested ideas in this regard.

References

Alchian, A. A., and Demsetz, H. (1972). "Production, Information Costs, and Economic Organization." 62 *American Economic Review*: 777–95.

Anderson, Gary M. (1989). "Penance and Property Rights: The Enforcement Contract by the Medieval Church." Manuscript, California State University, Northridge.

Anderson, Gary M., Robert E. McCormick, and Robert D. Tollison (1983). "The Economic Organization of the English East India Company." 4 *Journal of Economic Behavior and Organization*: 221–38.

Appleby, Joyce O. (1984). *Capitalism and the New Social Order: The Republican Vision of the 1790s*. New York: New York University Press.

Arias, Gino (1905). *Il sistema della costituzione economica e sociale italiana nell' eta dei communi*. Turin: Roux e Viarengo.

Atiya, Aziz S. (1962). *Crusades, Commerce and Culture*. Bloomington: Indiana University Press.

Azzi, Corey, and Ronald Ehrenberg (1975). "Household Allocation of Time and Religiosity: Replication and Extension." 85 *Journal of Political Economy*: 415–23.

Battalio, R. C., J. H. Kagel, and D. N. MacDonald (1985). "Animals' Choices Over Uncertain Outcomes: Some Initial Experimental Results." 75 *American Economic Review*: 597–613.

———— (1986). "Risk Aversion in Rats Under Varying Levels of Resource Availability." 100 *Journal of Comparative Psychology*: 95–100.

———— (1991). "Animals' Choices Over Uncertain Outcomes: Further Experimental Results." 101 *Economic Journal*: 1067–84.

Bautier, Robert-Henri (1971). *The Economic Development of Medieval Europe*. London: Thames and Hudson.

Becker, Gary S. (1981). *A Treatise on the Family*. Cambridge, Mass.: Harvard University Press.

———— (1985). "Public Policies, Pressure Groups, and Deadweight Costs." 28 *Journal of Public Economics* (Dec): 329–47.

Bentham, Jeremy [1790] (1879). *An Introduction to the Principles of Morals and Legislation.* Reprint, Oxford: Clarendon Press.

Berman, Harold J. (1983). *Law and Revolution: The Formation of the Western Legal Tradition.* Cambridge, Mass.: Harvard University Press.

Blair, Roger D., and David L. Kaserman (1983). *Law and Economics of Vertical Integration and Control.* New York: Academic Press.

Blumenthal, Uta-Renate (1988). *The Investiture Controversy: Church and Monarchy from the Ninth to the Twelfth Century.* Philadelphia: University of Pennsylvania Press.

Bold, Frederick, and Brooks B. Hull (1994). "Hell, Religion, and Cultural Change." 150 *Journal of Institutional and Theoretical Economics*: 447–64.

Bork, Robert H. (1978). *The Antitrust Paradox: A Policy at War With Itself.* New York: Basic Books.

Boswell, John (1994). *Same-Sex Unions.* New York: Villard Books.

Boyd, C. E. (1952). *Tithes and Parishes in Medieval Italy.* Cambridge, Mass.: Harvard University Press.

Brinig, Margaret F., and Steven M. Crafton (1994). "Marriage and Opportunism." 23 *Journal of Legal Studies*: 869–94.

Brundage, James A. (1982). "Crusade Propaganda." In *The Dictionary of the Middle Ages.* Vol. 1, edited by J. R. Strayer, 18–21. New York: Macmillan.

———— (1987). *Law, Sex, and Christian Society in Medieval Europe.* Chicago: University of Chicago Press.

Caves, Richard E., and William F. Murphy, II (1976). "Franchising: Firms, Markets, and Intangible Assets." 41 *Southern Economic Journal*: 572–86.

Chandler, Alfred D., Jr. [1962] (1966). *Strategy and Structure.* Reprint, New York: Doubleday.

———— (1977). *The Visible Hand: The Managerial Revolution in American Business.* Cambridge, Mass.: Belknap Press.

Christiansen, Eric (1980). *The Northern Crusades: The Baltic and the Catholic Frontier, 1100–1525.* Minneapolis: University of Minnesota Press.

Christie-Murray, David (1976). *A History of Heresy.* London: New English Library.

Cipolla, Carlos M. (1963). "The Italian and Iberian Peninsulas." *The Cambridge Economic History of Europe.* Vol. 3, *Economic Organization and Policies in the Middle Ages,* edited by M. M. Postan, E. E. Rich, and E. Miller, 397–429. Cambridge: Cambridge University Press.

Clark, John M. (1939). *The Social Control of Business.* New York: McGraw-Hill.

Cleary, Patrick (1914). *The Church and Usury.* Dublin: M. H. Gill & Sons.

Clergeac, Adrien (1911). *La Curie et les beneficiers consistoriaux: Etude sur les communs et menus services, 1300–1600.* Paris: A. Picard.

Coase, Ronald H. (1937). "The Nature of the Firm," 4 *Economica,* n.s.. 386–405.

———— (1972). "Durability and Monopoly." 15 *Journal of Law & Economics*: 143–49.

Darby, Michael R., and Edi Karni (1973). "Free Competition and the Optimal Amount of Fraud." 16 *Journal of Law and Economics*: 67–88.

Davies, J. G. (1967). *The Early Christian Church.* New York: Doubleday.

Dawkins, Richard (1976). *The Selfish Gene*. New York: Oxford University Press.

De Roover, Raymond (1948a). *Money, Banking and Credit in Medieval Bruges*. Cambridge, Mass.: Medieval Academy of America.

——— (1948b). *The Medici Bank*. New York: New York University Press.

——— (1958). "The Concept of the Just Price: Theory and Economic Policy." 18 *Journal of Economic History* (Dec): 418–34.

——— (1967). "The Scholastics, Usury and Foreign Exchange." 41 *Business History Review*: 257–71.

Donahue, Charles, Jr. (1983). "The Canon Law on the Formation of Marriage and Social Practice in the Later Middle Ages." 8 *Journal of Family History*: 144–58.

Donkin, R. A. (1962). "Cattle on the Estates of Medieval Cistercian Monasteries in England and Wales." 15 *Economic History Review*: 31–53.

——— (1964). "The Cistercian Grange in England in the 12th and 13th Centuries, with Special Reference to Yorkshire." 6 *Studia Monastica*: 95–144.

Dosi, Giovanni (1988). "Sources, Procedures, and Microeconomic Effects of Innovation." 26 *Journal of Economic Literature*: 1120–71.

Duby, Georges (1978). *Medieval Marriage*. Translated by Elborg Forster. Baltimore: Johns Hopkins University Press.

Duncalf, Frederic (1969). "The Councils of Piacenza and Clermont." In *A History of the Crusades*. Vol. 1, edited by M. W. Baldwin, 40–53. Madison: University of Wisconsin Press.

Ekelund, Robert B., Jr., and Robert D. Tollison (1981). *Mercantilism as a Rent-Seeking Society*. College Station: Texas A&M University Press.

Erbstösser, Martin (1984). *Heretics in the Middle Ages*. Translated from German by Janet Fraser. Leipzig: Edition Leipzig.

Eusebius (1984; originally written ca. 324). *The History of the Church from Christ to Constantine*. Translated by G. A. Williamson. New York: Dorset Press.

Finucane, Ronald C. (1983). *Soldiers of the Faith*. New York: St. Martin's Press.

Fisher, Helen E. (1992). *Anatomy of Love*. New York: Norton.

Flint, Valerie I. J. (1991). *The Rise of Magic in Early Medieval Europe*. Princeton: Princeton University Press.

Frend, W. H. C. (1971). *The Donatist Church: A Movement of Protest in Roman North Africa*. Oxford: Clarendon Press.

Friedman, David D. (1980). "In Defense of Thomas Aquinas and the Just Price." 12 *History of Political Economy*: 234–42.

Fry, Timothy, OSB, ed. (1981). *The Rule of St. Benedict 1980*. Collegeville, Minn.: Liturgical Press.

Geary, Patrick J. (1990). *Furta Sacra: Thefts of Relics in the Central Middle Ages*. Princeton: Princeton University Press.

Ghiselin, Michael T. (1974). *The Economy of Nature and the Evolution of Sex*. Berkeley: University of California Press.

Gies, Frances, and Joseph Gies (1987). *Marriage and the Family in the Middle Ages*. New York: Harper & Row.

Gilchrist, J. (1969). *The Church and Economic Activity in the Middle Ages*. London: St. Martin's Press.

Gonzalez, Justo L. (1990). *Faith and Wealth: A History of Early Christian Ideas on the Origin, Significance, and Use of Money*. San Francisco: Harper & Row.

Goody, Jack. (1983). *The Development of the Family and Marriage in Europe*. Cambridge: Cambridge University Press.

Gottlieb, Beatrice (1980). "The Meaning of Clandestine Marriage." In *Family and Sexuality in French History*, edited by Robert Wheaton and Tamara K. Harevan. Philadelphia: University of Pennsylvania Press.

Hair, Paul (1972). *Before the Bawdy Court: Selections from Church Court and Other Records Relating to the Correction of Moral Offences in England, Scotland, and New England, 1300–1800*. London: Elek.

Hanawalt, Barbara A. (1986). *The Ties That Bound*. New York: Oxford University Press.

Hauser, Henri (1927). *Les debuts du capitalisme*. Paris: F. Alcan.

Helmholz, R. H. (1974). *Marriage Litigation in Medieval England*. Cambridge: Cambridge University Press.

Herlihy, David (1961). "Church Property on the European Continent, 701–1200." 36 *Speculum*: 81–105.

——— (1985). *Medieval Households*. Cambridge, Mass.: Harvard University Press.

Hill, B. D. (1968). *English Cistercian Monasteries and Their Patrons in the Twelfth Century*. Urbana: University of Illinois Press.

Hill, Rosalind (1951). "Public Penance: Some Problems of a Thirteenth-Century Bishop." 36 *History*: 213–26.

——— (1957). "The Theory and Practice of Excommunication in Medieval England." 42 *History*, 1–11.

Hilton, Rodney H. (1947). *The Economic Development of Some Leicestershire Estates in the 14th and 15th Century*. London: Oxford University Press.

Hitti, Phillip K. (1985). "The Impact of the Crusades on Moslem Lands." In *A History of the Crusades*. Vol. 5, edited by N. P. Zacour and H. W. Hazard. Madison: University of Wisconsin Press.

Homer, Sidney (1977). *A History of Interest Rates*. Rev. ed. New Brunswick, N. J.: Rutgers University Press.

Houlbrooke, Ralph (1985). "The Making of Marriage in Mid-Tudor England: Evidence from the Records of Matrimonial Contract Litigation." 10 *Journal of Family History*: 339–52.

Hull, Brooks B., and Frederick Bold (1989). "Towards an Economic Theory of the Church." 16 *International Journal of Social Economics*: 5–15.

Hyma, Albert (1937). *Christianity, Capitalism and Communism: A Historical Analysis*. Ann Arbor, Mich.: G. Wahr.

——— (1951). *Renaissance to Reformation*. Grand Rapids, Mich.: Eerdmans.

Iannaccone, Laurence R. (1988). "A Formal Model of Church and Sect." 94 *American Journal of Sociology*: S241–68.

Iannaccone, Laurence R., and Brooks B. Hull (1990). "An Introduction to the Economics of Religion." Manuscript.

Ingram, Martin. (1987). *Church Courts, Sex and Marriage in England, 1570–1640*. Cambridge: Cambridge University Press.

Jaeger, Lorenz (1961). *The Ecumenical Council, the Church and Christendom*. Dublin: Geoffrey Chapman.

Jordan, Edouard (1909). *De mercatoribus apostolicae camerae in XIII saeculo*. Paris: Thesim proponebat facultati litterarum Universitatis parisiensis.

Kamen, Henry A. F. (1985). *Inquisition and Society in Spain in the Sixteenth and Seventeenth Centuries*. Bloomington: Indiana University Press.

Kamien, Morton I., and Nancy L. Schwartz (1982). *Market Structure and Innovation*. Cambridge: Cambridge University Press.

Kaserman, David L., and John W. Mayo (1993). *Monopoly Leveraging Theory: Implications for Post-Divestiture Telecommunications*. Knoxville: University of Tennessee Center for Business and Economic Research.

Kelly, J. N. D. (1986). *The Oxford Dictionary of Popes*. New York: Oxford University Press.

Kieckhefer, R. (1976). *European Witch Trials: Their Foundations in Popular and Learned Culture, 1300–1500*. London: Routledge & Kegan Paul.

Klein, Benjamin, Robert G. Crawford, and Armen A. Alchian (1978). "Vertical Integration, Appropriable Rents, and the Competitive Contracting Process." 21 *Journal of Law & Economics*: 297–326.

Knowles, David (1948). *The Religious Orders in England*. Vol. 1. Cambridge: Cambridge University Press.

——— (1955). *The Religious Orders in England*. Vol. 2. Cambridge: Cambridge University Press.

——— (1963). *The Monastic Order in England*. Cambridge: Cambridge University Press.

——— (1969). *Christian Monasticism*. New York: McGraw-Hill.

Krueger, Hilmar C. (1969). "The Italian Cities and the Arabs Before 1095." In *A History of the Crusades*. Vol. 1, edited by M. W. Baldwin. Madison: University of Wisconsin Press.

Lambert, Malcolm (1977). *Medieval Heresy*. New York: Holmes & Meir.

Lane, Frederic C. (1966). *Venice and History: The Collected Papers of Frederic C. Lane*. Baltimore: Johns Hopkins University Press.

——— (1973). *Venice*. Baltimore: Johns Hopkins University Press.

Lane, Frederic C., and Reinhold C. Mueller (1985). *Money and Banking in Medieval and Renaissance Venice*. Vol. 1, *Coins and Moneys of Account*. Baltimore: Johns Hopkins University Press.

Langholm, Odd I. (1984). *The Aristotelian Analysis of Usury*. Bergen: Universitetforlaget.

——— (1992). *Economics in the Medieval Schools: Wealth, Exchange, Value, Money and Usury According to Paris Theological Tradition, 1200–1350*. Leidin: Brill.

Lawrence, C. H. (1984; 1992). *Medieval Monasticism*. London: Longman.

Lea, Henry C. (1883). "Excommunication." In *Studies in Church History*. 2d ed. Philadelphia: Russell.

——— (1894). "The Ecclesiastical Treatment of Usury." 2 *Yale Review*: 355–85.

——— (1896). *A History of Auricular Confession and Indulgences in the Latin Church*. 3 vols. Philadelphia: Lea Brothers.

——— (1971). "The Taxes of the Papal Penitentiary." In *Minor Historical Writings and Other Essays by Henry Charles Lea*, edited by A. C. Howland. Port Washington, N. Y.: Kennikat Press.

Lecky, William E. H. (1897). *History of the Rise and Influence of the Spirit of Rationalism in Europe*. Rev. ed. 2 vols. New York: Appleton.

Le Goff, Jacques (1984). *The Birth of Purgatory*. Translated by A. Goldhammer. Chicago: University of Chicago Press.

———— (1988). *Your Money of Your Life: Economy and Religion in the Middle Ages*. New York: Zone Books.

———— (1989). *Medieval Civilization*. Cambridge, Mass.: Blackwell.

Leighton, Albert C. (1972). *Transport and Communication in Early Medieval Europe, A. D. 500–1100*. Newton Abbot: David & Charles.

Lekai, Louis J., OSCO (1953). *The White Monks: A History of the Cistercian Order*. Okauchee, Wisc.: Cistercian Fathers.

———— (1977). *The Cistercians*. Kent, Ohio: Kent State University Press.

Le Roy Ladurie, Emmanuel (1978). *Montaillou: The Promised Land of Error*. New York: Braziller.

Levack, Brian P. (1987). *The Witch-Hunt in Early Modern Europe*. New York: Longman.

Logan, F. Donald (1968). *Excommunication and the Secular Arm in Medieval England*, Studies and Texts 15. Toronto: Pontifical Institute of Mediaeval Studies.

Lunt, William E. (1934). *Papal Revenues in the Middle Ages*. 2 vols. New York: Columbia University press.

———— (1939). *Financial Relations of the Papacy with England to 1327*. Cambridge, Mass.: Mediaeval Academy of America.

———— (1962). *Financial Relations of the Papacy with England, 1327–1534*. Cambridge, Mass.: Mediaeval Academy of America.

Luthy, Herbert (1970). *From Calvin to Rousseau: Tradition and Modernity in Socio-Political Thought from the Reformation to the French Revolution*. New York: Basic Books.

Lynch, Joseph H. (1976). *Simoniacal Entry into Religious Life from 1000 to 1260: A Social, Economic and Legal Study*. Columbus: Ohio State University Press.

———— (1992). *The Medieval Church: A Brief History*. London: Longman.

Machlup, Fritz, and Martha Taber (1960). "Bilateral Monopoly, Successive Monopoly, and Vertical Integration." 27 *Economica*: 101–19.

MacKay, Charles [1852] (1980). *Memoirs of Extraordinary Popular Delusions and the Madness of Crowds*. Reprint, Toronto: Coles.

MacKinnon, Malcolm H. (1993). "The Longevity of the Thesis: A Critique of the Critics." In *Weber's Protestant Ethic: Origin, Evidence, Contexts*, edited by Hartmut Lehmann, 211–44. New York: Cambridge University Press.

Marshall, Alfred (1890). *Principles of Economics*. London: Macmillan.

Mayer, Hans E. (1972). *The Crusades*. London: Oxford University Press.

McLaughlin, T. P. (1939). "The Teaching of the Canonists on Usury." 1 *Mediaeval Studies*: 81–147.

McNeill, John T., and Helena M. Gamer [1938] (1990). *Medieval Handbooks of Penance: A Translation of the Principal Libri Poenitentiales and Selections from Related Documents*. Reprint, New York: Columbia University Press.

Michell, Robert, and Nevill Forbes, trans. (1970). *The Chronicle of Novgorod*. New York: AMS Press.

Morris, Colin (1963). "A Consistory Court in the Middle Ages." 14 *Journal of Ecclesiastical History*: 150–59.

Mundy, John H. (1954). *Liberty and Political Power in Toulouse, 1050–1230*. New York: Columbia University Press.

———— (1973). *Europe in the High Middle Ages, 1150–1309*. New York: Basic Books.

Muntz, Eugene, ed. (1878–82). *Les Arts à la cour des papes pendant le XVe et le XVIe siècles*. Vol. 3. Paris: Bibliothèque des ècoles françaises d'Athènes et de Rome, fascs. 4, 9, 28.

Murray, A. (1981). "Confession as a Historical Source in the 13th Century." In *The Writing of History in the Middle Ages*, edited by R. H. C. Davis and J. M. Wallace-Hadrill. Oxford: Clarendon Press.

Nelson, Benjamin N. (1947). "The Usurer and the Merchant Prince: Italian Businessmen and the Ecclesiastical Law of Restitution, 1100–1550." 7 *Journal of Economic History*: 104–22.

———— (1969). *The Idea of Usury*. 2d ed. Chicago: University of Chicago Press.

Newhall, Richard A. (1963). *The Crusades*. Hinsdale, Ill.: Dryden Press.

Noonan, John T. (1957). *The Scholastic Analysis of Usury*. Cambridge, Mass.: Harvard University Press.

North, Douglass C. (1981). *Structure and Change in Economic History*. New York: Norton.

———— (1990). *Institutions, Institutional Change, and Economic Performance*. Cambridge: Cambridge University Press.

———— (1994). "Economic Performance Through Time." 84 *American Economic Review*: 359–68.

North, Douglass C., and R. P. Thomas (1973). *The Rise of the Western World*. Cambridge: Cambridge University Press.

Oakley, Thomas P. (1932). The Cooperation of Medieval Penance and Secular Law." 7 *Speculum*: 515–24.

———— (1937). "Alleviations of Penance in the Continental Penitentials." 12 *Speculum*: 488–502.

———— (1969). *English Penitential Discipline and Anglo-Saxon Law in Their Joint Influence*. New York: AMS Press.

O'Brien, George (1920). *An Essay on Medieval Economic Teaching*. London: Longmans, Green.

O'Sullivan, M. D. (1962). *Italian Merchant Bankers in Ireland in the Thirteenth Century: A Study in the Social and Economic History of Medieval Ireland*. Dublin: A. Figgs.

Ordover, J. A., A. O. Sykes, and R. D. Willig (1985). "Nonprice Anticompetitive Behavior by Dominant Firms Toward the Producers of Complementary Products." In *Antitrust and Regulation: Essays in Memory of John J. McGowan*, edited by F. M. Fisher. Cambridge, Mass.: MIT University Press.

Otis, Leah L. (1985). *Prostitution in Medieval Society*. Chicago: University of Chicago Press.

Paris, Matthew (1872–83). *Chronica majora*. 7 vols. Edited by H. R. Luard. London: Longman.

Pastor, Ludwig (1949). *The History of the Popes from the Close of the Middles Ages*. 5th ed. Vol. 4, edited by F. I. Antrobus. London: Routledge & Kegan Paul.

Pautler, Paul A. (1977). "Religion and Relative Prices." 5 *Atlantic Economic Journal*: 69–73.

Payer, Pierre B. (1984). *Sex and the Penitentials: The Development of a Sexual Code, 550–1150.* Toronto: University of Toronto Press.

Pelikan, Jaroslav (1984). *The Christian Tradition.* Vol. 4, *Reformation of Church and Dogma (1300–1700).* Chicago: University of Chicago Press.

Peters, Edward (1971). *The First Crusade.* Philadelphia: University of Pennsylvania Press.

——— (1980). *Heresy and Authority in Medieval Europe.* Philadelphia: University of Pennsylvania Press.

——— (1988). *Inquisition.* New York: Free Press.

Pirenne, Henri (1937). *Economic and Social History of Medieval Europe.* New York: Harcourt, Brace.

Posner, Richard A. (1976). *The Robinson–Patman Act: Federal Regulation of Price Differences.* Washington, D. C.: American Enterprise Institute.

——— (1980). "A Theory of Primitive Society with Special Reference to Law." 23 *Journal of Law & Economics:* 1–53.

Power, Eileen (1941). *The Wool Trade in English Medieval History.* Oxford: Oxford University Press.

Prawer, Joshua (1972). *The Crusader's Kingdom: European Colonialism in the Middle Ages.* New York: Praeger.

Redman, Barbara J. (1980). "An Economic Analysis of Religious Choice." 21 *Review of Religious Research:* 330–42.

Reynolds, T. S. (1984). "Medieval Roots of the Industrial Revolution." *Scientific American* (June): 123–30.

Riley-Smith, Louise and Jonathan (1981). *The Crusades: Idea and Reality, 1095–1274.* London: Edward Arnold.

Robbert, Louise B. (1985). "Venice and the Crusades." In *A History of the Crusades.* Vol. 5, edited by N. P. Zacour and H. W. Hazard. Madison: University of Wisconsin Press.

Robertson, Hector M. (1933). *Aspects of the Rise of Economic Individualism: A Critique of Max Weber and His School.* Cambridge: Cambridge University Press.

Rodes, R. E., Jr. (1977). *Ecclesiastical Administration in Medieval England: The Anglo-Saxons to the Reformation.* Notre Dame, Ind.: University of Notre Dame Press.

Rogers, James E. T. (1963). *A History of Agriculture and Prices in England. Volume 1: 1259–1400.* Oxford: Clarendon Press.

Rosenberg, Nathan (1978). *Perspectives in Technology.* London: Cambridge University Press.

Rubin, Paul H. (1978). "The Theory of the Firm and the Structure of the Franchise Contract." 21 *Journal of Law & Economics:* 223–33.

Runciman, Steven (1951). *A History of the Crusades.* Vol. 1, *The First Crusade.* Cambridge: Cambridge University Press.

——— (1952). *A History of the Crusades.* Vol. 2, *The Kingdom of Jerusalem.* Cambridge: Cambridge University Press.

——— (1954). *A History of the Crusades.* Vol. 3, *The Kingdom of Acre.* Cambridge: Cambridge University Press.

——— (1982). *The Medieval Manichee: A Study of the Christian Dualist Heresy.* Cambridge: Cambridge University Press.

Russell, Josiah C. (1948). *British Medieval Population*. Albuquerque: University of New Mexico Press.

Schulte, Aloysius (1904). *Die Fugger in Rom 1495–1523*. Mit studien zur geschichte des Kirchlichen finanzwesens jenerzeit, Vol. 2. Leipzig: Duncker and Humblot.

Schumpeter, Joseph A. (1954). *History of Economic Analysis*. Edited by E. B. Schumpeter. New York: Oxford University Press.

Seward, Desmond (1972). *The Monks of War: The Military Religious Orders*. Hamden, Conn.: Archon Books.

——— (1978a). "Marriage Theory and Practice in the Conciliar Legislation and Diocesan Statutes of Medieval England." 40 *Mediaeval Studies*: 408–60.

——— (1978b). "Choice of Marriage Partner in the Middle Ages: Development and Mode of Application of a Theory of Marriage." 1 *Studies in Medieval and Renaissance History*, n. s.: 3–33.

Sheehan, Michael M. (1971). "The Formation of Marriage in Fourteenth-Century England: Evidence of an Ely Register. 33 *Mediaeval Studies*: 228–263.

Smith, Adam [1776] (1937). *An Inquiry into the Nature and Causes of the Wealth of Nations*. Edited by E. Canaan. Reprint, New York: Random House.

Smith, Charles E. (1972). *Papal Enforcement of Some Medieval Marriage Laws*. New York: Kennikat Press.

Snape, Robert H. (1926). *English Monastic Finances in the Later Middle Ages*. Cambridge: Cambridge University Press.

Sombart, Werner (1915). *The Quintessence of Capitalism*. New York: E. P. Dutton.

Southern, R. W. (1970). *Western Society and the Church in the Middle Ages*. Baltimore: Penguin Books.

Spengler, Joseph J. (1950). "Vertical Integration and Antitrust Policy." 58 *Journal of Political Economy*: 347–52.

Tanner, J. R., C. W. Previte, and Z. N. Brooke, eds. (1926). *The Cambridge Medieval History*. Vol. 5. New York: Macmillan.

Tawney, Richard H. (1926). *Religion and the Rise of Capitalism*. New York: Harcourt, Brace.

Telser, Lester (1960). "Why Should Manufacturers Want Fair Trade?" 3 *Journal of Law & Economics*: 86–105.

Tentler, Thomas N. (1977). *Sin and Confession on the Eve of the Reformation*. Princeton: Princeton University Press.

Thomas, Keith (1971). *Religion and the Decline of Magic*. New York: Macmillan.

Thompson, James W. (1928). *An Economic and Social History of the Middle Ages*. New York: Century.

Throop, P. A. (1940). *Criticism of the Crusades*. Amsterdam: Von Swets & Zeitlinger.

Thurston, Herbert (1913). "Relics." In *Catholic Encyclopedia*. Vol. 12, 734–38.

Tierney, Brian (1955). *Foundations of the Conciliar Theory: The Contributions of the Medieval Canonists from Gratian to the Great Schism*. Cambridge: Cambridge University Press.

——— (1972). *Origins of Papal Infallibility, 1150–1350*. Leiden: Brill.

Trevor-Roper, Hugh R. (1972). *Religion, the Reformation and Social Change*. London: Macmillan.

Troeltsch, Ernst (1931). *The Social Teachings of the Christian Churches*. 2 vols. Translated by O. Wyon. New York: Macmillan.

Tullock, Gordon (1967). "The Welfare Costs of Tariffs, Monopolies, and Theft." 5 *Western Economic Journal*: 224–32.

Tyerman, Christopher (1988). *England and the Crusades, 1095–1588*. Chicago: University of Chicago Press.

Ullman, Walter (1972). *A Short History of the Papacy in the Middle Ages*. London: Methuen.

Urban, William (1975). *The Baltic Crusade*. DeKalb: Northern Illinois University Press.

Vernon, J., and D. Graham (1971). "Profitability of Monopolization by Vertical Integration." 79 *Journal of Political Economy*: 924–25.

Viner, Jacob (1978). *Religious Thought and Economic Society: Four Chapters of an Unfinished Work*. Edited by J. Melitz and D. Winch. Durham, N. C.: Duke University Press.

Vodola, Elisabeth (1986). *Excommunication in the Middle Ages*. Berkeley: University of California Press.

Wardrop, Joan (1987). *Fountains Abbey and Its Benefactors, 1132–1300*. Vol. 91. *Cistercian Studies Series*. Kalamazoo, Mich.: Cistercian Publications.

Weber, Max (1930). *The Protestant Ethic and the Spirit of Capitalism*. Translated by T. Parsons. New York: Scribner.

———— (1963). *The Sociology of Religion*. Boston: Beacon Press.

White, Andrew D. (1896). *A History of the Warfare of Science with Theology in Christendom*. 2 vols. London: Macmillan.

White, Lynn T. (1978). *Medieval Religion and Technology: Collected Essays*. Berkeley: University of California Press.

Williams, D. H. (1990). *Atlas of Cistercian Lands in Wales*. Cardiff: University of Wales Press.

Williamson, O. E. (1975). *Markets and Hierarchies: Analysis and Antitrust Implications*. New York: Free Press.

Wrigley, Edward A., and R. S. Schofield (1981). *The Population History of England, 1541–1871*. Cambridge, Mass.: Harvard University Press.

Zippel, Giuseppe (1907). "L'Allume di Tolfa e il suo commercio." 30 *Archivio della R. Societa Romana di Storia Patria* 5: 389.

Author Index

Alchian, A. A., 53
Appleby, Joyce O., 174
Arias, Gino, 118
Atiya, Aziz S., 144
Azzi, Corey, 5

Battalio, R. C., 12n.3
Bautier, Robert Henri,148–49
Becker, Gary, 5, 87–88, 107,
    108n.1, 126
Bentham, Jeremy, 164n.5
Berman, Harold J., 17, 24, 39n.3,
    63, 67, 69
Blair Roger D., 47–49, 58n.9
Bold, Fredrick, 5, 64
Bork, Robert H., 91
Boswell, John, 108n.1
Boyd, C. E., 36
Brinig, Margaret F., 108n.1
Brundage, James A., 88, 97, 100,
    109n.10, 110n.16, 133

Caves, Richard E., 58n.7
Chandler Alfred D., Jr., 39n.5
Christiansen, Eric, 146

Christie-Murray, David, 80n.23,
    81n.25
Cipolla, Carlos M., 125
Clark, John M.,126
Cleary, Patrick, 114
Clergeac, Adrien, 118
Crafton, Steven M., 108n.1

Darby, Michael R., 13n.13
Davies, J. G., 175
Dawkins, Richard, 12n.3
Demsetz, Harold, 53
DeRoover, Raymond, 41n.15,
    109n.10, 114, 125–26,
    129nn.3, 4, 130nn.12, 13
Donahue, Charles, Jr., 99, 100,
    102, 105, 111n.24
Donkin, R. A., 45
Dosi, Giovanni, 153–54, 161
Duby, Georges, 98–99,
    110n.13
Duncalf, Frederic, 143, 145

Ehrenberg, Ronald, 5
Ekelund, Robert B., Jr., 36

197

Subject Index